D1110916

I JUST RAN

OTHER BOOKS
BY SAMUEL HAWLEY

Speed Duel: The Inside Story of the Land
Speed Record in the Sixties

The Imjin War: Japan's Sixteenth-Century Invasion
of Korea and Attempt to Conquer China

America's Man in Korea: The Private Letters
of George C. Foulk, 1884–1887

Inside the Hermit Kingdom: The 1884 Korea
Travel Diary of George Clayton Foulk

I JUST RAN

Percy Williams,
World's Fastest Human

SAMUEL HAWLEY

RONSDALE PRESS

I JUST RAN
Copyright © 2011 Samuel Hawley

All rights reserved. No part of this publication may be reproduced, stored in a retrieval system, or transmitted, in any form or by any means, without prior written permission of the publisher, or, in Canada, in the case of photocopying or other reprographic copying, a licence from Access Copyright (the Canadian Copyright Licensing Agency).

RONSDALE PRESS
3350 West 21st Avenue
Vancouver, B.C. Canada V6S 1G7
www.ronsdalepress.com

Typesetting: Julie Cochrane, in Granjon 11.5 pt on 15
Cover Design: Julie Cochrane
Front Cover Photo: Percy Williams in 1928, moments after winning the
    100-metre Olympic gold medal (BC Sports Hall of Fame and Museum)
Back Cover Photo: Percy Williams in 1928, winning the 200-metre Olympic
    gold metal (BC Sports Hall of Fame and Museum)
Paper: Ancient Forest Friendly "Silva" (FSC) — 100% post-consumer waste,
    totally chlorine-free and acid-free.

Ronsdale Press wishes to thank the following for their support of its publishing program: the Canada Council for the Arts, the Government of Canada through the Canada Book Fund, the British Columbia Arts Council, and the Province of British Columbia through the British Columbia Book Publishing Tax Credit program.

Library and Archives Canada Cataloguing in Publication

Hawley, Samuel Jay, 1960–
  I just ran: Percy Williams, world's fastest human / Samuel Hawley.

Includes bibliographical references and index.
Issued also in electronic format.
ISBN 978-1-55380-126-9

  1. Williams, Percy, 1908–1982. 2. Runners (Sports) —
Canada—Biography. I. Title.

GV1061.15.W55H39 2011   796.42'2092   C2011-903006-3

At Ronsdale Press we are committed to protecting the environment. To this end we are working with Canopy (formerly Markets Initiative) and printers to phase out our use of paper produced from ancient forests. This book is one step towards that goal.

Printed in Canada by Marquis Book Printing, Montreal, Quebec

CONTENTS

Prologue

c%

THE REPORTERS CLUSTERED round the young sprinter after the race and the question they kept asking was: How did you *feel* just before the gun sounded? He answered politely but the intrusiveness grated. "What a fool question," he groused to his coach after the scrum finally dispersed. "How does anybody feel before a race — scared as blazes."[1]

It was more or less how all six runners had felt as they took their marks that July afternoon for the hundred-metre final of the 1928 Amsterdam Olympics. The fear had taken hold the night before as they lay in their beds trying to cope with their nerves and had only gotten worse as race time drew nearer. A lot of coaches held that being scared was a good thing for a runner, a necessary building up of emotional tension that could then be unleashed in one almighty effort. But that didn't make it any easier to bear — certainly not in that final hour in the dressing room, or in that lonely walk down the tunnel that led to the track, or in those last few moments when you strip to your shorts and stand exposed to the thousands and wish you were somewhere, *anywhere*, else.

The six runners had endured two rounds of qualifying heats the previous day and the semifinals two hours before, a winnowing that had seen eighty-one others fall by the wayside. For one of the finalists a gold medal lay at the far end of the track. For the rest it would be, quite literally, the agony of defeat. It had rained earlier that day; the sky was leaden and the air chilly, far from ideal conditions for sprinting. They dug their start holes in the damp cinders at the chalk line, then took off their warm-up gear and did some final limbering, trying to control the surging adrenalin as they waited to be called to their marks. To the watching crowd the two Americans on the outside, Wykoff and McAllister, seemed good bets to win. So did the muscular figure of London in lane four, representing Britain, and the German ace Lammers in two.

As for the young man in lane three — a Canadian, was he? — he appeared hopelessly outclassed. At 126 pounds on a five-foot-seven-inch frame, he was surely too scrawny for such top-flight competition. Then there was the matter of his experience: he didn't have any, at least not in the big time. This meet was his first taste of international competition.

No, all things considered, the young man didn't have much of a chance. He was probably down there falling to pieces under the pressure, poor kid.

But he wasn't falling to pieces. He was scared, all right, pacing back and forth like a caged lynx, his heart beating a hole through his chest. But he was holding it together, repeating to himself the words his coach had used to soothe him moments before in the change room: *It's just another race. It's just another high school race.*

The six runners were called to their marks. The set command. The crack of the gun. A flurry of pumping legs and arms and then that slight figure emerging in front to breast the tape and claim gold with a leap. Pandemonium in the stands, a delight that transcended borders that such an unlikely youngster had won. And in the press box grinning journalists shaking their heads and beginning to scribble, muttering incredulously: "Who *is* this Canadian kid?"

∞

The kid was Percy Williams of Vancouver and he wasn't finished. Two days later he captured the two-hundred-metre gold medal as well, completing the Olympic sprint "double," the Games' most glamorous feat. The following winter he swept the US indoor track circuit, silencing critics who claimed his Olympic wins were a fluke. In 1930 he broke Charlie Paddock's nine-year-old world record for the hundred metres, setting a new mark that would stand until the advent of Jesse Owens. In 1932 he returned to the Olympics to defend his double sprint crown, something never before successfully accomplished. And in between he engaged in an ongoing speed duel with some of the fleetest men on the planet, arch rivals Frank Wykoff and Eddie Tolan foremost among them — a battle for track supremacy and the title World's Fastest Human.

Yet through it all he remained a reluctant hero and very much an enigma. When pressed to explain his secret for winning, he would only shrug and say, "I just ran."

Percy Williams was showered with such acclaim in his day that he was almost as well-known as contemporaries Babe Ruth and Jack Dempsey, a remarkable degree of fame for a runner, particularly one who so assiduously shunned the spotlight. It wasn't just his athletic prowess that attracted all the attention. Percy's own story, the quintessential underdog tale, was immensely appealing. He wasn't the product of some top-flight collegiate track program. He wasn't a member of a renowned athletic club. He didn't have a big-name coach or any powerful backing. He was just a kid from nowhere with a talent for running, discovered and pushed to stardom by a man named Bob Granger who earned his living mopping floors at a school. The unlikely pair lacked the basic facilities that were elsewhere taken for granted, Percy doing most of his running on grass fields and dirt tracks. They had no money. To get Percy to the nationals in Toronto they had to raise funds themselves to buy him a train ticket while Bob worked in the pantry car for his passage. They didn't realize that nobodies like them weren't supposed to have a chance and so they doggedly kept at it — until they made it all the way to the top.

And there was more. There was something about Percy himself that the press and the public found irresistibly attractive. He was clean-cut and clean-living, delicate yet tough, vulnerable yet resolute, obedient to his coach and his father, devoted to his mother, loyal to his hometown and nation — the embodiment, in short, of qualities that allowed just about everyone to see in him whatever it was that they yearned for. Even the dourest of officials and sharpest of promoters couldn't help getting just a little maudlin over Percy. He was so touchingly shy; so humble despite his talents; so much the epitome of the amateur tradition, an athlete who did a little training after school — shockingly little, by today's standards — and still became a champion.

It all added up to make Percy more than just a media sensation. Inevitably, he also became a symbol. For Canada he was the flesh-and-blood representation of how the country viewed itself and what it wanted to be: an underestimated nation that could hold its own and even beat its domineering, often-resented American cousins. And for Vancouver, Percy was expected to be even more — not just the Canadian David standing up to the American Goliath, but the West Coast David standing up to the arrogant East. He was the symbol of a vibrant, fast-growing city that would no longer be overlooked, a city whose time had come.

The fond perception of Percy as a shy, unaffected kid who became a champion and stumbled into the spotlight wasn't far from the truth at the time of his 1928 rise to stardom. In the years that followed, however, while the public image still lingered, the private Percy started to change. He had never much liked running to begin with — it was Bob Granger who drove him — and the fame that it brought him, coupled with the expectations of hometown and country, soon turned into a torment. But worst of all was the disillusionment it led to, the sense that everybody was trying to take advantage of him, to use him in one way or another. It would turn him against the amateur sports establishment and leave him distrustful of others. It would even turn him against the man who made him, his coach.

The story of Percy Williams is not just a Cinderella tale of an unlikely hero who came out of nowhere to conquer the track world. It is also the grittier inside story of the life of a sports legend in a world in many ways far removed from our own; of what happened to a naïve, sensitive, naturally gifted young man who attained superstardom and passed through the meat grinder of fame — and of what happened along the way to his mentor Bob Granger. It was a journey that would shape the rest of their lives.

At the start of our story, however, all that lies in the future. First Percy has to start running — and Bob has to catch him.

CHAPTER 1

The Runner

HE WAS A BEAUTIFUL little boy. He had an angelic face and big blue eyes and curly blond hair that his mother kept long. She liked to dress him up in all sorts of outfits to satisfy her theatrical nature: as a sailor like his great-grandfather, as a concert violinist in a neat tuxedo, as an Indian chief, as Cupid armed with a bow. He was the only child in a house filled with adults, his parents and grandparents and uncles, and they all loved him. He was their Percy.[1]

Percy was an active youngster, always on the go in the yard chasing the family's shaggy Newfoundland dogs, Rover and Queenie, displaying a surefootedness that his father found pleasing. You're going to be a fine athlete, he would say to Percy, and Percy would beam. He beamed even more when his uncles made him mascot of their lacrosse team and took him along to games outfitted with a pint-sized team sweater and lacrosse stick. He wanted to play on a team too, when he grew up.

He was also smart — and perceptive. He noticed the smells the men in the household brought home every day after work, the paint and thinner wafting off his grandfather's jacket, oil from the rail yard on his father, cigar factory tobacco on Uncle Harry. He was intimately familiar with the different looks of the women who raised him, their indulgent smiles that made him feel safe, his grandmother's warning arched brow that usually preceded a "that's enough Percy," his mother's pursed lips when she was doing the household accounts. He noticed how Granddad became boisterous and red in the face when he had a drink in his hand, and how his mother would bloom when the house was filled with people for the luncheons and card parties and musical evenings she took such delight in, and how his father on those occasions would fade into the background and sometimes slip out the back door.

It never occurred to him, however, that his father would one day move out.

∽

It was the eve of the Great War in Vancouver — a city that was not at end of the world perhaps, but you could see it from there. At least that's how Easterners seemed to view the British Columbia town, three thousand miles away on the other side of the prairies and the Rocky Mountains and some of the continent's most imposing forests. There might have been some truth in the joke fifteen years before, when the city was just a generation removed from a lumber camp, an outpost of tree stumps and dirt roads and unpainted houses. But it had done a lot of growing since then. New industries and businesses had been established and were flourishing alongside the sawmills; a construction boom was underway; streets were being paved; sewers dug; streetcar lines and residential neighbourhoods built. And immigrants were flooding in, mainly from eastern Canada and Britain, quadrupling the population. For these men and women Vancouver was a land of promise blessed with congenial weather, exotic in its wilderness and mist-shrouded mountains yet reassuringly British, part of the Empire's All Red Route that now encircled the globe.

Percy Williams' grandparents, Harry and Selina Rhodes, were part of that influx, arriving from Newfoundland, which was then a colony of Britain. Harry was an interesting character. He told stories of how he had been born at sea, the son of a St. John's sea captain named Richard Rhodes, and how he had grown up to a life of adventure, in some accounts as a sailor aboard an Arctic whaler, in others as an interpreter posted in Spain working for his father's trans-Atlantic trading business. He married Selina in the mid-1880s and they had their first child, Charlotte Sophia, Percy's mother, in 1887. Three sons followed: Harry Jr., Lyon and Archie. The family emigrated to BC in the early 1890s and eventually settled in Vancouver, where Harry found employment with BC Electric Railway as a streetcar washer and painter.[2]

Harry and Selina's daughter Charlotte, or "Dot" as most called her, was by this time a pretty girl of sixteen, fair-haired, blue-eyed and scarcely five feet tall, with a beautiful singing voice that she strove to improve with lessons. Her father's stories of seagoing adventure and distant ports had left her with a longing for a life that would not be ordinary, a longing she expressed in a poem a few months before her 1904 marriage to Percy's father: "When twilight draws your curtain back / And pins it with a star / Remember she who wrote these lines / Though I may wander far."[3]

She had chosen for her husband an Englishman named Frederick Edward Williams, a plasterer's son born in Norwood, Surrey, who prior to settling in Vancouver had spent time at sea just like Dot's grandfather and father. The Rhodes family wholeheartedly approved of the young man. Since immigrating to BC and starting out as a lowly cigar roller, he had worked his way up to the position of electrician at the Canadian Pacific rail yards and was earning a good living. He could come across as sober and staid and was most definitely shy, but there was a fun-loving side to him as well, particularly when he was on the playing field with Dot's brothers — they jokingly called him "the Jock" — or horseback riding in the BC wilderness he loved. He married Dot on December 14, 1904, when he was twenty-five and she seventeen. Four years later, on May 19, 1908, Percy Alfred Williams, their first and only child, was born.[4]

Harbingers abounded on the day Percy came into the world — at least in the pages of the *Vancouver Daily Province*. Dot, recovering in the Nurse Roycroft Home, was perhaps in no condition to notice, but had Fred turned to the horoscope section that Tuesday he would have been given a start. "An extremely unsettled mind will militate against the worldly success of the boy born this day," read the alarming prediction. "Much may be saved him if he is educated for a profession that he really desires." The sports page, meanwhile, contained a report on Canada's prospects at the upcoming Olympics in Stockholm, with the name of Bobby Kerr at the top of the list. The Hamilton sprinter would go on to win the gold medal in the two hundred metres, bronze in the hundred and accolades as Canada's greatest Olympian to date.[5]

Percy's parents had a strained marriage, possibly right from the start. The early separations would not have helped: the months Fred spent away from home working in Seattle the year before Percy was born, the lengthy trip Dot made to Newfoundland to show her baby to her Maritime relations, each chronicled with the exchange of anxious postcards, particularly from Fred. "I have been to the P.O. every day but got nothing," reads one of his messages from Seattle. "Do you not like writing any more?" And two months later: "Coming again. Don't kick. Let me know if I am writing too often."[6] The separations soon ended but were replaced by other factors that weighed on the marriage: Dot's insistence that they live with her family; her chafing at being a stay-at-home housewife; Fred's reserved, undemonstrative nature that permitted him to sign letters to his wife with only a chilly "good bye." Whatever lay at the heart of it, they were not happy together.

In 1915 Percy was attending Macdonald Elementary School and living on Keefer Street on the north side of the inlet known as False Creek. Fred was now working for BC Electric Railway in its nearby Prior Street maintenance barns, the job he would hold for the rest of his life, servicing the streetcars that his father-in-law Harry's crew would then wash and repaint.[7] Grandma Selina spent most of her day in the kitchen, helped by Dot with the cooking. She was a seer and sometimes spoke of having strong premonitions. Uncle Harry and Uncle Archie were still living at home, the one working in a cigar factory, the other a plumber. Grandpa Harry was getting on, sixty-one and a bit stiff in the joints, but he could usually be relied on to toss a ball in the yard. He had been a keen athlete in his youth and still liked to attend local games and roar out advice from the sidelines. His nickname was "Old Sport."

It was in 1920 that Percy's father moved out. Percy was twelve. In April he was sent away for the summer term to a boarding school in Victoria, what is today St. Michael's University School. "I arrived O.K. and am having lots of fun," he dutifully wrote to his mother after settling in, pleasing her by signing himself "Yours lovingly, Percy Williams" in a mature hand.[8] When he was brought back home in July, it was to a new house at 196 Twelfth Avenue West in the Mount Pleasant district on the south side of False Creek, a big, sprawling place with a flight of steps in front and a large upstairs balcony flanked by diamond-shaped windows that looked like eyes. It would remain his home for the next thirty years. He arrived to find his father gone, living at the Stratford Hotel and no longer part of the family, and his mother working outside the home for the first time in her life, managing the box office at the Empress Theatre just a few blocks from their old Keefer Street house. She was now coming home late most evenings full of excitement, bubbling over with talk of actors Charles Royal and Ray Collins, leading lady Edythe Elliott, set designer Eddie Eddie and all her wonderful new friends, how many tickets had been sold and what new plays were being planned and the thousand other interesting things that took place behind the curtain.

And then there was the new name she mentioned perhaps more than the others: George B. Howard, the actor who headed up the stock company based at the Empress. He was a flamboyant fellow, twenty years Dot's senior, a widely admired raconteur who wore a diamond tie pin and drove a nice car. Dot was dazzled by him, and so was Percy. And when he died the next year it hit her very hard. It happened following the week-long run of the play *Cappy Ricks* which George was headlining against the advice of his doctor, a physically demanding role that kept him at centre stage and required a good deal of shouting. The effort was too much for his heart. He collapsed and died the following week. Fifty-nine years later, when Dot followed George into the hereafter, Percy would quietly bury her alongside him.[9]

Percy's parents never divorced after Fred moved out. Dot kept his name and they simply lived apart for the rest of their lives, the separation a source of embarrassment that would never be mentioned in the press.[10] Percy would see his father regularly in the years that followed, spending occasional weekends with him hunting and horseback riding. But it wasn't the same. With Fred no longer part of the family, Percy drew very close to his mother and she came to rely emotionally on him. After Percy's rise to fame, newspapers would often comment on how young she looked, how vivacious she was, how attractive she appeared in smart dresses and hats and scarves — and how she didn't look at all like Percy's mother, but more like his "sweetheart."[11]

∽

Percy was now attending junior high school at Simon Fraser and was already starting to show the first glimmers of speed. It had begun while he was away at boarding school in Victoria in the summer of 1920, when he won the hundred-yard dash for boys under thirteen in the University School annual athletic meet, setting a school record of 12 4/5 seconds. He received a little silver medal for the effort and proudly took it home to show his family, his very first athletic prize.[12]

Percy graduated from Simon Fraser in 1923, fourth in his class of forty-seven, and in the fall entered King Edward High School, a mile west of his house on Twelfth Avenue at Oak Street.[13] King Edward — or King Ed as it was known to its students — was an imposing place for the delicate grade nine student. Set in a large three-storey building of cut stone with a pillar-flanked entrance and cupola dome on the roof, it took a serious approach to learning, placing boys and girls in separate classes to keep their minds focused. And it was just as serious about its athletics, with a playing field behind the main building and teams competing for school honour in a wide range of sports. Before Percy's speed could be much noticed, however, he fell ill with what was diagnosed as rheumatic fever, an episode that kept him out of school for a time and badly frightened his family. The crisis was weathered and Percy survived, but the doctors gravely informed Dot that his heart had been damaged and that he would likely never again be able to participate in sports.

They were wrong. Within months of recovering from his illness, Percy began running in earnest.

It all started when King Edward's history and English literature teacher, Emslie Yeo, who did double duty as physical education instructor, set the grade ten boys to running relay races one afternoon. "There was this youngster," Yeo remembered, "a pale, slim lad of no more than 115 pounds, who just seemed to float away from everybody. I went over to him and said, 'Williams, why aren't you turning out for the track team?'" To which Percy replied, "I'm just not interested in track, sir."

That was how Percy honestly felt: he didn't particularly like running. His interests lay more in rugby and tennis, target shooting on the inter-high team and being a cadet. To Coach Yeo, however, lack of interest was no excuse for not contributing to the fight for school honour. "Tell him he owes it to the school," he instructed the track squad. "Tell him it's his duty; that he owes it to you fellows. Coax him. Bully him. Shame him. But get Williams out here!"[14]

Whatever was said, it worked. Percy was soon on the team, outfitted in a baggy sweatsuit with a large blue "K" and "E" on the chest, and an ill-fitting pair of borrowed spiked shoes on his feet. "You're in high school," he would later muse. "You have a physical education class. You run a relay race and you get sweaty and you stay that way all day. The teacher who ran the races probably gets you for one of your other classes. He asks you to run for your school. You're in high school, you can't let the school down. That's how it is. They force you to run."[15]

The King Edward track team didn't receive much expert coaching, even by the standards of the mid-1920s. Training sessions consisted of the older boys passing on what they knew to their younger teammates, with Emslie Yeo in his suit and starched collar and Charlie Chaplin moustache dropping by occasionally to provide what guidance he could. For a new boy like Percy, however, it was the start of an education. He experienced his first sessions of "bounding," a form of exaggerated running in which the runner springs high with each stride, trying to remain airborne as long as possible between footfalls, one of the earliest exercises to be developed specifically for sprinting. He was shown how to dig toe holes in the track and how to launch himself out of them from a crouch stance. He learned how to break in a new pair of track shoes when he finally got them, stiff leather uppers with spikes riveted into the soles, by soaking them in water and lacing them on wet. And he began to harden himself to the discomfort of sprinting, for spikes in Percy's day were about as unforgiving as any footwear ever invented, guaranteed to blister and chew up the feet.[16]

Other than that, Percy just ran races against his teammates and tried to go as fast as he could. And for the moment that was enough. Right from the start he established himself as one of the fastest boys on the team and within a matter of weeks was in the finals of his first serious competition, the annual Vancouver and District Inter-High School Track Meet.

The Inter-High was held on May 22 on the only purpose-built running track in the city, at Brockton Point in Stanley Park, overlooking the harbour. It was a wretched facility really, a pot-holed, six-lane stretch of grass with a significant rise at the start for the short sprints, and for the longer races an equally rough dirt oval, just four lanes wide, the unfortunate boy on the outside running with the wooden paling of the grandstand practically scraping his arm. To Percy, however, it was the big-time. Chalk lines had been freshly drawn, officials were swarming about, the aroma of popcorn and peanuts wafted in the breeze and the grandstand was packed with several thousand students, cheering and roaring out school songs to the accompaniment of a jazz band. His whole family was there too, caught up in the excitement and shouting out encouragement, Grandpa Harry just about beside himself.

Competing at the intermediate level, Percy had survived four days of elimination rounds to earn a spot in the finals of two events, the 100-yard and 220-yard dashes, often referred to as the "century" and "furlong." He was up against the fastest boys from nineteen schools across the city, but the real competition was expected to come from King George High, King Ed's arch rival in all things athletic. Percy did well in the century, running second to his teammate "Dutchy" Grimmett on the six-lane sprint track. The furlong, run on the dirt oval, was tougher.

A downpour had left the track sloppy, the wet dirt clogging Percy's spikes. Having to leap over puddles didn't help either. He nevertheless managed to finish second again behind Dutchy — a not-so-close second this time.[17]

It was a rollicking triumph for the King Ed team and the school, one-two finishes in both the dashes. Percy had done his bit. The "Georges" were vanquished. The "Eddies" had bragging rights as the fastest team in the city.

With that the track season ended and Percy got on with his life. There were his studies to attend to, the steady grind that had returned him to the honours list after the missed time and mediocre grades he had suffered during his illness.[18] Then there was tennis, which he was becoming quite good at, his continuing membership in the cadets, where he was on the shooting team and would soon be company adjutant, and the rugby he hoped to start playing again. He much preferred rugby to running.

He was also starting to show signs of sharing his mother's taste for looking his best, with an appreciative eye for a nice suit and a good pair of shoes, and his wavy hair, darker now that he was older, carefully slicked back with tonic, and glossy like a movie star's. He was sixteen and on his way to becoming the sort of young man to attract female attention. He had inherited his father's shyness, however, and outside his circle of friends tended to be quiet and reserved and easily embarrassed.[19]

Good things were once again expected of Percy at the start of the next year's track season. What he displayed in those early practice sessions, however, wasn't just good — it was great. He hadn't grown much and hadn't done any sprinting in nearly ten months, and yet his speed had dramatically increased. His teammates were soon bragging that in training "our Percy" could run a hundred yards in close to ten seconds flat, what track aficionados called "even time." The claim was met with skepticism at rival schools, particularly at King George. But Percy didn't let his friends down. Although now competing in the tougher senior division, he sailed through the elimination rounds leading to the annual Inter-High track meet. And at the Inter-High he dominated, winning both the century and furlong and for the first time attracting attention in the papers: the *Daily Province* referring to his "splendid form," and the *Sun* hailing him as "a comer in the sprints" and "the class of the meet."[20]

Percy seemed a likely prospect to set new meet records at the Inter-High the following year as a grade twelve student. And in all likelihood his running career would have ended there, with a satisfying little flourish preserved for posterity in a footnote, had it not been for a part-time janitor who mopped the floors at King George High. He had watched Percy intently at the elimination trials that spring of 1926 and again at the Inter-High. His name was Bob Granger and he would change Percy's life.

CHAPTER 2

The Coach

❧

BOB GRANGER WAS OBSESSED with sports. He lived and breathed competition. In his youth he had been a first-rate athlete, at least according to the stories he told: running and swimming in epic races, playing Homeric games of rugby and lacrosse and hockey, pushing himself in water polo and rowing until his heart nearly burst.[1] Then, when his competitive days were over, he turned his attention to coaching. He coached the rugby team and the track squad at King George High School, helped out in the University of British Columbia's fledgling sports program, coached swimmers at the YMCA and offered private training in the art of sprinting, of which he was making a study. He had in fact devoted his whole life to athletics. He was a bundle of sporting energy. A phenomenon. A spark plug.

He was also broke. Bob had nothing to show from his days as an athlete beyond a handful of medals and a few small newspaper clippings. As for his coaching, it paid nothing. To bring in some money he took whatever jobs he could find. In 1926 he was working as a part-time janitor at King George High. He was thirty-one years old, unmarried, living at home with his parents.

Bob's mother and father, Robert Sr. and Margaret Granger, hailed from Scotland. They had left their homeland in the early 1880s for a sojourn in South Africa where the first four of their children were born, then continued on to British Columbia in 1891 where they added five more to the family. Robert Dow Granger, forever after known as Bob, came along in 1895, the third of four sons. By 1915 the family was living on Cardero Street on the edge of downtown Vancouver, Robert Sr. earning a good salary as chief clerk in the land registry office. Eldest son Walter was married, raising a family and working in a bank. The second eldest, John, was an accountant for the telephone company. The youngest, George, would become an insurance agent.[2]

As for Bob, he started out well enough, a freckle-faced, red-haired clerk at the Royal Bank, nineteen years old with his foot on the first rung. But after that it was a different job every year, clerking in one office after another, then slipping into more casual work as he got increasingly involved with coaching. On the field and track he had boundless intensity and focus, a coaching genius to the young athletes he worked with. When it came to the more mundane concerns of life, however, earning money and settling down and saving, he seemed hopeless. Even his young protegés could see it and felt protective of him.[3] If Bob had any money, he would spend it — if he didn't lose it first. An appointment? Bob would be late or miss it altogether. He was a dreamer, wandering rather than marching through life, carrying with him little baggage and only one real goal: to make something of himself in the sports world. He had gone as far as he could as an athlete. Now he was determined to continue his quest as a coach.

By 1926 Bob had come to see the track as the most likely place to achieve his ambition. By scouting local talent and applying his growing knowledge of sprinting, acquired through private study and trial and error, he hoped to mould a champion. One of his early prospects was Harry Warren, a University of British Columbia senior who made up for any lack of natural ability with dogged determination. Harry, however, had just been awarded a Rhodes scholarship to continue his studies at Oxford and would soon be departing for England. With him gone, Bob placed his hopes on a young sprinter from Commercial High School named Wally Scott. Wally delivered, capturing both the intermediate boys' sprints at the 1926 Inter-High. The meet was a personal triumph for Bob. Of the top three performances in the intermediate and senior 100-, 220-, and 440-yard races, a total of eighteen spots, ten were captured by runners he coached.[4]

But Bob wasn't satisfied. He wanted the boy who had won the senior 100 and 220. He wanted Percy Williams.

∽

Bob had had his first glimpse of Percy at the previous year's Inter-High, where Percy ran second in the intermediate century and furlong. It had been a commendable performance but nothing to get too excited about. By early 1926, however, Bob was beginning to hear a lot of talk about the King Edward flyer, stories being put out by Percy's teammates that he could run the century in close to ten seconds flat, nearly half a second faster than the longstanding Vancouver high school record. It piqued Bob's interest but he took it with a large grain of salt. It sounded too much like idle teenage boasting. And what of this rumour that Percy had a leaky heart, and a dicky knee from an injury sustained playing rugby? That didn't make him sound very tough. And you needed to be tough to be really fast on the track.

Early in the spring of 1926, at the start of the track season, Bob caught wind of a race being set up by Percy's teammates to test their hero against Wally Scott, who by this point was privately training with Bob. Bob showed up at the after-school showdown on the King Ed track with little doubt that Wally would win. The sight of Percy, stripped to his shorts and singlet, only added to his certainty. As he would later tell it, "Compared with Wally Scott, who was a sturdy, well-proportioned youngster, Percy was a runt: under five feet six, weighing not more than one hundred and ten pounds, puny and spindly. That boy beat Wally? Never in the world!"[5]

But to Bob's amazement, Percy ran Wally to a dead-heat finish. The issue of superior speed unresolved, the two returned to the start line and after a short rest set out again. This time the finish was uncontested. Percy was the victor by something under a yard.

"What did they do it in?" Bob asked one of the timekeepers after the race, a tall fellow with a stopwatch in his hand.

"Nine and two-fifths seconds!"

Bob's heart skipped a beat. That was a new world record. Then he took a good look at the timekeeper and realized how young he was, just an overexcited teen who didn't know what he was doing. The real time was likely a full second slower. It really didn't matter. What Bob found amazing was that Percy had done so well despite the way that he ran. "He ran with his arms glued to his sides," said Bob. "He 'sat' on his stride, body erect, head bobbing, legs bent, seemingly pulling himself along with a foot action that called for almost no lift in his legs at all. As he neared the finish he 'broke' like a poorly trained trotting horse, and actually galloped the last few yards."[6]

The kid seemed a disaster. "I had never seen such a travesty of running form," Bob later concluded. "But neither had I ever seen, in all my years of watching track races, such a pair of legs! They moved like the pistons of a gasoline engine with somebody opening the throttle wider all the time."[7]

Ah, the legs. Percy's wonderful legs. Harry Warren, who would train with Percy that summer before heading off to Oxford, would speak of how "fluid" and "loose" they were in the knee joints.[8] Others would describe how Percy's legs seemed to pedal effortlessly along beneath his torso, giving the impression that he was floating down the track. In modern parlance, Percy seems to have had a natural ability to "relax" while he was sprinting, a deceptively simple-sounding concept that is very difficult to achieve on the track.

Any movement in the human body is accomplished by muscles working in opposition to each other. Bending your leg, for example, is performed by the quadriceps on the front of your thigh and the hamstrings on the back. Contract the quadriceps and the leg straightens; contract the hamstring and it bends. This action is of course key to running, but there are many more paired sets of muscles that come into play when a sprinter moves down the track: muscles in the calves, the feet, the buttocks, the hips, the torso and arms.

To run with maximum efficiency, it is important that when one muscle is contracting, the opposing muscle in the pair is relaxed. Achieving this while sprinting is known as being "relaxed." It is relatively easy to achieve during casual jogging, but in a sprint race it's a whole different matter. When making an all-out effort, pushing as hard as you can, the tendency is for muscles throughout the body to remain constantly tense, quads fighting against hamstrings and so on down the line, wasting precious energy, resulting in less speed, not more. When that happens a runner is said to be "tying up."[9]

In his race against Wally Scott, judging from Bob Granger's description, Percy tied up as he neared the tape. Before that happened, however, Bob beheld a startling glimmer of greatness. The King Ed student had a weak start, he didn't use his arms, he didn't lift his knees high enough and he was apt to lose form in the final few yards. But all that could be corrected through training. It was what Percy already possessed that caught Bob's eye, the amazing fluidity of his legs and the way he expended every ounce of energy when pressed. These were things Bob couldn't teach. They were a natural gift. As he put it, "I began to do some thinking."[10]

Bob's next encounter with Percy was in the middle of May, during one of the elimination meets to select finalists for the Inter-High competition. Bob congratulated him on another solid performance and offered a little advice. As Percy remembered it, he prefaced his comments with the brutal assessment: "You violate every principle known to the running game." Percy listened politely and said only, "Thank you, sir." He struck Bob as gentle and well-mannered. But there was something about his face, a firmness suggesting a foundation of strength underneath.[11]

Percy's dominance at the Inter-High was the final proof that Bob needed. Right there, on the field after the meet, he offered his services to Percy and invited him to join the Vancouver Athletic Club and begin serious training. Percy had been looking forward to a summer of biking and tennis and going to English Bay to swim and lie in the sun. Bob's offer, however, was too flattering to decline. To join the VAC and train alongside runners like Harry Warren, who he had known since childhood and looked up to — that would really be something.

Well, he told Bob, I'll have to ask my mother.

And so, toward the end of May 1926, Percy Williams began training with Bob Granger. Several times a week during his summer vacation, he took the streetcar across town and then hiked into Stanley Park to work with Bob and the Vancouver Athletic Club at the Brockton Point track. At other times he met Bob for private sessions on the baseball field at Athletic Park, surrounded by billboards advertising Coca Cola, Nabob Coffee, the White Spot Barbecue and BC Lumber.

The first thing Bob set out to do was to get Percy's priorities straight. From now on, he said, Percy was to play no more rugby and risk no further injury to his legs. His bad right knee was already enough of a problem. Dancing was out too. So was swimming, a particularly hard blow to Percy. It softened the muscles, Bob said.

With these ground rules laid out, Percy began to learn about the finer points of sprinting. A dash race, Bob explained, could be broken down into five stages: the start; the period of initial acceleration known as the pickup; the stride, from around twenty-five to eighty yards, where the runner builds up and then tries to maintain his momentum; the gather, where the runner draws on his last reserves to drive through the tape; and the finish, where he takes his last step. Percy needed work in all five stages.[12]

To begin with, he needed a more powerful start. Bob addressed this by having Percy dig his toe holes closer to the chalk line, thereby throwing more of his weight onto his arms so that his kick-off would propel him more forcefully forward. To respond more quickly to the gun, Bob stipulated that he take and hold a deep breath at the "set" command. Then, in that moment before the gun, he should focus not on his legs but on that first movement of his driving arm, leaving his legs to follow automatically.

Once the race was underway, there was little need for breathing. With deep breathing practice, that first breath should be enough to last to the fifty- or even the seventy-five-yard mark in a century dash, when a second breath could then be indulged in. This way, Bob explained, a runner was spared the distraction of breathing, the heaving in and out of the chest, wasting energy and cluttering up the mind. A discredited notion today, this was cutting-edge thinking in the 1920s, subscribed to by some of the top names in the game. Charlie Paddock, the most famous sprinter of the day, claimed that he ran most of his century races on just two lungfuls of air. "I never felt the need for a second breath," Charlie claimed, "until I was almost on the finish string."[13]

For the second and third stages of the sprint, the pickup and stride, Bob wanted Percy to raise his body up and lift his knees higher, overcoming his tendency to "sit" on his stride. He also needed to unglue his arms from his sides, moving them in a powerful pumping action from the shoulders. If this was done right, it would add significantly to the momentum generated by his legs.

The gather. Here lay Percy's greatest weakness, the one Bob noted in that race against Wally when he "galloped" in the final few yards. It was a common mistake with novice runners, and one that could only be corrected with training and experience racing. What you want to achieve, Bob said, is to maintain correct form all the way to the finish, even when you're pushing yourself to the limit in that closing drive. When you can do that in a century race; when you start making that extra effort work for you and not against you, you'll knock two-fifths of a second off your time. That's more than *twelve feet*.

The finish. In the twenties there were several moves that were regarded as useful in gaining a slight edge. First there was the "lunge," thrusting the torso forward at the tape, good for about a foot over a non-lunging opponent. Then there was the "shrug," a refinement of the lunge consisting of a forward lean coupled with a twist to thrust one shoulder forward and add a few extra inches. Finally, there was the "jump," developed by the incomparable Charlie Paddock. "It requires that the sprinter run high," Charlie explained, "'bounding' along. He must come down on the tape, gaining in speed and momentum as he makes his last leap." Charlie didn't generally recommend his jump finish, claiming only that it worked well for him. His critics called it showboating and of no use at all.[14]

Percy had a tendency to unleash a Paddock-style leap at the finish. He didn't do it consistently or consciously. It just happened sometimes. Bob considered the move needlessly risky, a drag on speed if mistimed or executed poorly, and he urged Percy to lunge or simply run straight through the tape. He had only partial success. In the years to come, when Percy was straining to the limit and running on instinct, he would occasionally find himself leaping like Paddock at the finish. It was a habit he would never be able to break completely.[15]

So much for lectures. It was time to get down to business. Bob spread a towel on the grass, motioned for Percy to lie down, extracted a jar of cocoa butter from his bag and started massaging his legs. It's all about keeping your muscles supple, he explained, working with surprising firmness. Less chance of injury and you'll run better. It was embarrassing for Percy at first but Bob clearly knew what he was doing. He was in fact decades ahead of most other coaches in his use of massage, a skill he had picked up solely through intuition and reading. And it seemed to work: when Percy stood up, his legs felt great.

Next, Bob set about with what he called "visualization." It was a technique he would use only with Percy, proceeding from the assumption that he was too delicate for the sort of training that more robust athletes like Harry Warren and Wally Scott could handle. First, he had one of the other VAC runners demonstrate the race elements Percy needed to work on: the proper starting crouch, the way to lead with his right arm coming out of the holes, how to raise his knees higher, how to move his arms with more power. Then Percy would try to incorporate these refinements into his own sprinting, running short dashes at three-quarter speed over just twenty or thirty yards under Bob's watchful eye. To further imprint correct form onto his brain, Percy was to practise these motions at home every day in front of a mirror. To build up his strength and flexibility, he was to skip rope and do stretching, calisthenics, push-ups and sit-ups.[16]

And that was it. In Bob's training regimen there would be no long stamina-building jogs for Percy, no weight training (a sure way to bind up the muscles, as any trainer in the 1920s would tell you), and surprisingly few century races and no furlongs run at top speed. As Bob saw it, big expenditures of energy were to be saved for meet racing. Starting in early June and continuing on through the summer, he accordingly entered Percy in every local event that came up, making real competition the core of his training.

First up was a weekly handicap meet organized by local sports impresario and Vancouver Athletic Club founder Bob Brown. Bob Granger was eminently familiar with handicap racing from his own days as a swimmer, competing in the floating enclosure at English Bay. As the strongest swimmer in the club, he sometimes started more than twenty seconds behind the others in a hundred-yard race, forced to swim his heart out to win.[17] For a race on a track, distance rather than time handicaps were employed, the runner considered fastest being positioned at the start line, or "scratch," the others taking their marks at various distances in front.

Percy was apprehensive when he showed up with his family at Brockton Point for that first Monday night meet, for he was about to run against seasoned athletes, the best in the whole province. He was entered in the fifty-yard event and the hundred. Because of his youth and inexperience he was accorded a handicap of two yards, starting between the stronger runners at scratch and the weaker ones at five yards.

Percy got away well enough in the final of the fifty, urged on by his mother and grandparents and Uncle Archie shouting themselves hoarse in the stands. His start lacked explosive power but it was getting better, and was good enough to keep him even. Then, in a display of acceleration that set Bob's heart to pounding, he surged ahead, opening up a sizable lead. As he neared the finish, however, it happened again, the speed-killing loss of form, the gallop. Percy managed to finish first but his lead had shrunk to mere inches. Much the same thing happened in the hundred-yard final, Percy surging out in front and then falling back as he neared the tape, this time to place second.

Bob was satisfied. Percy had run five races, a good session of sprinting that left him well exercised but not exhausted. His tendency to lose form toward the finish continued to be a problem, but one that Bob was betting would correct itself with training and as he ran more races.

And as for that moment of acceleration, that burst of speed that carried Percy away from the pack — that really stuck in Bob's mind. Witnessing that thing of beauty, he said, "I knew I had a gem."[18]

∽

Another solid performance by Percy in the following Monday night handicaps — it was the last time he would get a head start in a handicap race — and it was time for Vancouver's annual Police Sports.[19] The hundred-yard dash event was attracting entries from Vancouver, Victoria and Seattle, with the University of Washington track coach bringing up some of his talent, notably George Clarkson. It would be a step up in competition for Percy. Bob thought he was ready.

Percy wasn't so sure. "Me, run with those stars?" he exclaimed. "Why, I wouldn't have a chance. Clarkson is a 10-second man."[20] This early lack of confidence was typical for him. Bob would later claim that Percy wouldn't even agree to enter the race until he saw the prizes that were to go to the winners displayed in a storefront window that he and Bob happened to pass. They stopped to examine the hardware, in particular the attractive mantel clock that would go to the first-place finisher in the century event. "Gee Bob," said Percy. "I'd like to get that clock for my mother."

That was what it took, Bob said. With his heart set on the clock, Percy swallowed his reservations and went on to beat Clarkson and win first prize. Afterward, Percy seemed more excited about the prize than his victory. Trotting back up the track to his beaming coach, he blurted out, "Mom gets the clock!"[21]

Many years later Bob would tell a different story, shedding new light on the methods he used to motivate Percy. Percy, he said, "ran best on hate." To stoke his competitive fires before a meet, Bob made up stories about how Percy's opponents were bad-mouthing him, claiming he couldn't possibly win. On one occasion he even forged a letter belittling Percy, signing it with the name of a particular rival, then showed it to Percy and left him "stewing all night in his adrenalin" so that when he went out to race the next day he was determined to win.[22] Percy himself never directly confirmed any of this. In later years, however, he spoke of how Bob "egged me on, egged me on."[23]

To ensure that his budding star continued to get a steady diet of competition when there were no meets to enter, Bob started incorporating the handicap concept into their training sessions together. He invited some of Percy's high school track friends to join them, Bobby Gaul and Vernard "Pinky" Stewart and Geoff Inkster and others, forming a little group they called the Gang. There was never any doubt about it: Bob Granger was the boss and expected the boys to do what he said. At the same time, however, he made sure they had fun. He was generous with his time and with his money when he had it, buying track shoes and whatever other equipment they needed and treating them to meals. And he had a strange, beguiling manner about him, a way of losing himself in flights of fancy, regaling them with almost mythical tales of his past sporting glories, flattering them with nicknames from the track stars of the days: Paavo Nurmi, Joie Ray, Jackson Scholz and Charlie Paddock — and for Percy, already a hero to his schoolmates, the appellation "the Gazelle." "He was like a tin god to us kids," Pinky Stewart would say of Granger. "He could hold us spellbound with his stories about track." Pinky would also remember Bob's appetite: "Bob was a voracious eater — he could devour any number of steaks."[24]

Even the best runner in the Gang, Bobby Gaul, could not give Percy much of a challenge. With handicap racing, however, it didn't matter. By positioning Percy at scratch, Bobby at ten yards, and "Scholz" and "Nurmi" and "Paddock" as much as thirty yards out, Percy got all the competition he needed. It was an interesting method of training, not used much these days, but one of which Charlie Paddock — the real Paddock — would have approved. As Charlie saw it, being accustomed to coming from behind to win was the key to his own success as a runner. Like Percy, he was not particularly fast off the mark but once he got going he could work up incredible speed. Charlie liked it that way, ignoring the "experts" who said he needed to work on his starts. As he explained in his autobiography, *The Fastest Human*, an athlete who relies too much on a fast getaway is like a handicap runner who starts ahead of the others. In his mind he bases his chances for victory on his early advantage. If he then fails to achieve a flawless start or is subsequently passed, his advantage vanishes and with it his confidence too. "[He] says to himself, 'My advantage is wiped out. I'm gone,'" Paddock writes. "And he generally is."[25]

With his use of handicap racing, Bob Granger was habituating Percy to coming from behind to win — just like Paddock. Here lay the essence of the consistency of both runners. If they got away poorly in a race or found themselves lagging, it didn't shake them. It was what they were used to. Where other athletes upon realizing that they were trailing might feel a psychological letdown, for both Charlie and Percy it was just a signal to unleash that surge they possessed to shoot them into the lead. At their afternoon sessions at Brockton Point, Bob and his acolytes therefore were not simply giving their pal the Gazelle a meaningful workout. They were teaching Percy how to overcome a disadvantage to win.

∞

It was the middle of August and there was one final meet, the Caledonian Games, to close out the summer. University of Washington coach Hec Edmundson was coming up again from Seattle and this time he was bringing a squad that included George Clarke, his very best sprinter. Percy had by this point run two century races, on grass, in ten and one-fifth seconds, which pundits were quick to point out was equal to ten-flat on a cinder track.[26] Clarke, however, had a personal best of nine and four-fifths, and he was just back from the intercollegiate championships in Chicago where he had placed fifth in the hundred — making him the fifth fastest varsity sprinter in the entire USA. If running against Clarke's younger teammate Clarkson in the Police Sports had been daunting for Percy, the prospect of facing Clarke himself was downright appalling.

The Caledonian Games, a showcase for Scottish pastimes like piping and dancing and caber tossing mixed with modern track and field events, were held at Hastings Park that year, the biggest venue in the city. The track was normally used for horse racing. It was just plain dirt and remained scored with ruts and hoof marks even after raking. Percy was used to that. The American entries were not.

With Bob hovering nervously on the sidelines and the Gang hollering support from the stands, Percy got down to the business of working his way through the heats. He was stronger now after three months with Bob and a summer of racing, and made it easily into the finals. Standing in the lane beside George Clarke, however, it looked like he was about to meet his match. The powerfully built U of W runner, a "Greek god" as Bob called him, was a head taller than Percy, his knees coming up so high as he jogged on the spot that the thought passed through Percy's mind that he might get knocked under the chin if he ventured too close.[27]

One of the Gang, writing in the King Ed student paper, breathlessly described what happened next. "The runners came tearing down the horse racing track — neck and neck — the crowd amazed — spellbound — bewildered — the little schoolboy keeping up with the giant from the States — the great eight-foot strides of Clarke and the little flying strides of the Gazelle — now they are nearer — the crowd can't believe its eyes — the Gazelle is ahead — two feet in the lead — a whippet chasing a hare — then the last desperate burst for the tape — the last breathless moment — the almost paralyzed crowd jumping up in a sudden frenzy — a wild maddening cheer — desperate urges — 'Win!' — 'Win!'"[28]

Percy won. He was first through the tape with a Paddock-style leap, arms outstretched, Clarke trailing two feet behind. It was another ten-and-one-fifth-second finish for Percy, on a track that upon remeasuring was found to be two yards too long. As Bob saw it, that made Percy a ten-second runner, an "even time" man.[29]

As Percy was congratulated by the delirious Gang and collected his prize, Bob felt hugely satisfied. His protegé was shaping up nicely. Percy's starts were still nothing to brag about but his pickup and stride were close to perfection, his arms moving more effectively now, his legwork fast and fluid and performed seemingly without effort. And most important, he had overcome his tendency to gallop near the finish. He was not merely extending his smooth legwork all the way to the tape but was "changing gears" as Bob put it, using the energy he had saved in his coasting stride to launch a finishing drive, a final burst of acceleration when other runners had begun to slow down.[30]

It wasn't all peaches and cream, however. Handling Percy could be frustrating. Although polite and willing to follow instructions, he remained uncommitted to track and needed constant coaxing and urging. "I couldn't have cared less about running," he would later assert.[31] Then there was his lack of confidence. Despite everything Bob did to fire him up, spinning dreams of big meets and great honours and telling Percy how he would soon be able to challenge the world's top runners, Percy would just smile and shake his head and reply: Oh, I couldn't beat those fellows. As Bob privately complained in a letter to Harry Warren, "If that boy Williams had your backbone he would indeed be a real flier."[32]

Dealing with Percy's fragility was also a strain. Bob doled out his training in carefully measured doses, massaged his legs until his forearms burned and maintained a constant watch for overworked muscles, tendons and joints. But even that wasn't enough. On the evening following the Caledonian Games, Percy phoned to say his knee was sore. Feeling remorseful that he had pushed his boy too hard, Bob ordered a halt to training. That was it for track work for the rest of the year. The fall school term began and Bob tried to concentrate on his other athletes at UBC and King George High. He was anxious to get back to work with Percy but knew he had to be patient. He had a plan for his Gazelle — and it was a big one.[33]

CHAPTER 3

Hometown Hero

PERCY WAS RIDING IN the hills near Lytton, in the rugged BC interior to the northeast of Vancouver. Coming up here for a couple of weeks to stay with friends of the family had become a regular part of his life since the sickness, something to look forward to two or three times a year. His mother and his coach agreed that helping out at the camp was good for his heart, bringing in the hay and chopping wood and doing the sort of work that would toughen him up. And there was always time for roaming the hills on his horse Spot, armed with a rifle. That was something Percy particularly liked, heading into the wilderness with some of the fellows from camp or, like now, with his father. Fred Williams was just up the trail, leading the way.

Percy didn't know the details of why his parents split up. It was something no one talked about and he never questioned. He could see, however, the sadness it had left in his father, a sadness that he did not sense in his mother. And when he thought of Fred living alone in that hotel room it made him sad too. But he tried not to think about that. Being sentimental, after all, was just a form of weakness, a chink in the armour he was expected to wear as a man. That was one of the reasons why he liked it so much up here in the hills, going out riding. Complicated feelings, the uncertainties of life, that nagging vulnerability — all of it subsided and for a while everything became simple. It was just himself, his horse and his rifle.

He reined to a stop. Something had caught his eye, a patch of white under the trees off to the left. Now what do you suppose that is? he said, slipping to the ground and leading Spot off the trail.

It was a scattering of bones.

His father came back and they stood gazing at the bleached remains, mulling over possibilities. They concluded it must be an Indian burial ground.

They continued poking about the site for a while. Then Percy reached into his saddle bag and pulled out his camera. Hey Dad, he said, how about taking my picture.

He held the reins in one hand and struck a meditative pose, looking down at the jawless skull that he held in the other.[1]

∽

It was the spring of 1927 and Dot Williams had a new job. She was now cashier at the Capitol Theatre downtown, a cavernous 2,500-seat movie palace built in the grandest style, with carpeting, polished brass railings and velvet curtains of scarlet and gold. Featuring the latest films, vaudeville acts and musical performances by an in-house orchestra, the Capitol offered a gala entertainment experience for which patrons dressed up. They were being treated to some fine new pictures that season: John Barrymore in *The Beloved Rogue*; the boxing comedy *Knockout Reilly* with handsome Richard Dix; "Man of a Thousand Faces" Lon Chaney starring in *Mr. Wu*; and on one special evening a bathing beauty contest live on stage, the winner to represent Vancouver at the International Pageant of Pulchritude in Galveston, Texas. And almost as thrilling was that the Capitol's organ, where Sidney Kelland

▲ Percy Williams at about age three, with his father
Fred Williams. (BC SPORTS HALL OF FAME AND MUSEUM)

▲ Percy, age three, in a studio portrait, dressed as Cupid.
(BCSHFM)

▲ Percy easily leaving the competition behind in a childhood race. (BCSHFM)

A cartoon drawn by 12-year-old Percy ▶
during his term away from home at
St. Michael's School in Victoria, 1920.
(ST. MICHAEL'S UNIVERSITY SCHOOL)

◀ Percy holding a skull found
while on holiday in the interior
of BC, mid 1920s. (BCSHFM)

▲ Percy at centre training with Bob Granger, in the suit, and Harry Warren, far left. (CHARLOTTE WARREN)

▲ The King Edward High track and field team, 1927. Percy at centre in the "KE" top; Bobby Gaul the second boy to his right. (BCSHFM)

◀ Percy's high school graduation portrait. (BCSHFM)

▲ Percy floating to another victory at Brockton Point, 1927. (BCSHFM)

▲ Percy and Bob Granger outside the Williams' home. (BCSHFM)

▲ Bob Granger in his steward's outfit working his way to the Canadian Championships in Toronto. (BCSHFM)

▲ Disappointment: Percy loses to Cyril Coaffee in the 100-metre final, 1927. (BCSHFM)

▲ Percy wins the 100-metre final at the Canadian Championships, 1928. (BCSHFM)

◀ Percy, Johnny Fitzpatrick, Cap Cornelius and Buck Hester (left to right), Canadian Championships, Toronto, 1928. (CITY OF TORONTO ARCHIVES)

▲ Percy in his stance, wearing his Commerce High track togs, in 1928. (BCSHFM)

◄ Percy en route to the 1928 Olympics aboard the *Albertic*. (BCSHFM)

▲ Percy clowning around in Amsterdam, his arm around Doral Pilling. (BCSHFM)

◄ Percy returning to the dressing room after a preliminary 100-metre heat; Jack London looking off to the right. (BCSHFM)

worked his magic, was being replaced by a Wurlitzer being shipped out from the East, so big that it would take several railway cars to haul it. This notion of talking pictures about to become a big innovation — with Sidney on a Mighty Wurlitzer, who was going to care?

Percy was now a senior at King Ed High School, a local celebrity after his sprint triumphs the previous year. Every student from grade nine up knew all about the Eddies' very own Gazelle, "Motocrat Williams" — although if you were one of Percy's friends you also knew that his nickname was "Perce" or, more inexplicably, "Luke."[2] He had gone out for rugby at the start of the school year, no doubt to Bob Granger's immense aggravation, and had promptly twisted his ankle in his very first game. He contented himself with being the team's secretary-treasurer after that. He served as a school prefect, was company adjutant to the King Ed cadet corps and earned top shooting honours leading his team to victory in the inter-class rifle competition.[3]

He also formed a private club with his best friend Bobby Gaul and four others in his graduating class, complete with a custom-designed crest for their sweatsuits. They named themselves the "Hexamis," a Greek and French combination meaning "six friends." They hung out together and cultivated the latest slang, calling things they liked "nize" and "a beaner," brushing aside hogwash with "that's crushed apples," and adding emphasis to statements with "and how" or "eh what."[4] "Luke's" track shoes, meanwhile, gathered dust in the closet.

Bob Granger for his part was keeping busy with his unpaid coaching. In January 1927 he was "hired" to train the UBC track and field athletes, adding to the work he was already doing with the intermediate rugby squad, and then he took on coaching the ice hockey team as well.[5] For all this labour he wasn't paid a cent. As an editorial in the university's student paper bemoaned in March of that year, "This University is probably unique in that it is the only college of its size on the continent having no paid athletic coaches. All the men who guide the various Varsity teams give their services voluntarily, turning out regularly all season, in all kinds of weather, simply for the sake of the Varsity and love of the game."[6]

Bob loved the game, all right. He did have hopes, though, of a reward from UBC that would be more substantial than mere satisfaction. If he continued to build on his reputation as one of the hardest working and most versatile coaches in the province, there was a chance the university would appoint him their first paid coach when they finally came around to accepting that money had to be spent on athletics.

With this thought tucked away in the back of his mind, Bob gave UBC countless hours of his time, on the playing field, at the rink, on the track. He was even involved in the construction that spring of the university's new running oval, promised to be "one of the firmest and fastest tracks in the West," with a proper surface of crushed cinders laid down to the depth of nearly a foot.[7] With this fine new facility in the offing, he proceeded to drive the track team to a higher level, announcing regularly scheduled practices in place of the irregular, unsupervised workouts of the past. Everyone was to turn out at the track well bundled, "a heavy sweater or sweat shirt and a pair of long underwear over your outfit. Wool is preferable. Even when coming out to the workouts in early spring it is advisable to wear such an outfit." As the team would discover, Coach Granger was very particular that his athletes keep warm.[8]

While Bob's UBC track squad included a few talented runners, no one approached Percy's potential. Bob had been champing at the bit all through the fall and winter to get back to polishing his gem. He would remember the exact day they resumed their training together: Sunday, March 20, 1927.

Percy showed up looking fresh and healthy, a bit heavier than he had been the previous summer, around 120 pounds, and ready to run. They had two months to get ready for the first event on the year's agenda, the Inter-High competition — two months of carefully supervised training, lots of massages and double sweaters for warmth. Percy was like a thoroughbred racehorse now. He needed careful handling.[9]

He began the Inter-High with almost ridiculous ease. In the preliminary elimination rounds he took the top qualifying spot in both the century and furlong without even bothering to take off his sweatsuit, staying well within his limits and still winning by yards. It rained. It poured. The track was soaked. Racing conditions were horrid but it hardly seemed to matter. In fact, it *didn't* matter as far as Percy was concerned. Only times posted in the final Inter-High meet would be considered official, when the full complement of five timekeepers was on hand, along with all the inspectors and judges. That was when he would need a dry track.[10]

He didn't get it. Monday, May 23, was another rainy day. Percy glumly packed his gear into his bag, his new spikes on top, presented to him by Emslie Yeo with the words: "Here's something to help you break these records with, Percy." It didn't look like he would be breaking any records today, not with the Brockton Point track muddy and soft.

Out at the Point, after Bob's massage, Percy put on two pairs of sweatpants and four sweaters and stepped onto the track for a light warming-up session, only five minutes. Then it was back to the sidelines to lie immobile under a pile of blankets. The whole point, as Bob saw it, was to get Percy warmed up with the minimum expenditure of energy. When it was time for Percy to race, Bob even dug his starting holes for him.

First up was the hundred-yard dash. Released from his blankets, Percy was "warm as toast," and after two or three practice starts was ready to go. Bob kept him in the sweats and sweaters until the last moment. Then, as Percy was taking his marks, Bob raced down to the finish with his clothes so that he could re-bundle his boy the moment he was first through the tape.

Bob was still running when the gun sounded. He turned and saw with a jolt that Wally Scott was at the head of the pack. What was going on? Was his old student really that good? But then his eyes settled on Percy, flying up the side, well in front of Wally. He was coasting smoothly, and then came the changing of gears, the finishing drive, and suddenly he was yards in front of Wally, yards and yards in front of Wally. He rocketed through the tape with Bob hurrying to catch up on the sidelines, running awkwardly with an armful of sweats and wool sweaters.

The time was good. Three watches caught Percy at 10 seconds, one at 9 9/10, one at 9 4/5. The judges ruled it a ten flat, "even time," a new BC high school record. It would remain unbroken for thirty-four years. As the stands erupted with cheering, Bob got Percy back into his sweats and under the blankets.

The furlong race went just as well. Percy finished a long way in front of his nearest rival in 22 1/5 seconds, a provincial high school record by nearly one and a half seconds and a Canadian scholastic record to boot. But this was no longer mere high school running. Consider: three years before, at the 1924 Paris Olympics, Jackson Scholz had won the gold medal in the two hundred metres in the record time of 21 3/5 seconds, running under clear skies on a cinder track that was dry and fast. Percy had posted his time of 22 1/5 seconds over a furlong, a distance roughly 1.2 metres longer, and had run through mud to do it, at one point leaping over a puddle.

It was all the proof that Bob needed. His boy was ready to compete with the best in the world.[11]

ॐ

It was time to begin the campaign that Bob had been planning for Percy since the previous summer, the long march that would take them to the Olympics. The standards to qualify for the Western sectionals in Edmonton, leading to the nationals in Toronto, had just been announced in the papers. The times were slower than what Percy had just run in the rain. He was a shoo-in.[12]

The first step in the journey east would be the provincial championships, scheduled for Brockton Point on Saturday, July 23. Percy spent the day before quietly at home. He had orders from Bob not to overexert himself, so he didn't do much. It felt a bit funny, sitting around like this after having worked so hard to pass his grade twelve exams. They had been tough. More than half his classmates had failed at least one and were now cramming for the supplementals later that summer. But he had made it on the first try. That made him a high school graduate, with his whole life ahead.[13]

Of the opportunities that lay before him, most promising was an athletic scholarship to the University of Washington that track coach Hec Edmundson had first offered verbally and that Percy now had in writing. They had a program in commerce, which Percy wanted to study, and were promising to pay his tuition and all his expenses. Bob, meanwhile, was talking up the University of British Columbia, where Percy's presence on the track team would make the varsity Blue and Gold a serious threat. UBC, however, didn't offer athletic scholarships and lacked any sort of business program. All in all, Seattle was looking like his best bet.[14]

The day waned and Percy sat down to supper, then he checked what was on the Radiola. Some singing and banter on the CJOR dinner program, an orchestra on CFDC, the other local stations off the air. Around seven o'clock he heard a commotion in the street and followed Grandpa Harry and Uncle Archie outside. People were gathering to watch an enormous pall of smoke billow up from one of the False Creek sawmills. All that lumber down there, Grandpa Harry was saying. It's like a tinderbox. All it takes is a spark.

Percy gazed at the spectacle as the evening light faded and the flames were brought under control, then drifted back into the house and got ready for bed. Bob had told him to get a good night's sleep.[15]

∽

The provincial trials kicked off with the women's hundred-yard dash and the big men heaving the shot put and hammer. Then it was time for the men's century race. The list of entries was short, necessitating just two qualifying heats to pick the six for the final. Percy knew most of them, names like Urquhart, Cathcart, Oliver, Moffat, McLaren, men he had beaten in handicap races in which they were accorded head starts.

His first race, a qualifying heat for the final, was a cakewalk. He ran smart, maintaining his lead but otherwise coasting to conserve his strength, winning in the slow time of 10 4/5 seconds. Then, in the final, he opened up, winning in 10 1/5. It wasn't his best time but it equalled the qualifying standard for the nationals. So far so good. He then did the same in the furlong, an easy coasting run to get into the final, where he opened up to win in 22 4/5 seconds, again equalling the standard. He had qualified for the journey east.[16]

But then the provincial Olympic committee got together to make its selection of athletes and decided to send . . . no one at all. There wasn't enough money, they said. There was just enough to send one local official.[17] As the delegate packed his bags and bought his first-class ticket, Bob and Percy sank into disappointment.

Then they started doing some thinking. They weren't out yet.

The Olympic committee had clearly stated that it was lack of money, not lack of talent, which had prevented them from sending Percy to the nationals. No one questioned that he had met the standard. Why then couldn't he head east on his own? All they needed was money — and Bob had an idea how they could raise it. It came from a little piece in the paper, relating how Charlie Paddock had recently set a world record of 17 4/5 seconds in the 175-yard dash at a meet in Salt Lake City.[18]

Now, 175 yards was a pretty odd distance to run for a record. But it was vintage Paddock, practically the inventor of showmanship on the track. Not content to set records in the more conventional distances, Charlie made a career out of claiming titles that no one contested, "collecting records in wholesale lots" as his old University of Southern California coach Dean Cromwell once put it. He would turn out at big meets in a set of turquoise or burgundy or powder blue togs and proceed to thrill the folks who bought the tickets with a record-setting performance over 90 or 125 or 300 yards. At a particularly memorable event in April 1921, he managed to set four such records in one afternoon, three of them in a single race, sprinting through a succession of tapes. It was that spring that sportswriters began calling him "The Fastest Human."[19]

It wasn't just a matter of vanity. Charlie did it for self-promotion, to cultivate his reputation for speed so that the opportunities and offers kept rolling in and the appearance money stayed good. More than any other amateur athlete in the 1920s, he knew how the system worked — and he worked it with relish. "He was a great publicity man," mused rival Jackson Scholz decades later. "I envied him. I wish I had known something about that."[20]

So did Bob Granger. But he was learning. After doing a little calculation, he realized that Paddock's record over 175 yards wasn't really so fast and that Percy could do better. Percy at first was skeptical. After Bob broke it down on paper, however, extrapolating from the furlong times Percy had already posted, the idea didn't seem quite so far-fetched. As amazing as it sounded, maybe he *could* beat a Paddock record.

The attempt was made on August 9 at the second annual Vancouver and District Playgrounds Meet. After the scheduled slate of youth dashes and sack races, the wheelbarrow event, the baseball toss, the potato-balanced-on-a-spoon run, Percy stripped off his sweatsuit and thrilled the fans with a hundred-yard sprint to warm up. Then it was time to take a crack at the record. To furnish Percy with competition, two other runners started out in front at the fifteen- and twenty-yard marks. The gun sounded and Percy got away to an exceptionally good start, instantly gaining back two yards. They headed round the first turn, hit the hundred-yard mark on the straightaway and already Percy had taken the lead, seventy yards to go with no one left to chase. He wasn't used to pushing himself to the limit running solely against the clock but he managed to find that second gear and flashed through the tape in what Bob sensed was good time.

The timekeepers huddled. They had all caught Percy in exactly the same time. The distance was remeasured and found to be correct. And so the announcement was made: Vancouver's own Percy Williams had just run 175 yards in 16 4/5 seconds. It was a new record, shattering Paddock's mark by a full second. *Nize!*[21]

It didn't count, of course. For a record to be considered, special application had to be made beforehand to the Amateur Athletic Union and a host of stringent conditions met at the meet. But it did stir up the crowd, which had been the point, and was a good lead-in to Bob's appeal for funds to send this marvel, Vancouver's own Gazelle, to the nationals to show those Easterners the sort of boys they raised in BC. With these words ringing in the air, Pinky Stewart and Bobby Gaul and Percy's other friends stepped forward to pass the hat. It came back heavy with coins.

Unfortunately, they were mostly pennies and nickels and didn't add up to much. A second appeal was made at the Caledonian Games in August, where Percy won both the open century event and the handicap dash on the Hastings Park horse track. Another hatful of coins but still not enough. Finally, with time running out, the head of the Vancouver Athletic Club, Bob Brown, kicked in the rest.[22]

At last they had the money they needed, enough for a cheap upper berth for Percy on the Trans-Canada Limited bound for Toronto, leaving on August 15 at half past six in the evening. Bob managed to finagle a job on the same train, serving ice cream and washing dishes to pay his way.[23] They packed their bags and excitedly hurried down to the CPR station, seen off by Percy's family and friends and a small group of supporters. As the train pulled away and into the wilderness to the east of the city, Percy settled into his compartment and Bob put on an apron in the pantry car and got down to work.

There was just one more thing left to worry about: the Dominion Track and Field Championships and Olympic Trials were scheduled to begin in five days in Toronto — and it would take them five days to get there by train.

CHAPTER 4

Going East

THE TRANS-CANADA LIMITED chuffed to a stop in a cloud of steam at Toronto's Union Station. It was August 20, eight o'clock in the morning. Percy, the detritus of his five-day journey stuffed back into his bag, followed the other passengers out of the car, down the platform and into the station's vast marbled hall. The place had only opened a week before and still smelled of wet concrete. The noise of the swirling crowds echoed in the cavernous space.

Bob had work left to do in the pantry car and would follow along later. Percy would have to go ahead on his own. He first had to find his way to the downtown YMCA where he and Bob would be staying. Then he had to get to Varsity Stadium, wherever that was. The Canadian nationals and Olympic trials were scheduled to begin there in less than six hours.[1]

The trip out had begun with a tremendous burst of excitement, the first real trip for either Percy or Bob outside BC. A poster in Vancouver's

CPR Station had promised "The Rockies by Daylight," and that was what they got, magnificent mountain vistas stretching for miles and miles, jagged snowy peaks soaring high above a carpet of forest. Then, after Calgary, they got onto the prairies and the enforced idleness and lack of sleep began to take a toll on Percy. Bob, working in the pantry car, didn't fare much better. By the time they reached the Ontario border they were both feeling tired and stiff.[2]

The vast expanse of Lake Superior was the view out the window when Percy started on his first letter home. He had particularly wanted to use the elegant stationery with "Canadian Pacific Railway en route" embossed in red at the top. "Dear Mother," he carefully began, trying to steady his hand as the carriage swayed back and forth. "This train riding isn't what it's cracked up to be. It starts to get monotonous after a couple of days, especially the prairies. I never saw anything so flat in all my life. . . .

"Coming thru we stopped in Winnipeg. It seems to be a good sized town, it's just the right place for a Ford. There isn't one hill within miles. At Winnipeg we changed diners. I thought that would be tough luck as I had become friendly with the cook and waiters but the new diner is even better. I've only had three meals on it so far but they won't take my money for them. They are all good sports.

"This trip I had to have an upper berth on the train. Well, find someone who has had to sleep in an upper berth and ask them how they managed getting up and going to bed. It takes me half the night to get undressed and the remainder of the night to get back in my clothes. It's just like getting under a table to dress. It's too small to stand up so you have to lay down to dress.

"This running is a lot of applesauce. I won't be able to walk let alone run tomorrow. Riding in trains certainly stiffens a fellow. Bob says I should have been there a week ago to get some of the kinks out of my legs, but since there isn't any chance of me winning I shouldn't worry, I got a good trip out of it anyway."[3]

∽

There was a big turnout at Varsity Stadium at the University of Toronto. Track and field seemed to be popular again after the long decline brought on by the Great War. Nearly five thousand tickets had been sold, far more than expected, with complimentary programs in such short supply that spectators were offering to buy them from earlier arrivals. Down in front a row of seats was roped off. These were for the members of the Canadian Olympic Committee who would be attending to size up the talent. Percy found the dressing room and got into his Vancouver Athletic Club togs and his sweatsuit. No sign of Bob. He was probably somewhere in the stands. Out on the track Percy took a few short sprints to warm up, just enough to work up a light perspiration. From now on, Bob never tired of telling him, preserving his energy was the name of the game, staying warm and loose for racing with the minimum of work.

There was Bob. He had come down from his seat in the bleachers and was standing at the edge of the track. Now remember, boy, he said, you've got some work ahead of you and you'll have to run smart. There'll be three rounds in the century and three in the furlong. That's six races before we can go get some supper. You don't need to win your heats. Just race your man and qualify and get yourself into the next round. Save the precious energy as much as you can. Then give it all you've got in the final.

There were thirty-five men entered in the sprints, thirty-five of the best dash men in the country. Cyril Coaffee was at the top of the list. A strapping, thick-necked Winnipeg native, Cyril had a peculiar running style on account of a partially paralyzed arm that forced him to lean forward. Some pundits claimed that it was this disability that made him so fast, his tilt forcing him to develop tremendous driving power in his legs to keep from tumbling over. Whatever it was, his unorthodox form worked. Since the start of the decade he had reigned supreme as the fastest Canadian with titles in the 100- and 220-yard dashes, the former in 9 3/5 seconds, tying the world record set by Charlie Paddock in 1921.

As was the case with many of the nation's premier athletes, Cyril no longer lived in Canada. For the past five years he had made Chicago his home, where he was fixed up with a comfortable job and taken care of by the affluent Illinois Athletic Club in exchange for wearing their crest. He did most of his running in the States but returned to Canada for the nationals every year to defend his crown as the fastest man in the country. In August 1927 he was also back for a second reason: to secure a spot on the Canadian Olympic team that would be sent to Amsterdam the following year. Cyril had already represented Canada twice at the Olympics, at Antwerp in 1920 and Paris in 1924. On both occasions he had failed to get into the finals. Now he had his sights set on making his third Olympic team, a tremendous accomplishment by itself, and getting another chance at a medal. He was already thirty years old, so it would be his last chance.[4]

A second strong contender was George "Buck" Hester, a short, husky runner with a personal best in the century of 9 4/5. Another expatriate Canadian, born in Toronto and ostensibly from Windsor, Buck had actually grown up in Detroit, where he was named Michigan high school track and field athlete of the year for an unprecedented three years running, 1921 to 1923, and won a track scholarship to the University of Michigan. He earned his keep as a U of M Wolverine by winning two Big Ten athletic conference sprint championships and a spot on the Canadian Olympic team in 1924. Like Cyril Coaffee, Hester had been eliminated in the early rounds at the Paris Games and had returned home empty-handed. And like Coaffee, he wanted another chance. He was twenty-five years old and had just one more year at the U of M. His time on the track too would soon be over.[5]

Other strong contenders included Leigh Miller of Halifax, the fastest man in the Maritimes and one of the fastest in Canada as well. He reportedly had run the century in Nova Scotia in 9 3/5 seconds but the time was not recognized because meet standards were assumed to be suspect.[6] There was also James "Buster" Brown of Edmonton, winner of the century dash two weeks previously at the Western trials. Harley Russell and Campbell Maybee of the University of Toronto were hometown favourites. Russell, lately based in Chicago, was said to be in particularly fine shape. Fast times were also expected from Winnipegger Laurie Cohen, who had run a close second to Coaffee at the nationals the previous year.

Finally, there was the crew from the Hamilton Olympic Club, the richest and most prestigious athletic club in the country, with a total of thirty-five athletes and entries in almost every event. In the sprints their top men were Ralph Adams and Johnny Fitzpatrick. Johnny, at twenty a year older than Percy, was being especially touted. Well-built and ruggedly handsome, a hint of boxer Gene Tunney in his chiselled features, he had made a name for himself in high school on the Hamilton Collegiate Institute track squad and was now the HOC's premier sprinter. His praises were being sung even south of the border, where just the month before Johnny had won both sprint events at an inter-scholastic meet at the University of Pennsylvania. Penn track coach Lawson Robertson gushed afterward that "he is the greatest young prospect I have ever seen."[7]

The first event of the afternoon was the hundred-yard dash. Bob was back in his seat and Percy was now on his own. At a big meet like this coaches and trainers were not allowed on the field. The only people who could set foot on the track and the grass were the groundskeepers and the swarm of officials often referred to as "badgers" — the time-keepers, judges and inspectors with identification badges pinned to their blazers — and of course the athletes themselves. As Percy lounged in the shade on the edge of the field, Harley Russell won the first heat and Johnny Fitzpatrick the second. Then it was his turn. Percy began digging his holes. Back in Vancouver Bob had often done this for him. Bob had made a careful study of the ideal hole shape and knew the best way to craft them. Of the four other runners digging in the lanes beside Percy, the toughest competition would likely come from Buck Hester and Ralph Adams.

It wasn't Ralph's day. He got away to a terrible start. By the time he was up and out of his holes, Buck and Percy were a yard ahead and had the race to themselves, running almost even most of the way to the tape. In the last few yards Percy eased up, saving himself by coasting to a second-place finish, good enough to advance. To Bob, watching from the stands, his boy had done well. Percy had not shown his best form — understandable considering those five days on the train — but he had looked all right and had run a smart race. With the kinks now worked out, he'd likely show better in the semis.

Thirty minutes later Percy was back on the track to face Cyril Coaffee. Beating him would be a tall order. But this was a semifinal and so it wasn't about winning. It was just about advancing.

The wind had picked up. It was whipping the stadium flags and blowing straight in their faces. The gun sounded, the runners got away, and almost immediately Bob's heart sank. Percy was galloping again. Maybe he was unnerved by running against the Canadian champion and was trying too hard. "Imagine my feelings," Bob writes, "as he raced at the side of the great and graceful Coaffee in that style. True, he'd shown them better form in his preliminary, but in that semifinal, when the pinch came, he'd all but failed."[8] Cyril crossed the finish first in 10 1/5 seconds. Percy, struggling most of the way, came second.

Things now became confusing. At just about any major track meet, a second-place finish in a semifinal guaranteed a spot in the final. Most major meets, however, were held on tracks with six lanes. The Varsity Stadium track had only five. To accommodate this fact, meet organizers had adopted an awkward qualification process for the final: the winner of each of the three semis would advance, plus the second-place finishers in the two fastest races. This meant that Johnny Fitzpatrick, Cyril Coaffee and Laurie Cohen were in. They had won their semis. Buck Hester was also in as having placed second in the fastest race. That left one more spot — and Percy and Buster Brown equally deserved it. They had both placed second in semis won in ten and one-fifth.

The officials hadn't anticipated this. They went into a scrum and came up with two options: Buster and Percy could race each other for the remaining spot, or they could flip a coin. Of course it was no choice at all. The additional expenditure of energy required for a race-off would leave the winner too tired to be any good in the final. Buster and Percy chose the coin.

Percy lost.

It was a stunning setback. He had travelled all the way across Canada, a distance of nearly three thousand miles; he had run second in both his heat and his semi despite lack of exercise and sleep during the five-day journey, and here he was eliminated by a coin toss. Confused, embarrassed, disappointed, Percy did the only thing he could think of: he shrugged and accepted the decision without a word of complaint. Then, when the runners were assembling for the final, he jogged over to the start line to shake hands with Buster, a fellow Westerner, and wish him good luck. From their seats in the front row, the luminaries of the Canadian Olympic Committee looked on with nodding approval, impressed that a teenager would behave in such a gentlemanly fashion. That was what amateur athletics was supposed to be all about. The crowds in the stands were also impressed. As Percy shook Buster's hand, they started clapping.[9]

With Percy watching from the sidelines, Cyril Coaffee went on to win the final of the hundred in just a fifth off the world record, trailed by Johnny Fitzpatrick and Laurie Cohen. They had pushed Cyril hard, running into a headwind. Without the wind he likely would have equalled Paddock's record again.

Although Percy didn't breathe a public word of dissatisfaction about his coin-toss elimination, the experience rankled and he never forgot it. Recalling the episode a half-century later, details altered by the passage of time, it was clear that he felt bitter. "After the heats," he said in an interview in 1978, "six of us qualified for the final of the 100. Then one of the badgers suddenly discovered — I think he may have taken off one of his shoes and counted the toes to make sure — that the track had only five lanes, not six. But they had the solution. There were two runners from western Canada, Buster Brown of Edmonton and myself. So they tossed a coin to see which one of us would have to drop out. I lost. I didn't get to run."[10]

Percy still had one more chance, the 220-yard dash. It was to be run like the hundred, with that tricky business with the coin to determine who would get into the final. Percy, determined not to take any chances this time, pushed hard to win his preliminary heat with ease, then pushed harder still to win his semi, forcing second-place finisher Johnny Fitzpatrick into a coin-toss with Laurie Cohen to advance to the final. Whereas Percy's elimination from the century under identical circumstances had excited little complaint, a storm now erupted over Johnny. The large contingent from the Hamilton Olympic Club, led by its president, Bobby Robinson, raised a vehement protest. But there was no way around it. A coin had to be tossed and Johnny chose the wrong side. The folks from Hamilton were not at all pleased.[11]

The sun was low when Percy went to work on his starting holes for the two-twenty final, his fifth and last race of what had already been a gruelling afternoon. It was his last chance to show his stuff, time to unleash everything, burn off every bit of whatever energy he had left. In the lane beside him, Campbell Maybee still looked fresh. He was the only finalist who had not competed in the hundred. On the other side, Cyril Coaffee wasn't looking so good. He had run one more race than Percy, that tough century final, and was showing signs of fatigue. Cyril had in fact privately confided that he didn't think he had enough left for the furlong. "I think Fitzpatrick will win," he told one newsman. "I don't think I can beat him." But then Johnny got tossed.[12]

Percy got away poorly at the gun and was lagging right from the start. As the runners rounded the first turn and hit the seventy-yard mark he was already twelve yards behind, trailed only by Laurie Cohen. Then, with a burst of speed that had Bob up out of his seat, Percy surged and started closing the gap, reeling himself up to Maybee in the lead and Coaffee and Leigh Miller as if he were joined to them by a string.

But it didn't last. It couldn't. The lingering fatigue and stiffness from the train; the anxiety of the rushed journey; the exertion of the past four races — as Percy came into the stretch it all began to catch up. He reached down for his finishing drive but couldn't find it. He was done. His tank was empty. The gap was widening again when Coaffee began his kick and was first through the tape. Miller, challenging right to the end, was second, followed by Maybee. Percy was fourth.[13]

The day was over and for Bob it was a big disappointment. He knew that it would serve as valuable seasoning for Percy, but still . . . he had wanted to *win*. Percy was disappointed too. A year of Bob's infectious confidence, his egging on, his soaring predictions — it had all had its intended effect. Although Percy did not dare admit it, although a part of him feared it, he wanted to be a champion. He wanted those cheers that were being given to Cyril Coaffee.[14]

Still, he could not begrudge Coaffee his laurels. The meet for Cyril had been a triumph, another Canadian championship under his belt, another victory added to the more than 250 he had accumulated so far in Canada and the States. "It will be many years," enthused the *Hamilton Spectator*, "before Canada can boast of a sprinter to rival the smooth-running Winnipegger." As for his ambition of making his third Olympic team, the first Canadian ever to do so, *Toronto Star* sportswriter Lou Marsh was of the opinion that Cyril "seems to have done everything toward that end but hoist himself aboard the boat."

But there was something more about Cyril, something you had to be up close to see — up close where Percy was now. The way the man with the paralyzed arm pushed himself was a revelation. He was a champion because he had real guts. When the furlong final, his sixth race of the day, was over, Cyril was so exhausted that he had difficulty getting to a nearby tap for a desperately needed drink of water, and he had to lie on the grass for a time before summoning strength enough to walk off the field. Afterward, following the other athletes into the dressing room, he slowly stripped off his gear and stepped under the shower. And then he just stood there, trembling from the strain of the day.[15]

CHAPTER 5

Olympic Year

PERCY HAD A LOT OF thinking to do on the long trip back to Vancouver. He had been urged to remain in Toronto to see the sights and compete in a track and field extravaganza to be held in two weeks at the Canadian National Exhibition. He declined. It was almost September and the new school year was about to begin — and his plans for furthering his education had just been shot to pieces.

Bob wasn't with him. He was having the time of his life on his first trip to the East and didn't want it to end. He adored wandering about Toronto, exploring the city, and was keen to visit the Exhibition to study the top sprinters at the upcoming meet and to watch the Lake Ontario marathon swim, which he would find particularly exciting. "Believe me boy," he later wrote in a letter, "I arose at 2 a.m. and beat it down to the exhibition and parked on one of the seats right on the finish line. There were only 200 seats for 200,000 people. I stayed there till 10:10 p.m. Boy, some seat — never again." To keep himself in funds,

Bob found a job in a factory making boxes for meat cutters. "Some job, when I did get them finished the blame meat cutters wouldn't fit in."[1]

Arriving back in Vancouver, Percy had a decision to make. Attending the University of Washington with its generous scholarship offer was now out of the question — or so he thought after Olympic officials in Toronto warned him against going to the States. He might well have asked why, considering the number of athletes competing alongside him at the trials who were based in the US, first and foremost among them Cyril Coaffee.

Cyril in fact was at the heart of the problem. For all his talent and success, he stuck in the craw of the Canadian Olympic Committee. He was the epitome of what they regarded as the problem of Canada's best athletes being lured to the States, spending most of their time and talent in competition south of the border and returning home every four years to claim a spot on the Olympic team. It was a source of resentment that had been building for several years, and at that very moment the committee were doing something about it. At the COC meeting held in conjunction with the national trials it was decided that henceforth any athlete who resided outside Canada could be deemed ineligible to represent the country at international meets. If Cyril remained in Chicago, under the new rule he would be barred from the next year's trials and in turn the Olympics.[2]

And so would Percy if he allowed himself to be enticed to Seattle. The *Daily Province* put it plainly: "Williams was to have entered the University of Washington this fall, but through pressure brought to bear by the Canadian Olympic Committee, he was persuaded to remain in Canada so that he could try out for the Olympic team."[3]

Percy wasn't sorry not to go to Seattle. He was glad to remain in Vancouver. Attending university there, however, wasn't an attractive proposition. UBC had no program in business, which was what Percy wanted to study, and did not offer athletic scholarships, making the annual tuition and related expenses a burden for his family. He therefore decided against it, much to the disappointment of some, and opted instead for the High School of Commerce, which shared the familiar premises of good old King Ed. "Commerce" had an intensive business program for high school graduates, tuition-free to those from Vancouver, that crammed three years of study into one, just the thing for getting quickly started on a white-collar career. Within three weeks of his return home, Percy was hard at work studying bookkeeping and accounting and office procedures, business-letter writing and typing and Pittman shorthand.[4]

∽

Nineteen twenty-eight. The Olympic year. On March 10, a Saturday, Percy packed up his sweatsuit and took his spikes out of the closet and headed west on Twelfth Avenue to resume training with Bob. His intensive program at Commerce was keeping him too busy most days to travel across town to Brockton Point. For most of their sessions together they would meet on the baseball field at Athletic Park, a brisk thirty-minute walk from Percy's house and less than half that from school. It didn't have an actual track but the grass outfield was spacious and reasonably free of potholes.

Percy as usual was in less than prime condition at the start of the season. He hadn't run a race since the previous November, an indoor fifty-yard sprint at the Hastings Park horse arena, which he won in 5 3/5 seconds, tying Bobby Kerr's longstanding Canadian record. He had strained his leg at the meet, stepping in a hoof print hidden under the sawdust, necessitating a long break from training. When they met at Athletic Park Bob started him off gently with massages, some light jogging and a few starts, keeping a close lookout for signs of strain. And that was it. The Olympic campaign was on.[5]

Over at Commerce, meanwhile, an unexpected track obligation had arisen for Percy. Vice Principal Graham Bruce had just formed the school's first track team to take advantage of the fact that four of the city's best high school sprinters were now enrolled there: Percy Williams, Wally Scott, Dave Hendry and Bob Dixon. With these four boys, Bruce was confident laurels could be won for Commerce.

It was Coach Bruce who got Percy into his first competition of the season. In early May he took him and the rest of the squad down to

Seattle to compete in the annual Washington State Relay Carnival, a prestigious meet that attracted the top American high school and collegiate runners in the Pacific Northwest. Bob Granger went along. He wasn't expecting much from Percy, at least not yet. After five weeks of careful training his boy was only just at the point where they were chancing real bursts of speed in practice. As Bob saw it the meet was a tune-up, a chance to shake out the kinks, the first step in building Percy up through competition to the fine pitch he needed to attain for the more important work ahead.

Percy surprised him. He won his very first race of the season, a hundred-yard dash, in 9.9 seconds, bettering "even time" for the first time in his life. Then, after a short rest, he was back on the track to run anchor in the 4 x 220-yard relay. The Commerce squad won it easily, beating the meet record by more than two and a half seconds. "Broke two records, relay and hundred," Percy cabled excitedly home to his mother.[6] Coach Bruce was ecstatic as the team headed back to Vancouver, enthusing that Percy was going to be one of the world's greatest sprinters. Percy, reluctant as always, passed it off as a joke.[7]

Next up was the Inter-High competition. Percy hadn't expected to compete. He had thought that the previous year's Inter-High, when he ran as a King Ed senior, would be his last. Now, in May 1928, he found that he was eligible again to run, this time for Commerce. For Percy it was an anti-climax to his career as a high school runner and was not likely to offer the sort of challenge he now needed. The handicap racing he had resumed with Bob was really more useful, chasing down the "Leaping Whippet," the nickname Granger had given to Percy's training partner, Bobby Gaul.[8] As a member of the Commerce track team, he nevertheless had to do his duty. Coach Bruce was once again expecting great things.

Bruce got the victories he wanted. At the Inter-High finals on May 23, Percy won both the century and the furlong and his teammates took second and third, making it a sweep for Commerce. The Commerce squad then capped off the afternoon with a resounding win in the senior boys' relay, smashing the meet record by almost six seconds, the second-place team trailing far, far behind.[9] Coach Bruce was satisfied. But not everyone was. There were those who felt that Percy hadn't tried hard enough, particularly in the hundred; that he had exerted himself just enough to win and had not run his fastest, thereby demonstrating that he maybe lacked heart. "Williams practically loafed through the hundred," tut-tutted the *Daily Province*. "He did not run his best through the final 50 yards, never once trying his best," added sportswriter Robert Elson, a former King Ed track man. "For a man who is to represent British Columbia at the Canadian finals it was neither reassuring nor good testimony of his ability."[10]

Bob Granger publicly rushed to Percy's defence, making much of his slip at the start of the hundred and generally making the excuses, the "alibis," that Percy disdained. Privately, however, he must have been pleased at the knocks. When he came to Percy with a sorrowful look and showed him the Elson clipping, he knew that it was just what his boy needed to stoke up the competitive fires. The scowl that came over Percy's face — that scowl took them both one step closer to the Olympics.

The Inter-High was Percy's last appearance as a high school runner. He and Bob were also hoping it would be his last meet before he headed east to the Olympic trials, the trials that really counted, scheduled for Hamilton in just over a month. After his experience in Toronto the previous summer, Percy was determined that he would not be saddled again with the disadvantage of arriving at the last minute and having to run immediately after a fatiguing train journey. "Nothing less than a week would be sufficient to overcome this handicap," he had said upon his return to Vancouver.[11] By May 1928 he was hoping for even longer than that. A drive was already underway to raise the necessary funds for his trip, with Bob Granger starting a public subscription and the High School Athletic Association agreeing to donate a portion of the gate receipts from the Inter-High meet "in aid of the movement."[12]

The "movement." For the BC Olympic Committee this was getting out of hand. They could not have a popular crusade sending Percy to the trials, effectively pushing them out of the picture. Bob was curtly informed that if he did not cease his fundraising at once, Percy might be placed on the disqualified list. As for Percy going to the Hamilton trials, the committee, and *only* the committee, would send him. But first he would have to formally qualify — again — in the Vancouver trials on June 9.[13]

This was something for Bob to worry about. What if Percy won his races and met the standards as he had the year before, and then the committee again decided to send no athletes, only one of its fat-cat officials? What if he qualified and the committee then dithered and hemmed and hawed and didn't come up with train fare until the last moment, putting him again in the horrid position of having to step off the train and compete? And even if there weren't any hitches, how much time would that leave him to travel to Hamilton and get back into shape for the trials? Not enough.

As the June 9 deadline neared, Bob found that there was even more to fret about. The standards that Percy and his fellow local runners were expected to equal or surpass to qualify for the nationals had been announced and they were stiff, only a bit shy of the Olympic records.[14] Bob had no doubt that the times were within Percy's capabilities, assuming favourable conditions. But what if it was raining on the day of the meet? What if Percy was not running to form? What if he stepped in a hole and pulled a muscle? And what about the Brockton Point track? It was unfair to expect great things from athletes running on such an inadequate surface. The short-dash track was laid out on grass, for goodness' sake, and had a rise at the start and any number of potholes.

When reporter Robert Elson dropped by at one of Percy's training sessions a few days before the Vancouver meet, he found the young runner confident and just a bit feisty. "Tell the public," Percy said, "that I have every intention of showing Vancouver and the AAU officials that I am keen to go to Hamilton, and that I am worthy to represent this city there." This was something new for Percy, calling himself "worthy." Elson's earlier crack that he hadn't tried his best at the Inter-High meet was no doubt still rankling. As for Bob Granger, he seemed to be fretting. While conceding that Percy was approaching his peak after three months of training, he "pleaded . . . for recognition of the fact that the course at Brockton Point in the 100 yards dash is far from satisfactory and that Williams should be excused if he does not equal his Washington time. 'There is a heavy (for a sprinter) upgrade at the start of the 100 yards,' he said, 'and the course is full of small holes. It was one of these holes which was responsible for his bad start in the high school sports and which seriously endangers the legs of any sprinter. The 220 yards is probably the best course for Williams on the local track, but even it is unsatisfactory because of the double turns which slow up the runner.'"[15]

Yes indeed, Bob was nervous.

❦

The track events at the trials were laid out in metre distances, the Olympic standard. Instead of the century dash, Percy would be running the hundred metres, the equivalent of slightly more than 109 yards. The two-hundred-metre run would be more familiar, equivalent to 218 yards, just a stride short of a furlong. Times would be recorded using stopwatches delineated to the fifth of a second, the same as used at the Olympics, not the tenth-of-a-second watches commonly employed at American meets.

Percy had almost no competition in the hundred. He would be effectively running against the clock, one more thing for Bob to worry about. Percy had to make the Olympic standard, 10 4/5 seconds, just a fifth short of the Olympic record set by Don Lippincott in 1912 and tied by Harold Abrahams at the Paris Games in 1924 — and he had to do it without competition to push him, running on a lumpy grass track with an uphill slant at the start.

Percy didn't disappoint. To Bob's huge relief and to the delight of the crowd, he won the first hundred-metre race of his life in 10 3/5 seconds, tying the Olympic mark and establishing a new Canadian record, and missing Charlie Paddock's world record by a fifth of a second. And he did it running on grass. It was in fact probably the fastest time ever posted on grass, were such marks kept in the record books, the *Daily Province* enthusiastically noted. Percy wasn't quite as brilliant in the two hundred metres but he still won in 22 1/5 seconds, equalling the Canadian Olympic Committee's standard.[16]

Percy was in. He had earned his ticket.

✑

It was an outwardly boisterous group, and yet somehow solemn, that took Percy downtown a few days later, on the eve of his departure for the East and the trials. Bobby Gaul was there, and Geoff and Alf and Pinky Stewart and the rest of Percy's friends. They had each chipped in to buy their pal and their hero a new pair of track shoes. They headed to George Spalding's shop on Robson, the best sporting goods store in the city, and began scrutinizing the spikes on display. Money was no object, so Percy went with the priciest model, the "Foster," $7.50 a pair. He squeezed into two or three different pairs of size eights as the group looked on, and when he found the ones he liked, a little presentation was made. "These shoes," said one of the boys, "are going to be the first over the line in the final, Percy. Remember, we'll all be pulling for you." Returning home, Percy immediately set them to soak in a pail of water. He would need to work fast to break them in.[17]

Two more days and it was time to go, time to get back down to the CPR station and start on another adventure. Only one other BC athlete was being sent to the trials, "Big Mac" Archie McDiarmid, a Vancouver fireman who excelled at heaving the hammer. Archie had been a member of the small Canadian team that competed at the 1920 Antwerp Olympics and was additionally acclaimed as a hero in Vancouver for his actions in the disastrous Royal Alexandra apartment building fire the previous year.[18] A crowd had gathered at the station to see them off, local Olympic committee and AAU members, city fathers, a contingent of fellow firemen and sportsmen and the firemen's band for Big Mac, and for Percy a big assembly of family and schoolmates and friends. His mother Dot was there, looking attractive, wearing her white fox stole in the middle of summer, and so were Uncle Archie and Grandpa Harry — and Grandma Selina, who had a glint in her eye. For she had had a premonition. It had come to her a few days before, that peculiar sense of glimpsing the future. She now was convinced that their Percy would win.[19]

Bob Granger was there too but he wouldn't be boarding the train. The committee hadn't had funds enough to send him. Don't worry, boy, he whispered, I'll be along. He was too broke to afford his own passage, so was arranging once again through a friend to work his way east in the dining car of a CPR train, hopefully leaving within a few days.

The conductor's cry sparked a final round of handshakes and back-slaps and shouts of Give 'em heck, Mac! and Do us proud, Percy! And with that the two athletes climbed on board and made their way to their compartment, where Percy this time had a lower berth. The train lurched forward and there was more cheering on the platform as he and Big Mac hung out the window, grinning and waving, the big griz-zled veteran squeezed beside the slight youth. Then they were gather-ing speed and leaving the yard and heading out of the city, the line following the Fraser River Valley through Maple Ridge and Mission and Dewdney, where Percy sometimes went hunting for pheasant.

It was growing dark now. There was nothing to see through the window except his reflection. Percy settled back in his seat and listened to Big Mac's tales of the Antwerp Games, laughing at his account of how he had carried a bare pole in the opening ceremonies because no one could find a Canadian flag. Mac was a good travelling companion, always full of fun, armed with a bottle of brandy to get on the good side of the train conductors and attendants.[20]

Finally, with the excitement of the day subsiding and the prospect of his first fitful night's sleep just ahead, Percy took out the pocket diary he had brought along to record his impressions of the trip for his mother, smoothed it open to the page marked June 15 and wrote his first entry: "Was there a crowd to see us off? Boy, and how! I only hope it will be for a good reason."[21]

CHAPTER 6

The Trials

HAMILTON CALLED ITSELF the Ambitious City, and when it came to track and field the name certainly was apt. It had the finest athletic field in the country, the recently completed Scott Stadium, and a population of enthusiastic meet-goers who could be relied on to fill it. And when they did, they came to root for the runners and jumpers and heavers from the city's own Hamilton Olympic Club, Canada's leading athletic club and the only one on par with the big outfits in the United States. HOC-affiliated athletes dominated Canadian track and field. In the upcoming trials, the vast majority of competitors would be from Ontario, and of these most would wear the black and yellow HOC crest. Hamilton was so far ahead in athletics that Hamiltonians, HOC president Bobby Robinson at the forefront, couldn't resist a little crowing — which the rest of Canada, led by Toronto, could not help but resent.[1]

Percy and "Big Mac" Archie McDiarmid arrived in town on June 20 and were put up in a shared room at a bed and breakfast.[2] Big Mac immediately got down to the stadium with the Vancouver fire department's fine brass hammer and started heaving, two sessions a day for the week. He liked to train hard. Percy inspected the track and found it top-notch, six lanes all round, easy turns at the corners, the expertly laid cinder surface smooth and firm. It had turned rainy and the HOC runners were complaining about the oval being slow, but to Percy it seemed just fine, much better than the grass and dirt courses he was used to. J.R. "Cap" Cornelius, coach of the 1924 Canadian Olympic team and now heading up the pre-meet training camp, soon had him into his togs and working out alongside the HOC sprinters. A highly regarded physical education instructor and coach at Hamilton Collegiate Institute, Cornelius had been a captain in the Canadian army in the Great War, hence the nickname. The Scotsman believed in regimented drilling and vigorous workouts. He soon had the boys sweating.

Bob Granger showed up two days later, having worked his way east in a CPR dining car. "After cutting and serving pies, cakes, cheese and various other edibles from the diner's larder for five days," he wrote afterward, only half-joking, "I felt, when I 'resigned' at Hamilton, that I at least had a trade now that I could fall back on in an emergency."[3] Out at Scott Stadium he observed with a jolt Percy being run up and down the field in the heat of the summer. Cornelius clearly didn't know how his boy should be handled. Percy had already been worked up to a very fine pitch and required just light work to maintain his condition, saving his energy for the upcoming trials. Bob immediately stepped in and took over his training.

On the following day they showed up at Scott Stadium and spent a long time just sitting on the grass, studying the other runners in action. There was a lot of talent on the track. Most of the country's top dash men were now in town and hard at work. Percy was particularly eager to examine how they started, which he and Bob now considered the point in his game most in need of improvement. He couldn't quite get his initial arm action perfected, coordinating the forward motion of his right arm with his legs as he shot out of his holes. After Bob identified those runners with the finest starts, Percy studied them intently, engaging in "visualization," trying to imprint their movements onto his brain.[4]

It was only after a long period of this entirely passive form of training that Percy finally got down to some work. He stretched for a while, did a little jogging, took a few starts. Then Bob gave his legs a massage and that was it. On the days that followed they went through the same routine, Percy spending long periods simply watching the other runners, not doing more than thirty minutes of actual work himself.

That got the local track experts talking: Cap Cornelius, the HOC crowd, the officials in charge of the trials, the Olympic Committee members who would be selecting the team. Percy, they believed, wasn't doing enough training. There was no doubt that he was fast. In practice he showed remarkable acceleration, shooting ahead of the top HOC runners. But he usually eased up after just forty yards, and repeated the exercise only a few times before lying down for one of Granger's massages — the HOC runners didn't get massages — or heading off to the showers. That might be well and good for an exhibition dash man, a prima donna who was done in after only one race. Competing in the trials, however, wasn't just about speed. It was also about endurance, surviving the grind of preliminary heats and semifinals and still having enough left to come on strong in the final. Did this Vancouver flyer have the stamina for that? It didn't seem likely considering the lackadaisical way that he trained.

It all served to compound the general skepticism that already existed in Ontario over reports that had filtered east about Percy, especially about that Olympic-record-tying 10 3/5 seconds he had supposedly run in the Vancouver trials. Even if the standards at that meet weren't suspect — and to many that remained a big "if" — what sort of grind had Williams endured before posting that time in the final? For that was what he now would be facing. Considering the lightness of his workouts, it seemed probable that in real competition he would use up all his energy in the heats and semis and have nothing left for the final, just as in the previous year.[5]

Daily Province writer Robert Elson was on the scene in Hamilton, sending stories home by cable, and came to Percy's defence. Percy, he wrote, "is a man of peculiar temperament and ability and hard work here would have a tendency to make him stale."[6] "Stale" was the term used for what would later be known as being over-trained or burnt-out, and was precisely what Bob Granger feared. It was a hard sell, however. The handful of Westerners at the trials had high hopes for Percy but to Ontarians he seemed too uncommitted, too young, too soft. When the crunch came in the finals, a more durable runner surely would beat him, someone like Johnny Fitzpatrick or Buck Hester or Cyril Coaffee.

Yes, Cyril Coaffee. He was back. The Olympic committee had decided not to enforce the rule it had passed the previous summer, that Canadians residing outside the country would not be eligible to represent it in international competitions — the same rule that had prompted Percy to turn down the University of Washington scholarship offer. Cyril had simply ignored the ruling and showed up, turning out at Scott Stadium in his old 1924 Canadian Olympic jersey and thereby making it hard to deny him.[7] The committee decided to let the matter drop. The former Winnipegger was determined to make his third Olympic team and he seemed a sure bet. Buck Hester, a long-time resident of Detroit, was similarly in the clear. He had just graduated from the University of Michigan and had been taken in by the Hamilton Olympic Club and would run in their colours.

The trials got underway on Saturday, June 30, with an opening ceremony modelled after the Olympic Games. The athletes, clad in their shorts and jerseys, marched in lockstep into the stadium under leaden skies and through intermittent showers, led by a bevy of officials in white shirts and boaters and a kilted Highlander carrying the flag out in front. The Ontario contingent was by far the largest, outnumbering all the other provinces combined, the majority of the athletes wearing the HOC crest. Marching behind the BC placard were just Percy and Big Mac, Percy in his Vancouver Athletic Club singlet and wrinkled Commerce High shorts, Mac looking old enough to pass for his grand-dad. The athletes formed up in ranks and speeches were made and the athletes' oath taken. A thousand homing pigeons were released, circling above the stadium for a time before getting their bearings and heading off to their cotes. Then it was time to begin.[8]

Percy won his preliminary heat in the hundred metres without having to exert much effort, followed by Buck Hester and Campbell Maybee. Buck was coasting at the end, content to qualify, and didn't challenge. After an hour's rest in the dressing room Percy was back for his semifinal. It too went without a hitch, a second-place finish this time, behind Johnny Fitzpatrick and ahead of Ralph Adams. Percy had had to extend himself more but still had not unleashed his full speed. Then it was back to the dressing room to rest again for the final while Bob did more work on his legs. He was feeling nice and relaxed when a Western Union delivery boy stepped into the room with a cable. It was from Bobby Gaul, just a line containing one of their private slang words. The Hexamis, it read, were expecting him to "run like a Fung." That made Percy smile. He was still smiling when he headed back out to the track.[9]

Percy was the last finalist in the hundred to appear at the start line. The clouds were parting and the track was almost dry but the wind had picked up and was now blowing straight in their faces. Whoever won, the winning time would be mediocre. He laced on his spikes, took just one practice start and was ready to go. A keen eye in the stands could just make out the tension grip blocks in his palms, a sprinting aid Bob had suggested he try, round pieces of wood held in place by rubber bands around the back of his hands. They would serve as a reminder to Percy to keep his hands relaxed as he ran, halting the "tying-up" process that typically started with clenched fists before radiating throughout the body, slowing a runner down the harder he strained.[10]

Percy was in lane three. To his left, on the inside, were Cyril Coaffee and the Maritimes' Leigh Miller. The Hamilton Olympic Club entries were on his right: Buck Hester, Ralph Adams and Johnny Fitzpatrick. Normally Cyril, the national champion, would be the runner to beat. But Cyril was running injured. The problem was a tendon in his leg. He had pulled it two weeks before and it was now giving him trouble after the strain of the previous two races. The crowd was rooting for the HOC sprinters, with Johnny favoured to win, followed by Buck. Percy was considered a long shot. "He'll have to break a record to beat Fitzpatrick," people were saying.[11]

All six runners got away evenly at the sound of the pistol. Percy accelerated and slipped into his stride, edging into the lead at the halfway mark even though he seemed to be coasting, Johnny and Buck fighting it out a half stride behind. Then came Percy's kick, his highest gear, that point in a race when he ran like a Fung. He was surging now, chin tucked in, arms pumping strongly but still relaxed, the grip blocks cradled lightly in his hands, Johnny and Buck falling back, showing signs of strain as they tried to keep up. They neared the tape and suddenly Percy's head went back and with one final effort he was across the line in first, followed by Johnny second, Buck third, Ralph fourth.

The men with the watches went into a huddle. Hamilton had gone all out and there were seven of them. Low and high times were discarded, the mean was determined, and it was good. Percy had won in 10 3/5 seconds, tying the Olympic record, the same time he had posted three weeks before at the BC trials. A gaggle of reporters were around him in an instant, barking out questions. How did you do it, Percy? How did you beat Fitzpatrick? What's your secret? Percy, still panting, a lick of hair askew, couldn't give them much of an answer. "I just ran," was all he could think of to say.[12]

No one took much notice of Cyril Coaffee. The dethroned champion had finished last. As the reporters continued to fire questions at Percy, Cyril limped off the field and headed for the showers, his Olympic hopes dashed. His downfall left Percy completely unmoved. "Defeated by the Western Gazelle for the first time in 8 years," he would write in his meet program beside Cyril's picture. "20 cigarettes a day didn't produce enough smoke for this old boy in the final."[13]

A little ceremony followed to honour Percy's victory. He stood on a dais flanked by Johnny and Buck, the provincial flag of BC was raised and at the sound of a bugle Percy gave the raised-arm Olympic salute, his tension grip blocks still in his hand. Standing there, the eyes of the stadium on him, his victory seemed all the more remarkable, for he really did appear to be just a boy. Although only a year younger than Johnny, his face still had the roundness of youth and he was not nearly as filled out through the chest. And his legs were slender. Compared to Johnny's sturdy pins, Percy's were lean and sinewy, his calves accentuated by the narrowness of his knees and ankles, his veins and tendons showing.

The day's program finished with the running of the ten thousand metres. It was won by Johnny Miles, his mother watching through field glasses from the veranda of their house, which had a view of the track.[14] Then it was off to a banquet laid on by the city for all the athletes, a loud and lengthy affair filled for Percy with congratulatory backslaps and handshakes and words of acclaim. By the time he got back to his room his head was swimming with all the praise that had been heaped on him and the assurances that he was in — that his ticket to Amsterdam was already safe in his pocket.[15]

⚬∾

Dear Mother:

I guess my place on the team is about cinched. They say that after the show I made Saturday that I can't be kept off the team. Tomorrow we run again. It doesn't matter whether I win or lose. . . .

It has been the funniest experience I have ever had. The coach here is one of the Scotch men who believe in the Big 'I' and little 'u,' and he was dead set against the method of training I use. Bob figured out that he was trying to give me twenty times too much work to do, so I just loafed all the time I have been here. He claimed that I wouldn't be able to last out three heats of the hundred metres but I didn't say I could or couldn't and since the race when I beat out both of his boys he hasn't said hardly a thing to me. . . .

I had an invitation last night, while we were at a banquet the city put on for us, to stop off on my way back from Amsterdam, and run in the Toronto Exhibition sometime in September. I don't know but that sounds sort of optimistic to me. I'm not even there yet.[16]

⚬∾

Percy in fact wasn't quite yet on the boat. The Olympic Committee was planning to take four sprinters to the Games and had decided that they would pick only all-rounders, athletes who could compete in the hundred and the two hundred and then in the relays. Calls were coming from several quarters, moreover, that Cyril Coaffee be put on the team based on his past performance. If that happened, Percy still could be bumped. To guarantee himself a spot, he had to place at or very near the top in the two hundred, his weaker event.[17]

Monday, July 2, was blistering hot. In the five-thousand-metre race, five of the fourteen entrants were unable to finish. Percy drew the innermost of the staggered lanes in his first-round heat of the two hundred, starting furthest back with the other runners angled out in front to his right — out in front where he could see them and pace himself better. At the gun he stuck close to Ralph Adams ahead in the lane beside him and concentrated on running an efficient, energy-conserving race. Ralph won it. Percy coasted across the finish in second, good enough to advance. The semis unfolded in much the same fashion, Percy again in lane one on the inside, again tracking the man Bob had identified as his fastest opponent. This time Percy finished first, still running within his limits, still holding a bit back.

The final brought him up against almost the same line-up he had faced in the hundred: Ralph Adams, Johnny Fitzpatrick, Buck Hester, Leigh Miller. Only Cyril Coaffee wasn't there. He had gamely turned out for the two hundred despite his bad leg but hadn't stood a chance. He was eliminated in the first round. The sixth spot was now occupied by S.J. McKechenneay from Montreal. Percy's toughest competition, Johnny, Ralph and Buck Hester, the HOC runners, had the three inside lanes. Percy, starting in front in lane four, wouldn't be able to see them.

The finish was extremely close, almost a dead heat. It was Percy and Johnny first through the tape together, followed by Ralph and Buck a half-stride behind. Who had won it? Up in the bleachers several people seated around Bob Granger were saying that Johnny seemed to have had the edge, and with a sinking feeling Bob figured they were probably right. The timekeepers and finish judges stayed in their huddle for quite some time before the decision was conveyed to the meet announcer at his microphone.

"Attention please," he began, waiting for the buzz in the stands to subside. "In the two-hundred-metre final. First," — and a long pause — "Williams of Vancouver."

Percy had won it in twenty-two seconds. Johnny had placed second, Ralph third, Buck fourth.

The air now filled with praise for Percy — and this time it was praise from the East. *Toronto Star* sportswriter Lou Marsh raved that Percy had "the makings of another Charlie Paddock." Bill Hewitt in the same paper began his piece with, "They grow 'em big and they grow 'em fast in the Far West!"[18] The *Hamilton Spectator* labelled Percy "a sensation." Bobby Robinson, HOC president and manager to the Olympic team, called him "a real wonder."[19] Nick Bawlf, a Cornell University coach who had come up for the trials, claimed that he was "one of the greatest sprinters I have ever seen."[20]

At the Toronto *Evening Telegram*, meanwhile, sportswriter Ted Reeve was moved to break out his really snappy prose, the good stuff. "Say it with sweet Williams," he began his column. "The boys who came back from Hamilton last night with their conversash cluttered up with split seconds were talking of Williams more than anything else. He was the big thrill. A year ago the same lad slipped off a train at Toronto just in time to catch a bucket of Java and wiffle a waffle or two before biffing up to Varsity Stadium to compete in the big local meet." On that occasion, Ted continued, Percy missed his chance at the century due to a coin toss. But did he let it get him down? "Not so, Bolivia. He went back to the Coast, bore down on his track dusting, and returned this year with a burst of hasty hook and knee action that makes him a dangerous opponent in the sprints to anyone in the world."[21]

Expectations were suddenly running high for Percy. And no one's were higher than Bob Granger's. In a dispatch cabled to Vancouver and published in the *Daily Province* on July 3, he blurted out his cherished dream in the very first line. "I believe," he boldly declared, "that Percy Williams will win the Olympic 100 metres for these reasons." He proceeded to list them, one by one: that his boy had won the hundred at the trials in Olympic-record-tying time despite running into a headwind; that he had faltered slightly in his ending drive, which cost him a tick; and that he would do even better at Amsterdam because the tougher competition there "will draw him out to the utmost, something no sprinter in this country can do at the present moment." When all the facts were considered, Bob concluded, it was clear that Percy had everything that was needed to win a gold medal. Whether he actually succeeded or not "will depend entirely on the care he receives."[22]

Bob added that last bit because it was looking like he wouldn't be the one caring for Percy. With the Olympic Committee having turned down his offer to accompany the track team to Amsterdam as trainer — they didn't have the money to buy him a ticket — it looked like Bob had gone as far as he could go, and that Percy would have to be entrusted to the care of Cap Cornelius and his rigorous notions of training. Bob accepted it at first, but not for long. On the night before he was to return to Vancouver, his meagre supply of money almost exhausted, he awoke at two o'clock and lay staring at the ceiling for hours, stewing about what Cornelius might do to his boy.

By dawn Bob had made up his mind. He was going to get to Amsterdam one way or another, "even if I had to swim there." He headed to the Western Union office and started sending cables to Vancouver, to Dot Williams and anyone else who he thought could raise money.[23]

∽

For a week after the trials Canada's new Olympic track and field team attended a training camp sponsored by the Hamilton Olympic Club, turning out every day in their newly issued red-edged shorts and jerseys with a maple leaf and "Canada" on the chest. For Percy they were days of tedium, with nothing to do but read and hang around and pretend to work for Cap. "I'm just about fed up on this place," he would write his mother. "There's nothing to do and too much time to do it." The one redeeming factor was his new teammates. Percy thought they were "just great."[24]

Archie McDiarmid hadn't made the cut. He was on his way back to Vancouver. Percy had urged him to drop in to see his mother and tell her about the trials.[25] That left Percy the only BC man on the team, one of four sprinters. The other three, Johnny Fitzpatrick, Buck Hester and

Ralph Adams, were all members of the Hamilton Olympic Club —
Cap Cornelius' "pets," Percy would call them, but he liked them just
the same. A fifth man, an alternate, was to join them in England on the
way to the Games — none other than Bob's old student and Percy's
former training partner Harry Warren, whose presence at Amsterdam
wouldn't cost the committee a ticket. It was an unexpected piece of
good news.

The large proportion of Hamilton athletes and officials selected for
the team did not pass without comment. The Toronto press was openly
resentful and the accusation was made that Hamilton was hogging the
show. The *Hamilton Spectator* brushed the complaints aside as a "child-
ish squeal."[26] And indeed, it was hard to deny that the Olympic Committee had chosen the team wisely. The fact that it included so many
Hamilton-affiliated men was really just a reflection of the Ambitious
City's success in track and field. It did more than any other Canadian
town to develop local talent. It had the best facilities and the most
active officials, and the biggest and best-financed athletic club in the
country, the HOC, with nearly a thousand dues-paying members, and
was generous in sponsoring athletes from anywhere in Canada who
wanted to train with the club and wear its colours. So sure, Hamilton
dominated the team. It dominated because it had most of the best athletes.[27]

Bob Granger was still in camp, trying to raise money. Percy slipped
him a few dollars to keep him going. Bob accepted it, although it
caused him some anguish.[28] They tried to have their usual light workouts together but it wasn't easy with Cap Cornelius intent on whipping
everyone into shape, radiating red-faced indignation every time Percy
loped through his practice races at what was obviously less than full
speed. Bob and Percy were in fact both developing an intense dislike
for the narrow-chested former army officer and his boot-camp approach to training: sturdy legs and stout hearts and that sort of thing.
"The boys are stripped in my office," Cap had stated some years
before, explaining how he set out to mould high school athletes, "and
I take their height, chest and weight measurements, then chest expansion and all the other physical tests. Then, in three months they come

in again, and if there's no improvement, I want to know the reason why."[29] To Cap, the young Vancouver sprinter was doing nothing to improve. He was lazy, a loafer who would be taught a well-deserved lesson in Europe when the real tests started.

Percy for his part considered Cap something of a buffoon. In his Olympic trials meet program he wrote in the third person alongside Cap's photo: "Coach of the Canadian team, but gets on Percy's nerves with his I, I, I — I hold every record, I will break everything etc. About the only thing he could break is china. He's all right, but would be better off teaching Sunday School."[30]

∽

Finally the big day arrived, July 10, when Canada's Olympians started on their journey. Percy and his teammates boarded the train at Hamilton station just before noon, clutching their labelled bags, laden with gifts of oranges and packets of paper and envelopes for writing letters. They had been enjoined in one of the after-dinner speeches at a banquet earlier that week "that no matter how old a man was, he never grew up to his mother," and should therefore remember to write home often. They headed first to Toronto, where they met the six-member women's team that had been selected at trials in Halifax — this would be the first Olympics where women would compete in track and field — and then the whole party continued together to Montreal, where berths awaited them on the White Star liner *Albertic*.[31]

The Canadian team, fifty-one athletes and a dozen officials and chaperones and coaches, made a convivial party as they swarmed up the gangway and started getting to know the ship, their home for the next week. They were headed by Olympic committee president Pat Mulqueen, who had come aboard minus his Olympic straw boater, eaten by a horse during the team's whirlwind Montreal tour. Cap Cornelius was the acknowledged expert on ocean travel, this being his fourteenth Atlantic crossing. "He knows all the stokers by their first name," joked reporter Lou Marsh, who was accompanying the team. Also very much in evidence was feisty team manager Bobby Robinson, a gentleman farmer, dynamo athletic enthusiast and *Hamilton Spectator* sportswriter whose confidence in the team was unbounded. Before leaving home he had placed several bets of a year's supply of potatoes that Canadian runners would bring home gold medals. The Dutch consul in Hamilton took him up on the outcome of the marathon, wagering an equal value of cheese. At the moment, Bobby was livid. The boxes containing the Olympic parade uniforms for the opening ceremonies had just been delivered and a third were missing. He started firing off cables.

Among the athletes, ace eight-hundred-metre runner Phil Edwards attracted a lot of attention. A student at New York University, born into a well-to-do family in British Guiana, Phil had been invited by Bobby Robinson to join the HOC and compete in the trials since British Guiana was not fielding a team of its own. Phil was the first black man many of the Canadians had ever personally met — "black as anthracite" Percy privately noted — and his flamboyance and intelligence and obvious good breeding quickly shattered any *Amos 'n' Andy* notions they held. When he appeared on deck it was usually in something quite splendid: cream-coloured plus-fours, sharkskin socks, two-tone golf shoes, flashy ties, a cane in hand and sometimes a monocle just for fun, a present from his NYU classmates.[32]

Marathon runner Percy Wyer, ninety-five pounds and five-feet-nothing, was the smallest member of the team, and the oldest. He called Phil in his finery "Burlington Bertie." Everyone called Wyer and his six-foot steeplechaser pal Art Keay "Mutt and Jeff." Middle-distance runner Dave Griffin got everyone going with his turkey-red beret and matching knee socks. The socks, he announced, were family heirlooms, passed down from his granddad. Among the women, star runner Myrtle Cook seemed a jumpy, nervous sort, a thoroughbred of a sprinter, while high jumper Ethel Catherwood, the gorgeous "Saskatoon Lily," had the boys falling all over themselves. She was five feet ten and proclaimed that there were only two things in the world she was afraid of: swimming, and being seen with a man who was shorter than her.[33]

Percy, our Percy, didn't make much of a splash. For the most part he stayed on the sidelines wrapped in his warm black sweater, casting cautious admiring glances at Ethel, whose angelic face, he wrote his mother, "would stop an eight day clock."[34] He was becoming chummy with two fellow west-of-Ontario outsiders, Jimmy Ball, a department store pharmacist from Winnipeg who specialized in the four hundred metres, and Doral Pilling, a javelin thrower from Cardston, Alberta. Jimmy was somewhat like Percy, with a similarly lightweight frame and quiet disposition, but several years older. Doral was different, big and loud and outgoing and a bit of a hellraiser. There was something about him, though, that was very attractive, a welcoming openness, an easy jocularity, a gift he seemed to have for enjoying life to the fullest. He and "Perce" soon became very good friends.

Bob Granger, meanwhile, was racing about on shore, seeing the sights in between frequent trips to the telegraph office. Back in Hamilton his cabled entreaties to Vancouver had resulted in the dispatch of a small sum that he had used to follow the Olympic team to Toronto and then Montreal. The *Albertic* was now about to sail and Bob still had not received the more substantial amount he needed to pay his way across the Atlantic. Pushed to the furthest extremity, his baggage somehow found its way on board and was carried along with the Canadian team to Quebec City while Bob himself, as he enigmatically put it, followed along "by other means than by the St. Lawrence River" — means that he insisted did *not* include stowing away. In any event he continues: "As the ship docked and I walked on board, [the ship's officers] tried to collect for the passage from Montreal. However, I managed to get my passport and baggage ashore just in time, and bade the team 'Bon voyage.'"

After watching the *Albertic* sail away down the St. Lawrence toward the Atlantic, Bob headed once again to the telegraph office. He was three thousand miles from Vancouver and had another four thousand miles to go to get to the Olympics. And he was once again broke.[35]

CHAPTER 7

American Juggernaut

✑

AS PERCY AND THE Canadian Olympic team were leaving Montreal aboard the *Albertic*, the *President Roosevelt* was steaming out of New York harbour with an enormous banner on its side proclaiming that "America's Olympic Teams" were aboard. Consisting of a battalion of 350 athletes and a battery of officials and coaches and masseurs and attendants and trainers, the American contingent would be the largest at the Games after the Dutch, so large that the entire ship had been chartered to serve as a floating gymnasium for the ocean crossing and then as a dockside hotel to house the team in Amsterdam.

Leaning against the rail, watching the New York skyline disappear in the haze, were some of the fleetest men in the world, the cream of American talent who had risen to the top at the recent tryouts in Boston. The youngest of them was Frank Wykoff, an eighteen-year-old high school sensation who had shot to national prominence the year before and was now being praised to the skies. He was America's version of

Percy Williams, only much more famous. Percy and his fellow Canadians by this point knew all about Wykoff and had followed the American trials closely. Frank and the Americans, conversely, knew virtually nothing of Percy.

Frank had been born in Des Moines, Iowa, in 1909, the son of a plumber. His family moved to Glendale, California, around 1917 and he went on to attend Glendale High School, where he joined the track team and made a name for himself as a speedster. Things really took off in April 1927, when he ran the century in 9.7 seconds and then again in 9.8, world-class times from a high school junior.[1] And he was just as fast in the furlong, posting a time of twenty-one seconds flat in May — a new world record, had it not been disallowed due to a slight tailwind. To an even greater degree than was happening with Percy up north in Vancouver, Frank's spectacular performances had the home crowds cheering and boasting — and the track establishment in the East muttering that seventeen-year-olds simply couldn't run that fast.

In the spring of 1928 Frank, in his final semester of high school, was hard at work with his Glendale High coach, Normal Hayhurst, preparing for the Olympic trials. By now the papers had him sounding pretty confident, proclaiming that he was out to dethrone fellow Californian Charlie Paddock as the new sprint king. Charlie didn't appreciate such boasting from someone so young and responded that he thought it unlikely Frank would make the Olympic team. And so a rivalry was born, with Frank reportedly "peeved to such an extent that he is determined to win a berth on the team even if he has to humble Paddock to do so."[2]

The first step in Frank's march to Amsterdam was the Western Olympic tryouts at the LA Coliseum on June 16, where he would go head to head in the sprints against Charlie Paddock in what was being billed as the "Race of the Century." Facing Paddock was intimidating. Watching him saunter up to the start line, smiling and waving to a cheering crowd of forty-five thousand, wearing his custom-made track suit and what the papers were touting as his "winning shoes," Charlie didn't look like any other sprinter Frank had competed against. He was more like a movie star. In fact, he *was* a movie star. He had appeared in a string of Westerns and campus comedies, most famously in *College Flirt* alongside Paramount star Bebe Daniels, with whom he was widely reported to have had a romantic attachment. Charlie's latest picture, a loosely autobiographical movie entitled *The Olympic Hero*, had just opened in theatres the day before. He starred in it as a sprinter named "Charley Patterson."[3]

And yet up close, stripped to his shorts, Charlie didn't look like much. A French doctor who once examined him noted that he had a slight curvature of the spine, a drooping shoulder, shoulder blades that protruded and defective nasal passages that caused him to breathe through his mouth. And finally, he was what was politely known as husky — or as the French doctor put it, "plainly fat. . . . Paddock's arms and shoulders remind one of a 40-year-old matron in décolleté. In short, I have never seen any sprinter so poorly set up for speed. But, nevertheless, he is the fastest man in the world."[4]

At the start line for the hundred-metre dash Charlie went through his pre-race ritual as Frank warily watched out of the corner of his eye. First he had to find a piece of wood to touch for good luck, a railing or hurdle. Then, as the runners settled into their lanes, he positioned his hands well out in front of the chalk line, slowly drawing them back before the second command was given. It was something he often made a point of doing, occasionally attracting the ire of the starter in the process — and perhaps giving his opponents' concentration that little tweak that could throw them off. (*Is he cheating? Can't the starter see that?*)[5]

Then, unexpectedly, Charlie rose up in the "set" position before the command was given, taut and ready to spring while the others still had a knee on the ground. He said afterward that his coach recommended it, but it seemed like a mind game. It might have thrown off other runners, particularly ones so much younger and more inexperienced than Charlie. But Frank kept his cool. Getting off to one of his famous lightning starts, he led throughout the race, beating off Charlie's even more famous lightning finish to claim first place in 10 3/5 seconds, equalling the Olympic record. Then he turned around and did it again, winning the two hundred metres in 20 4/5 seconds, tying Paddock's own world mark and bettering the Olympic record by almost a second. Charlie trailed in second, one and a half yards back.

It had been a bad afternoon for Charlie. He was not used to losing, certainly not on his home turf in Southern California, where his string of consecutive victories extended all the way back to 1916. "I just didn't have the old push at the finish," he said. "I felt so good before the race that I sort of suspected something was going to happen, for I generally feel rotten before things start." He had qualified for the national trials, though, and still had a chance of making a third trip to the Olympics, the first sprinter ever to do so.[6]

As for Frank, he was riding high and feeling cocky. "I used to think that Paddock had great starting form," he told a reporter as he got ready for the big trip east. "He has changed it since, and I don't think much of it. I don't see how a man who has been running for fifteen years could get such a sloppy start as Paddock had last Saturday. I don't think so much of the flying finish either."[7]

The national Olympic trials were scheduled for Boston, starting on July 7 at the Harvard University track. Competition in the sprints was expected to be fiercer than ever. As one pundit was overheard saying to Olympic head coach Lawson Robertson, of Scottish extraction, "Robbie, those sprint finishes will be closer than the whole Scotch nation."[8] In addition to Wykoff and Paddock, top University of Southern California sprinter Charlie Borah was back in condition and taking the train east to compete. In the 1926 nationals Borah had placed first in the century and second in the furlong and in 1927 had been respectively second and first. He had also tied Paddock's world record in the century — twice. Jackson Scholz of Missouri, gold medal winner in the two-hundred-metre dash at the 1924 Paris Olympics and in the sprint relay at the 1920 Antwerp Games, was coming up from New York, where he ran for the New York Athletic Club and worked as a pulp fiction writer. At thirty-one he was the oldest sprinter in the field, and had competed many times before at the nationals in the sprint finals. Like Paddock, Jack was out for an unprecedented third Olympic journey. Other strong contenders included sophomore Claude Bracey from the Rice Institute in Texas, Karl Wildermuth from Georgetown U., Ohio State's George Simpson, former Cornell star Henry Russell, now with the Penn Athletic Club, and University of Nebraska "Husker" Roland Locke, holder of the furlong world record of 20.5 seconds.

And then there was Bob McAllister, the twenty-nine-year-old New York City policeman known as "The Flying Cop." Unlike just about all the other sprinters in contention, McAllister had never been to college and had not come up through the athletic scholarship system. He had joined the police force right out of high school, training in his spare time with a local club affiliated with the Knights of Columbus. He was deadly at the shorter distances, holding a number of indoor dash records — including those for the 110-, 120-, 130- and 150-yard dashes, all of which he set in a single Paddock-style attention-grabber, breasting through a succession of tapes. McAllister had never made it to the Olympics, however, and he was determined to get there. He ran to win and was a tough competitor in every sense of the word, renowned for his banter at the start line — what a later generation of athletes would know as trash-talking.[9]

McAllister was also tough off the track. In the early 1920s he fell afoul of the corrupt politicians of Tammany Hall who ran New York and soon was facing trumped-up perjury charges stemming from a liquor raid in which it was alleged he unlawfully kicked in a door. He managed to avoid prison that time, but an accusation of accepting bribes from a bootlegger immediately followed, then a charge of murder in the shooting death of a car thief. McAllister spent nearly a year locked up in the Tombs awaiting trial over that one, his police career in ruins and his life in peril, but in the end he was found not guilty. Then he had to fight for nearly two years just to get his job back, supporting his family by driving a bus and singing Irish ballads in vaudeville in his beautiful baritone voice.[10]

By 1928 "Flying Cop" Bob McAllister knew all about overcoming challenges. Getting on the Olympic team and winning a gold medal in Amsterdam would be just one more. After everything he had so far endured, he had come to believe that he was destined to win.[11]

❧

The Harvard track was wet from an early morning rain on the first day of the trials in Boston. The sun was now out, however, so the meet organizers decided to postpone the start of the running events until half past three to give the cinders time to dry. For the contestants entered in the sprints, what lay ahead would be gruelling. In the hundred-metre competition, four rounds were to be run that afternoon: two rounds of elimination heats, then the semis, then the final, continuing on into the twilight. Those surviving into the final would be sprinting all afternoon. The two hundred metres would be run the next day, three rounds this time, again featuring some of the fastest men in the world. On the plus side, the US Olympic committee, unlike its cash-strapped Canadian counterpart, had not had to stipulate that sprinters hoping to make the team had to qualify in both the hundred and two hundred metres. They would be selecting four men for each event, a total of eight. Several runners had therefore decided to focus on the event in which they felt strongest.

For Frank Wykoff that was the hundred, and he established himself as a star from his very first heat. "When I took the mark," he said, "I never felt so good. I was keyed up to the limit. I thought that gun would never bark. But when it did go, so did I."[12] He won in the Olympic record-tying time of 10.6 seconds. He did it again in the second round, another first-place finish, another 10.6, and then again in his semifinal, trailed by Bob McAllister and Henry Russell, George Simpson limping in last with a pulled muscle. In the other semi, meanwhile, Charlie Paddock found himself eliminated in a controversial decision, the judges forced to come up with placings for four runners, including Charlie, who all crossed the finish locked in a dead heat. With only the first three finishers advancing to the final, someone had to go. After a long, see-sawing debate, that someone was Charlie.[13]

It was getting dark when the final was run. Incredibly, Wykoff won again in 10.6 seconds, the fourth race for the day in which he had posted that time. He now had his ticket to Amsterdam. "Flying Cop" Bob McAllister in second was on the boat too, one step closer to that destiny he talked of so often. Barring something unexpected, so were Henry Russell in third and Claude Bracey in fourth. Not so for Jackson Scholz. He had finished sixth and was out.[14]

Both Paddock and Scholz were back on the track the next afternoon for the two hundred metres. They still had one more chance to make the team and they intended to take it. This time they both got through the heats and semifinals to qualify for the final, doing so in better than Olympic time, Paddock getting a big cheer from the crowd upon winning his semi, a little salve after his hard luck the previous day. It had been eight years since he had run in his first national championship sprint final, eleven years for Scholz. They were grizzled veterans by sprinting standards, well past their prime. But as they thundered around that last turn and up the straightaway and on through the tape, it was Paddock second and Jackson Scholz third, behind the winner, Charlie Borah. They had made it. They were both going to their third Olympiad — although to compete at a distance that had not been their first choice.[15]

But then again, maybe Paddock wasn't going after all. In the wake of the meet, a conflict erupted that threatened to prevent him from making the trip. For Charlie, it was just the next in a long line of controversies that had dogged his career, another fracas to turn the press from hailing him as "The Fastest Human" one week to disparaging him as "Good-Time Charlie" the next. Most of his trouble stemmed from the fact that he was so much in the spotlight, always attracting attention, and that he was so outspoken, notorious for flouting the all-powerful Amateur Athletic Union. In 1923, for example, the Union overlords told him he was not to compete at the student games in Paris. Charlie responded in a newspaper column that he would go wherever he liked, and he went. The AAU suspended him for it. In 1925, after a fight in which he won reinstatement, Charlie was next accused of padding meet expense claims. That resulted in accusations of professionalism and another big row. Then he was raked over the coals for writing about sprinting while making his living as a sports reporter, supposedly another violation of the amateur rules. There were also his public lectures on sprinting. The man was making money on them, he was supporting himself on them, and that wouldn't do.[16]

And then there was his latest film, *The Olympic Hero*, released the previous month. In it Charlie not only played a champion sprinter, he was shown actually *running*, making him a professional by AAU standards since he had obviously been paid. Charlie managed to beat that charge down just days before the trials with affidavits from the film's producer and exhibitor stating that he had not received a cent. He had starred in the film, Charlie asserted, because he liked acting and wanted to help out his friends. It was awfully hard to believe but just as hard to disprove.[17]

Unguarded comments got Charlie into trouble as well. He would sometimes make highly suggestive cracks like: Another year of this amateur running and I can retire! And just the month before, in June 1928, he had caused a commotion by revealing on a radio show that the American sprint squad at the 1924 Olympics had cooked up a scheme to wear out Britain's Harold Abrahams in the hundred-metre final by taking turns making false starts. They never went through with it, but that this had even been contemplated led to charges of unsportsman-like conduct.[18]

Now, in July 1928, with Charlie just nicely qualified for the team and packing his bags for the voyage to Amsterdam, all the past accusations coalesced into a howl of protest both in America and Europe that someone so clearly professional should be allowed in the Games. It was looking like he would be bumped, replaced by Roland Locke, world-record holder in the furlong, who had not made the team.[19]

∽

It was a hugely confident American team that sailed into the Atlantic aboard the *President Roosevelt* on July 11. The competition at the Boston trials had been brutal. Good men, great men, had fallen by the wayside in a process that sportswriter Walter Trumbull said "closely followed Mr. Darwin's theory." The end result of this survival-of-the-fittest struggle, he concluded, "is that we are sending a team of champions to Amsterdam and that in practically every event, it will take supermen to beat us."[20]

Of course, as in any Darwinian struggle, the trampled losers were not all that happy. Just before the *Roosevelt* cast off, the coach of the New York Athletic Club bulled his way on board with three of his eliminated athletes, including Roland Locke. A verbal skirmish ensued before General Douglas MacArthur, head of the Olympic Committee, was able to ease the irate coach and his three charges back down the gangway.[21] Later, when the *Roosevelt* was well out at sea, four other eliminated athletes were discovered to have stowed aboard, among them runner Frank Hussey. They were confined to the brig until friends and supporters came up with the cost of their fare to Europe. Bob McAllister, a friend of Hussey's, helped raise $130 for his ticket.[22]

Out in the Atlantic the track team was working hard to keep in shape. A small cork-topped track had been constructed on the promenade deck and Frank Wykoff, Charlie Borah and the others were limbering up for a workout. Jackson Scholz had already finished his session and was leaning against the rail, placidly smoking a stogie. He had smoked for years and never gave it a thought. Lawson Robertson, the team's head coach, spotted the bad example and scurried over. "For God's sake, Jack," he hissed. "Don't smoke cigars around the track. If you're going to smoke them, smoke them in your cabin."[23]

And lo and behold, there was Charlie Paddock, jogging around in another of his outlandish outfits. He had made it after all. The arguments had been long and heated when the Olympic Committee met to finalize the selection of athletes but in the end General MacArthur led a majority in backing Charlie, arguing that there was no reason to block him as the AAU had not rescinded his amateur status. To do otherwise, he said, would amount to "athletic lynch law" based on "whispered innuendo." Committee vice president George Wightman, who had organized the trials, was so offended by Paddock's retention that he resigned on the spot. When Charlie heard the news he couldn't resist getting in a dig. "Wightman of Boston and the American athletes are now even," he said. "We athletes helped him put over the Olympic fund [by appearing at the trials and selling tickets] and now he is going to help us by not being on the ship."[24] The whole episode would continue to rankle with Charlie. A year later he penned an exposé of amateur track in which he accused the AAU and the Olympic Committee of exploiting him and his fellow sprinters at the Boston trials "much the same way as Barnum & Bailey would their paid performers."[25]

Below deck Charlie was sharing a stateroom with Frank Wykoff and Charlie Borah. It seemed a well-intentioned grouping. All three, after all, were sprinters and from California, and all three were connected to the University of Southern California, Paddock as an alumni, Borah as a current student, Frank intending to enrol in the fall as a freshman. But despite their similarities they were not very chummy. To middle-distance runner Nick Carter, occupying the fourth bunk in the room, watching these three rivals interact made for an interesting show all the way across the Atlantic, "being very careful not to agitate each other. Being friendly, but not overly friendly."[26]

When it came to training, the three sprinters generally went their own way, Wykoff working with Glendale High coach Normal Hayhurst, Borah with USC coach Dean Cromwell, Paddock with "Dink" Templeton of Stanford. It wasn't easy for any of them to stay in shape on board the ship. With the makeshift track so small and sharp metal corners protruding all around, any real sprinting was out of the question. The best they could manage was starting practice, jogging, calisthenics and walking — difficult enough with so many athletes vying for space. Apart from that, it was just a question of putting in the time, waiting for the eight days to pass that would get them to Europe and onto solid ground for a real workout. Fortunately, there were lots of things to do: friends to visit, card games to play, movies and music and dancing in the evenings, loafing with a book, a little illicit poker, trying not to get in trouble with the army of sharp-eyed officials.[27]

And the food! The *Roosevelt* might not have been the grandest ship on the ocean but it had a well-stocked larder and cooks who knew how to fix tasty meals. For Frank, Jackson, the two Charlies and their teammates, the trip to the dining room three and four times a day was always something to savour — so much so that they had to be careful not to put on weight.

As it turned out, some would have more success with that than others.

CHAPTER 8

Amsterdam

PERCY HAD SEEN A STRIP of grey on the horizon from the deck of the *Albertic* that morning, during Cap's mandatory calisthenics, before being released for another fine breakfast. "I guess this is the last day on the boat," he wrote to his mother as he sat in the lounge. "We sighted land this morning. I think it's Ireland, at least everything looks green.

"Last night we had a concert and a mock trial which provided a great deal of fun. I was called on as a witness and had to give evidence against one of the head officials of the team. The whole thing was a scream from start to finish. We got to bed some time after midnight as training rules were relaxed for this one night.

"I was pretty lucky on the trip over; wasn't seasick once. Some of the other boys were pretty sick and I will admit feeling 'queer' once or twice, but I never missed a meal. The meals on the boat are great. Anything you want and no check to pay at the end of it.

"We started out by training three times a day. Then it was cut down to once a day when it got rough. Now it has gone up to twice a day again. This riding on a rolling ship makes a fellow kind of weak at the knees but I guess I'll get over my sea legs after a couple of days on shore. . . .

"I've had an invitation to run at the Toronto exhibition when going back. I don't think I will, though. Some of the boys have asked me to stop over for a week at Winnipeg and then at Calgary. I don't think I will."[1]

∽

The voyage across the Atlantic had not been entirely happy for Percy. He had had fun with his teammates, but he was not getting along with Cap Cornelius, the coach. It was Cap's notions of rigorous training that were the source of the tension. Weather permitting, a typical day under Cap's regime consisted of a session of calisthenics before breakfast, jogging and starting practice at mid-morning, then another workout in the afternoon. It was more training than Percy wanted to do, more than he felt he should be doing — a lot of counterproductive wear and tear now that he was already in the peak of condition. He complained about it to the team officials and was allowed some discretion with his workouts. Cap didn't approve. If Percy lacked the stamina to keep up with his teammates in training, what chance would he have at Amsterdam, competing against the best in the world? Despite Percy's winning performances in the trials, Cap was convinced that he would fade at Amsterdam, and that Johnny Fitzpatrick, whom he had coached all through high school, was Canada's best hope in the sprints.[2]

The Canadian team disembarked at Southampton shortly after dawn on July 19 to a welcoming speech from the town's robed mayor. Then it was up to London by train, where Harry Warren joined the party, much to Percy's delight. With Bob Granger no longer with him, it was good to see a familiar face from home. After a whirlwind tour of the city, the track team headed to Stamford Bridge stadium for a short workout, their first chance in more than a week, and did some actual running. Then it was off to Harwich to board another ship, this time the Channel ferry, for the crossing to Amsterdam, where they arrived in the middle of the night to put up at the Holland Hotel.[3]

Percy awoke the next morning and looked out the window to find himself over an alley lined with drinking establishments that was clearly in a bawdy part of the city. The bars had been closed and silent when the team arrived but would soon be lively again, player pianos pumping music into the street that would continue, accompanied by the shouts of noisy revellers caught up in the carnival spirit of the Olympics, until one o'clock in the morning. The hotel itself, the Holland, where the bulk of the Canadians were staying, was cramped and seedy, the small rooms packed with beds. Percy was sharing his room with three others: Harry Warren, Doral Pilling and four-hundred-metre runner Stanley Glover. Percy, the lightest of the four, got the flimsy cot that was stowed under one of the beds during the day. A toilet and sink were down the hall. There was also a tub somewhere, two in fact, to be shared by fifty people. On the whole, Robert Elson discreetly reported, the team was "comfortable, but not sumptuously housed."[4]

It could have been worse. The British team was struggling with conditions at the Lloyd Hotel beside the railway yard down by the docks, the officials in single and double bedrooms, the athletes in an adjoining structure divided into areas containing as many as sixty bunks each — what one newspaper described as "a railway shed fitted specially."[5] Filtering in through the windows came the chug and screech of trains and the sounds of stevedores and ships being unloaded, a round-the-clock cacophony that prevented the higher-strung of the athletes from getting much sleep. The best they could do was to draw up a schedule for switching beds, allocating the bunks in the quieter rooms to those who had yet to compete.[6]

Amsterdam was a lot of fun for Percy and his teammates. "All we do here is run," he complained to his mother, but there was still a lot of time to explore the city. One day after their workout half the team went out and bought wooden shoes and spent the rest of the day clunking around, their boisterousness peaking sometime in the evening when they started dancing the Charleston in the middle of the street, blocking traffic. Then Jimmy Ball had the idea of getting everyone to autograph his pair of clogs. That seemed like a good idea and so everybody did it and there followed an orgy of signing. One night the team decided to do something about the noise in the streets that was keeping them awake and they started flinging pails of water out the windows, dousing the drunken revellers from the neighbouring bars who congregated around the hotel entrance. That caused a commotion and had the police on the scene.[7]

And then there were all those encounters one had in a foreign city — encounters that sometimes revealed a hard edge in Percy. "Last night," he wrote to his mother, "we went into a big department store and learned there that a word that sounds like 'escullay' means hello. Well, we were walking through the store and there was a dumb-looking girl standing behind the counter and we all said 'escullay.' There wasn't even a flicker of recognition that she understood what we were saying and one of the fellows said that maybe we had the wrong word, but I said that the only reason was that she was dumber than the usual run of people. In fact we call them anything we want and they can't understand. But I had no sooner said this than she gave me a dirty look and then politely said that she understood me perfectly well, and she said this in perfect English and ended up with saying something about the Hollanders not being as simple as they looked. About this time I started laughing and heading for the door. This is only one of the funny things we have run into. There are thousands of others."[8]

Doral Pilling, meanwhile, couldn't resist buying a gun cane, a shotgun disguised as a walking stick that sporting Dutchmen carried on their country rambles to bring down small game. Hurrying back to the Holland Hotel, he and Percy decided that they had to test fire it then and there, out the window and into the brick wall on the other side of the street. That turned out to be a bad idea. Within minutes an agitated crowd had blockaded the hotel entrance and the police were again summoned. "Don't let it be said that we were calm and collected," Doral later recalled of his and Percy's frantic scramble to hide the evidence, "for we weren't, and we were surely glad to see the policeman knocking on other doors to make enquiries. You can hardly imagine the things we did, but remember we were in the prime of life, with worlds of pent-up energy and nothing to do except what we wanted. How could you have it better?"[9]

∽

Amsterdam's newly built Olympic Stadium was in the southern part of the city, a bus ride across town from the Holland Hotel. It was an impressive structure, larger and more striking than any stadium in Canada. It had been constructed on marshland, the area first drained and firmed up with thousands of piles, then elevated six feet with a million cubic yards of fill. The structure itself was of reddish brick. In front of the main entrance stood a hundred-and-fifty-foot-high tower where a flame would, for the first time, burn throughout the Olympics.

Inside, there was seating for forty thousand spectators in bleachers extending all around the field, roofed over on both sides at the middle, exposed to the sun and elements everywhere else. The grass field at the centre, where the field events would be held and most of the games played, was of newly laid sod, emerald green and untouched. Around it was a running oval, six lanes wide. The Dutch planners had wanted it to offer a colour contrast with the field, so the top layer consisted of crushed red brick, not grey cinders. Encircling the track was a larger outer ring of concrete for bicycle racing with alarming banks at the corners. It was white like the bleachers, furthering the pleasing colour contrasts.

There was just one thing wrong: the track wasn't finished. The Games began in less than a week and it was still a sunken trough for most of its length, the final layer of crushed brick yet to be laid. It was, Canadian team manager Bobby Robinson delicately put it, "not quite up to the standard that is looked for in competition of this kind."[10] American coach Lawson Robertson was somewhat sharper. "Deplorable, deplorable," he said. "It is the worst I ever saw in all my Olympic experiences and all the other arrangements here are just as bad." The Dutch by now were working round the clock and made assurances that the track would be ready in time for the opening ceremonies on July 28. "But it takes a year to make a good track!" Robertson moaned.[11]

With work still underway on the track, the Olympic Stadium remained off-limits and the athletes had to do their training elsewhere, mainly on a nearby patch of ground that passed for a field. Coach Cornelius immediately got the team to work, doing real sprinting now, and lots of it. Percy once again held back. His knee was sore, he said, and he was convinced that to do everything Cornelius prescribed would do him more harm than good.[12]

Having Bob Granger there would have helped. "Things were just the same then," Percy bitterly recalled many years later. "There was lots of room for the officials but not for the athletes and coaches."[13] After more than two years together, he had come to rely on Bob for a lot — not just for the personalized training program and the massages that kept his legs loose, but for more intangible things as well: the motivation Bob provided, the focus he instilled, his pep talks, his hovering protection, his infectious confidence that Percy was a winner. It had all been important in getting Percy this far and now he didn't have it. As Percy finished his workout and followed the team onto the bus for the ride back to the Holland, he was depressed and his confidence was slipping away.

⁂

Later that evening, Harry Warren returned to the Holland from an after-dinner constitutional with a big smile on his face. Guess who's here, he said, opening the door to the room he shared with Percy. He stepped aside to reveal a red-haired figure in a rumpled suit, clutching a suitcase and grinning. It was Bob.

Hello, Perce, he said. I told you I'd make it.

Back in Quebec City, the funds Bob needed to continue on to Europe, $250, had arrived not long after the Olympic team sailed down the St. Lawrence. Dot Williams had been instrumental in raising the money. She had come to put a lot of faith in Bob's coaching, viewing him as essential to her Percy's success. But she also knew that in just about every other aspect of his life Bob was fumbling, impractical and "hopeless," in need of all the help he could get.[14] After receiving a cable assuring him the money would be forthcoming, Bob booked third-class passage aboard the Canadian Pacific liner *Minnedosa*, the next trans-Atlantic steamer leaving Quebec City after the *Albertic*, and just managed to purchase the ticket at the last moment when the money finally arrived. He then made a mad dash in a taxi down to the dock and leaped on a departing tender to take him out to the *Minnedosa*, which was already in midstream — only to discover that he had misplaced his ticket. "Just as I was contemplating whether to confess then or take a stowaway's chance," he says, "the excited French Canadian taxi driver came rushing down the dock waving the precious ticket in the air. He stooped and tied it to an iron bolt and threw it aboard."[15]

With Bob now on the scene, the officials in charge of the team accepted his offer to help in exchange for a bed at the Holland — though he would have to look after his own transportation home after the Games. He was appointed trainer to the track and field athletes, to serve under Coach Cornelius. Bob could accept Cap's authority with regard to the other athletes, and he willingly provided whatever support was required and put in long hours giving massages. When it came to Percy, however, he brooked no interference. A blow-up with Cornelius followed, when Cap insisted that the runners compete in time trials just days before the Games were to begin. Bob had something to say about that — and he could be forceful when he was worked up. With that, Cap washed his hands entirely of Percy, warning that he would only have himself to blame when he lost. "Williams is taking his labors easy," reported team manager Bobby Robinson after things had cooled down. "He has not had his sweat suit off since leaving Hamilton and his methods of training are different to all others. The officials permit him to use his own judgment with the responsibility all his own."[16]

Even though it was now just days to the start of competition, there were things Bob Granger still wanted to work on with Percy. His first and foremost concern remained Percy's start, the arm action that he felt was not quite coordinated with the legs. Curiously, he chose to do a lot of his work with Percy at the Holland Hotel, in Percy's bedroom, making a space between the beds and having Percy launch himself out of his crouch and into a mattress held by his roommates. He put Percy through sessions of this every day leading up to the Games — once to Percy's great embarrassment, when a group of Dutch women watching from a window across the street started laughing.[17]

As Bob dramatically tells it, things finally clicked for Percy when they were at the workout field together and stopped to watch the American women sprinters practise their starts. "Suddenly Percy clutched my arm. 'Bob, they've got the arm action we've been working for. I see it now. I can do it. Come on.' Athletes are like that. You work and work at something and you think you'll never get it, and then some curious little thing happens one day, and you find yourself."[18] Bob would call this new and improved starting form of Percy's, a combination of Bob's guidance and Percy's instinct, a "shooting start." Most other sprinters, he said, launched out of their starting holes with a "driving start," taking two or three short, stabbing steps before getting into their full stride. Percy, thanks to his light bodyweight and strong, sinewy legs, was able to "shoot" out of his holes with such force that he was into full striding from practically his first step.[19]

∞

"Mes Chers Enfants," Percy began his letter to Bobby Gaul and his Hexamis friends. "Everything here is uckle buckle. Yesterday I met a lot of fellows on the American team, Paddock, Scholtz and some others.

"This place may be all right for some people but I think it's the bunk. Vancouver is bad enough but there's foreigners here any and every place you go. They gawk and stare at us but the best of it all is that we can stand up before them, look straight in their faces and tell them to go to Eagle Lake, and I'm telling you we certainly tell them off.

"Talk about cheap, good gosh, you can get suits here for 8 guilders 75 cents. This is exactly $3.50 in our money, and they are good suits, three piece and everything. I'm buying an expensive one and so are about three other fellows. Pilling, Glover, Jimmy Ball and I went into a store and ordered suits for all of us. Pretty expensive too, 25 guilders 25 cents. This is just a shade under ten dollars. The suit is an English whipcord. Not Bad Eh?

"I'm rooming with Stan Glover, Doral Pilling and Harry Warren now. We picked up Warren in London. Doral is a great big fellow and he and I go around all the time together. If we get into a row I'm sure he can get us out. He was boxing champ at his school for awhile. Bob Granger blew in yesterday. I certainly was glad to see him.

"Doggone but I wish I was up at Ethle's camp this weekend. All we do here is run, in the morning and at night. It seems to put a rough edge on your temper. The slightest little thing makes you mad. They say a fellow is in good shape if he's that way. Well maybe, but I doubt it."[20]

∽

With more and more athletes converging on Amsterdam in the lead-up to the Games, workout space was at a premium and tensions were high. On some days Percy and his teammates were scarcely able to do any sprinting, the makeshift track at the practice field being so crowded.[21] The presence of the Americans came to be a source of particular resentment and not a little jealousy, their team so large and so well-funded and taking up such a great deal of space. When they showed up for a training session, Bobby Robinson observed, it was "an impressive sight. They drove up in huge cars and a host of 150 track athletes swarmed over the field, accompanied by an army of coaches and trainers, including a regiment of negro rubbers and attendants. The Americans make a noise wherever they go and they make other nations look small when it comes to placing a team in Olympic competition."[22]

At first the Canadians kept their complaints private. But then it all burst forth, prompted by a report that the US team had been privately admitted to the Olympic Stadium and allowed to train on the unfinished track. The rumour was overblown. A few American athletes *had* managed to beg their way into the stadium one afternoon and had taken a brief turn on the finished portion of the oval.[23] It was a small thing but it riled the other national teams just the same. The Canadians, led by Pat Mulqueen, went down to the stadium the following day to demand a session on the oval as well, but they were denied entry. The French were similarly rebuffed and got into a fight with a stadium guard that resulted in a French official being struck in the face. Suddenly everyone was steaming at the Americans, all the resentment now out in the open. "The Americans are plainly not popular," wrote Lou Marsh in the *Toronto Star*. "The other nations here all seem to resent the United States' display of wealth and power and a characteristic desire to exhibit smartness in obtaining privileges denied others. . . . Smaller nations are evidently afraid to make an official complaint regarding the stadium, but not so with Canada. P.J. Mulqueen says Canada is not afraid of the United States, either in the committee room or on the field."[24]

Mulqueen wasn't fooling around. Brushing aside the cautionary warnings of some of the other team officials, he and Bobby Robinson lodged a protest, charging that the Americans were getting special treatment and demanding similar access for Canadians to the stadium track. When the track was finally completed and the Canadian team allowed some workout time on it on July 26, it was hailed as a great victory back home, the *Toronto Star* trumpeting in a page-one headline splashed across all eight columns: "Canada Wins Same Olympic Rights as US."[25]

All in all it was a typically contentious start to another Olympics, outraged badgers engaging in verbal battles in defence of their athletes, while the athletes themselves quietly focused on the real competition. From Percy's perspective, the hard-won workout on the new track was literally a washout, a torrential downpour sending him and his teammates scurrying for cover shortly after the start of their session. That was the extent of his exposure to the new track. The next chance he would have to step on it would be in the hundred-metre dash itself.

∞

On Saturday, July 28, Percy got into his cream-coloured flannel team suit with scarlet maple leaf on the pocket and headed to the stadium for the opening ceremony of the Ninth Olympic Games. Team officials had decided that he and the other sprinters would sit out the parade as it might tire them unduly before competition, which for them began the next day. Several other nations, including the US and Britain, were keeping their runners out as well. As the rest of the team assembled outside the stadium's Marathon Gate and formed up for the parade, Percy, Johnny, Buck and Ralph made for the athletes' section in the stands and settled down to watch the spectacle.

Percy had his camera safely hidden in his pocket. He wasn't supposed to have it. The firm that had purchased exclusive photographic rights for the Games was so determined to protect its monopoly that it had guards posted all around the stadium, scanning the crowd through binoculars for anyone trying to sneak a picture. Two thousand cameras would be seized. Percy had unwittingly gotten into trouble with a guard when he took out his camera during his stadium visit two days before, and had returned to the hotel feeling insulted and angry. He was now determined to get that shot.[26]

The ceremony began at two o'clock with the arrival of Prince Consort Henry, who would open the Games on behalf of Holland's Queen Wilhelmina. He took his seat in the royal box to a fanfare of trumpets and the entire stadium rose as a massed choir sang the Dutch national anthem. Outside, there was a last-minute scramble for tickets for the few seats remaining.

Another blast of trumpets and the march-past began of the forty-seven nations in competition, a total of more than five thousand officials and athletes, the largest in the history of the Games, and representing the most countries. The Greeks were in the lead, the start of an Olympic tradition. They were followed by the surprisingly large team from Argentina, then the Australians, the Belgians, and the Bulgarians in military-style outfits, carrying swords.

Then came the Canadian contingent, bulky heavyweight wrestler Earl McCready carrying the placard, rower Joe Wright with the flag, officials next and then the athletes, all marching in lockstep, three abreast in thirty-five rows. Earl's stride was a bit off and Fred Marples, a badger, was incessantly swabbing the sweat from his brow, but the overall effect was of pleasing precision. They stepped smartly up the track in a compact mass and in front of the royal box the men removed their straw boaters, Joe dipped the flag and everyone did a crisp eyes-right. That drew an ovation from the crowd and had Percy and the boys on their feet, clapping and cheering.

On and on it went: the Cubans, the Finns, the Germans sombrely clad in white trousers and black jackets, the team from Great Britain headed by a burly Highland piper, a solitary figure from Haiti, the Indians resplendent in blue turbans.

No sign of the French. They were boycotting the opening and were threatening to withdraw from the Games altogether over that poke in the snout received by one of their badgers. The Dutch authorities had momentarily appeased them with promises that the offending guard would be fired, but when the French team showed up for the opening ceremony, there the man was, still defiantly at his post. They went storming away.[27]

The end was almost in sight when the US contingent appeared through the Marathon Gate. The front of their column made a full half-circuit of the track before the entire team was in view, the crowds looking on in silence, then breaking into applause as they beheld the full size of the team. The Americans' marching was a bit straggly, the Canadians cattily noted, the women's shoes didn't match and the men "looked as only a collection of U.S. college men can look." They saluted military fashion but did not take their hats off.[28] Then came "Suisse" and "Afriq du Sud" and, finally, there were the Dutch, last into the stadium as was customary for the host nation. They made their circuit of the track to the loudest ovation of all, saluted the royal box and took their place on the field for the speeches and anthems and the Olympic oath and flag-raising.[29]

And then it was over. In twenty-four hours the real show would begin.

∽

It was evening now. Aboard the *President Roosevelt* anchored out in the harbour the mood of the American team was buoyant and expectations were high. General MacArthur in one his speeches to the athletes set the tone succinctly. "We are here," he said, "to represent the greatest country on earth. We did not come here to lose gracefully. We came here to win — and win decisively."[30]

Prospects seemed particularly rosy in the sprints. It was widely assumed that the US had such a strong team with Wykoff, Bracey, McAllister, Paddock, Scholz and the rest that multiple dash medals were certain. It could almost be mathematically proven, some newspapers argued, by comparing the results of the Olympic trials in Boston with those from the qualifying meets in other nations. American athletes in almost every instance were faster. Canada for some reason was not included. The one Canadian runner that the Americans had viewed as a threat was Cyril Coaffee. They were surprised that Cyril had not made the team.[31]

The sprints of course weren't going to be a complete cakewalk for the States. The stiffest competition was expected to come from the Germans, returning to Olympic competition after a sixteen-year absence that had begun with the Great War. By all accounts they were doing great things with scientific methods of training. "It is the mechanics of muscle," explained Joseph Waitzer, German national track coach. "For instance, it was considered that dash men should run on their toes. That is wrong. It violates the fundamental law of mechanics of the body. The body has two kinds of muscles — antagonist and synergist — those that work against the motion and those that travel with it. If the former are overworked it causes weakness and ultimate collapse."[32]

It sounded like the Germans knew what they were doing. They had four ace sprinters in competition, all trained by Waitzer. They were George Lammers, Richard Corts, Hubert Houben and Helmut Koernig. The Americans would be watching them closely.

❧

At the Holland Hotel a subdued air hung over the Canadian sprinters. They were feeling it now, that build-up of tension before a big meet, nagging low-grade anxiety occasionally cresting into a wave that had to be pushed firmly down. Bobby Robinson had just dashed off his latest dispatch and cabled it to the *Hamilton Spectator*. Within a few hours the folks back home would be reading it in their evening newspaper. "The strain is a terrific one on the boys," he observed, "but they are receiving every attention and will give their utmost for the Maple Leaf. It is do or die now."[33]

In the Holland's dining room Percy finished his dinner, which was thankfully not as greasy as those first few meals, before the team had asked for more Canadian-style fare, lighter on sauces. Then he got out his diary and made his brief daily entry: "The big opening. Spectacular? Boy, I'll say so. Speeches, parade, pigeons, etc. Took a picture I wasn't supposed to. It wasn't so bad. It happens tomorrow."[34] "It" was the start of competition. Percy was trying not to think about it. He started his evening stretching routine.

Ten o'clock curfew. Time for the team to go up to their rooms. Percy pulled his cot out and lay down but he and the boys continued talking. There wasn't much point trying to sleep until the noise eased in the street below. Worst of all was the mechanical jazz organ in the beer hall on the ground floor of the Holland. The manager had agreed to shut it off one hour before the usual one o'clock closing. That meant it still had two more hours to play.

Midnight. Bobby Robinson, Bobby Kerr and Bob Granger went out to ask the other neighbourhood bars to keep a lid on the noise, pleading that the Canadian athletes were in bed and needed their sleep. Some agreed to curtail the racket. Others were less obliging. Granger kept at them. Upstairs in Percy's room the talk had died down. Percy remained very still in his bed down close to the floor. Its short legs had a way of collapsing when he rolled over. He lay quietly in the darkness, staring up at the ceiling, listening to the sounds of the city drift in through the window along with the breeze.

▲ The 1928 Olympic 100-metre final. Percy, fourth from left, pauses from digging his start holes. (BCSHFM)

▲ The start. From left to right are Frank Wykoff, Bob McAllister, Jack London, Percy Williams, George Lammers and Wilfred Legg. (BCSHFM)

▲ The finish of the Olympic 100-metre final. From left to right are Frank Wykoff, Bob McAllister, Jack London (silver), Percy (gold), George Lammers (bronze) and Wilfred Legg. (BCSHFM)

◀ Percy, moments after winning the 100-metre Olympic gold medal. (BCSHFM)

Percy being ▶ carried by Phil Edwards (left) and Brant Little after winning the 100-metre gold medal. (BCSHFM)

Percy, in the near ▶ lane, on his way to eliminating Charlie Paddock, third from left, in the Olympic 200-metre semi-finals. (PADDOCK, *TRACK AND FIELD*)

▲ Percy winning the 200-metre Olympic gold medal. From left to right are Johnny Fitzpatrick, Jackson Scholz, Helmut Koernig, Walter Rangeley, Jacob Schuller and Percy. (BCSHFM)

▲ Percy, embarrassed as he's cheered. Doral Pilling and Bob Granger on the left, Cap Cornelius at back on the right. (BCSHFM)

▲ Percy and his mother Dot Williams smiling to the crowds
at his Vancouver homecoming, September 14, 1928. (BCSHFM)

▲ Percy, Bob Granger and young "Spuddie" Millar with the
Graham-Paige coupe car presented to Percy by the mayor of
Vancouver, on behalf of the city. (BCSHFM)

◀ Phil Edward, Percy and Johnny Fitzpatrick (left to right) in February 1929 during the US indoor track season. (BCSHFM)

▲ Percy at the wheel of a big Packard during the month he spent in Hamilton selling cars, March 1929. (BCSHFM)

▲ A rare flash photo of Percy, wearing Vancouver Athletic Club colours, winning an indoor race, February 1929. (BCSHFM)

The wrapper from an "Our Percy" ▶ candy bar, one of several products to cash in on Percy's sudden fame. (BCSHFM)

▲ Percy (far left) with Johnny Fitzpatrick, members of the Canadian women's sprint relay team (centre) and high jumper Ethel Catherwood (far right), Vancouver, July 1929. (BCSHFM)

▲ Percy beats Frank Wykoff in a preliminary heat prior to the "Century of Centuries," July 12, 1929. Johnny Fitzpatrick is second from the left. (BCSHFM)

◀ Handshakes between Frank Wykoff, Eddie Tolan and Percy Williams (left to right) after the "Century of Centuries," Vancouver, July 13, 1929. (BCSHFM)

Percy in his prime circa 1929, posing ▶ with a proud Emslie Yeo, the King Edward High teacher who had first coached him in track. (BCSHFM)

CHAPTER 9

The Hundred Metres

∽

SUNDAY, JULY 29. Day One. Percy put in a long morning of anxious waiting, then joined the rest of the team for a lunch nobody wanted. Phil Edwards, who would be competing in the eight hundred metres, barely touched his food before jumping up to continue his pacing. Percy managed to stay seated and quietly ate his meal but his nerves were jangling too. Johnny Fitzpatrick beside him, usually a gregarious fellow, remained silent and solemn. Bob Granger, on the other hand, was uncharacteristically loud, storming about the slowness of the service, but when his meal came all he could do was push the food about on his plate.[1] He was a nervous wreck. "I couldn't sit still," he said, "couldn't even stand still. I must have walked ten miles uselessly before the time came for the start of the first heat."[2]

Reporter Robert Elson stopped by Percy's table and laid a hand on his shoulder. "I wonder where one could see a track meet this afternoon?" he joked, trying the ease the tension.

Percy smiled. "Oh yes," he said, playing along, "there's a Sunday school picnic out in one of these stadiums here." Then a more serious look came over his face. "It's hard to believe all this. You know, when I was a kid I used to read about the Olympic Games, but I thought only heroes came to these affairs."[3]

They arrived at the Olympic Stadium at one o'clock and made for the dressing room under the stands. It had been drizzling on and off all morning. The track would be wet for the first day of racing, wet and slow and what the runners called "heavy." A total of eighty-seven athletes from thirty-four countries were entered in the hundred-metre dash, more than any other Olympic hundred before, more than any other for the next forty-four years. It would take sixteen heats to accommodate them all in the first round, the first two finishers in each advancing. The run-offs were to begin at 2:45.

Percy was scheduled to run in heat twelve, an hour into the proceedings. As usual he remained in the dressing room until the last possible moment before heading onto the field. He didn't know a thing about any of the other four runners he was facing, men from Czechoslovakia, Lithuania, Portugal and France. (Yes, the French were back.) A British official was doing the starting, giving the commands in English. Percy, the practice against the mattress evidently having helped, got away to a good start, two yards in the lead by the time they were up and running, and he held it right through to the finish, clocked at eleven seconds. Only the Czech, Vykoupil, was able to stay near him. The others were completely outclassed.

The remaining three Canadian sprinters advanced as well, Johnny Fitzpatrick winning his heat, Buck and Ralph running second in theirs. Johnny's win in particular raised a few eyebrows when he edged out the German Richard Corts, widely regarded as one of the best sprinters in Europe. The four American sprinters, meanwhile, Wykoff, McAllister, Bracey and Russell, all won their heats. So did the Germans Houben and Lammers.

The first round was over. Fifty-five athletes had been eliminated, thirty-two were left. It was time for round two. There would be six heats.

Johnny was up first and again he advanced, running second behind South African Wilfred Legg in a very close finish that took the judges some minutes to decide. McAllister and Russell won heats two and three, trailed by the Germans Corts and Houben. The winning times were getting a bit faster now, mostly 10 4/5.

Percy's turn came in heat four. Again he was up against runners he had never heard of: an Argentine, another Frenchman, a Cuban and that lone athlete from Haiti he had seen in the parade the day before, no one posing a serious challenge. He coasted to another comfortable win.

Buck and Ralph didn't make it, both finishing last in their heats. Ralph lost his race fair and square. As for Buck, he had had terrible luck. As the runners were nearing the finish, a gust of wind caught the tape from a just-completed eight-hundred-metre race that officials had left lying around and blew it out across the track, causing Buck and another man to misjudge the finish and ease up too early. Bobby Robinson, bashing out a story up in the press box, was hopping mad, and Pat Mulqueen stormed out on the field to demand that the race be re-run. The Americans responded with equal vigour that nothing of the sort should be done. Their man Henry Russell had won it and he shouldn't have to win twice because of some mistake the Canadian made. That stoked Mulqueen's temper even hotter and he was eventually ordered off the field, proclaiming as he went that Canada would *not* be attending the Los Angeles Olympic Games in 1932.[4]

Back at the Holland Hotel that evening the Canadian team was roundly congratulating Percy. They had been hoping for good things from him and so far he had delivered. At dinner he got everyone laughing when he blandly responded to Doral Pilling's gushing on how fast he'd run: "Oh, I didn't run so hard." They all thought Percy was being modest but Bob Granger knew he was just stating a fact. From his seat in the stands he had noted that Percy had won his heats without fully opening the throttle.[5]

That was it for Percy's first day of competition. Of the eighty-seven runners who had started, seventy-five had fallen by the wayside. Twelve were left and Percy was among them. "My ideals of the Olympic Games are all shot," he wrote in his diary. "I always imagined it was a game of heroes. Well, I'm in the semifinals myself so it can't be so hot."[6] Bob gave his legs a rubdown and delivered another pre-bed pep talk, then headed out to patrol the street, making sure that it stayed quiet. His boy needed his rest.

∽

The Americans were pleased. All four of their sprinters had survived the first day of competition and were going into the semis, a perfect record. The Germans had looked tough, just as expected. Three of them, Corts, Houben and Lammers, were still in competition. Jack London, competing for Great Britain, had also emerged as an unexpected threat, edging past Frank Wykoff in their second-round heat to tie the Olympic record. Canada's Percy Williams had won his heat in the same time, 10 3/5, running against relative unknowns, but at a reported 126 pounds he seemed too slight to get much further. All things considered, the chances of American gold in the final were looking very good, with maybe a silver or bronze in the bargain.

The Olympic track, though, was a cause for concern. The American runners had found it too soft for their liking — certainly too soft for setting records. That dimmed hopes for Frank Wykoff. Frank had a floating style of running, those who seemed to know what they were talking about were saying, and a floating style worked best on a firm track, where his feet could bounce like rubber balls off the surface. In any event Frank seemed to be off his form. He had struggled in his heats, not the same athlete who had run so smoothly at the trials in Boston. Maybe it was the extra weight. It was being whispered that he had gained eighteen pounds on the trip over.

With the team's confidence in Wykoff slipping, some of the pundits aboard the *Roosevelt* were now looking to Bob McAllister as America's best chance for gold in the hundred, the long-shot "Flying Cop" who had made the team despite predictions that he was past his prime. Bob, the reasoning went, was a driving rather than a floating sprinter who dug in like a plough horse when he ran down the track. The soft surface at the Olympic Stadium favoured a driver, so Bob was their man.

McAllister himself certainly thought so. So did his trainer, Jake Weber, who claimed that Bob's form on the first day of competition had never been better. "Run like that tomorrow," he assured Bob that evening, "and you'll be the first Yank to equal or break the Olympic record of ten-three. I expect great things of you."[7] The Flying Cop's destiny was now looming large. He continued to speak of it often.

∽

Monday, July 30. Day Two. The hundred-metre semifinals were the first event on the card. There would be two heats, scheduled to begin at two o'clock, the first three runners in each advancing. Percy was in the first, Johnny Fitzpatrick in the second. It had rained overnight and the track remained heavy. In the dressing room Bob Granger advised Percy to do the bare minimum of warming up for his semi so as to conserve energy for the final. He was also to switch from one knee to the other as he dug his start holes, as using only one knee might strain it and throw him off form. It hardly bore mentioning that he wasn't under any circumstances to bend over while digging. As Bob had told him many times before, this stretched out muscles that needed to be kept taut.

They could hear McAllister talking loudly on his side of the room, getting himself worked up for the race. "I'm destined to win this 100-metre race before I retire," he proclaimed, "and raise a family of sprinters." The bravado ticked off Granger. He didn't like the Flying Cop and wanted to see him brought down.

Out on the track a German official, Franz Miller, had the pistol, so the start commands for the day would be given in German. Percy was now up against some very serious competition: Bob McAllister and his fellow American Claude Bracey; one of those scientifically trained Germans, Hubert Houben; and the South African Wilfred Legg, who had the day before beaten Johnny Fitzpatrick. Percy was in lane four, between the two Americans.

Herr Miller had a disconcerting way of starting. After issuing the "set" command (*Fertig!*) he paused for a long time before firing the pistol. Percy hung there coiled in his forward lean, waiting, waiting, but could not maintain the tension and was starting to ease back when the gun finally sounded. He got away to a terrible start, out of his holes behind everyone except the Argentine, Juan Bautista Pina. He was going to have to push to the limit. He accelerated and slipped into his stride, catching Houben at the halfway mark and then Claude Bracey. By the eighty-metre mark he was in overdrive and bearing down on Legg and McAllister in the lead, giving it everything he had. But so was the Flying Cop, "chest out, head up and his arms flying wildly like a Dutch windmill in a channel storm," as Granger described it. With a final surge Percy willed himself past Legg, but McAllister remained a foot in the lead, winning in 10 3/5.

McAllister was ecstatic. His destiny was unfolding according to plan. "It was the greatest race I had ever run in my life," he later wrote. "I felt like jumping with joy."[8] In the dressing room afterward he approached Percy and said he had been "easy pickings."[9] Now Bob Granger *really* didn't like him — although he noted with satisfaction the hard look that came over his boy's face.

Johnny Fitzpatrick hadn't made it. He had finished fourth in his semifinal and was out, leaving Percy the only Canadian going into the last round. With the exertion of the race having momentarily burned off most of his tension, Percy lay down on a rickety massage table of boards nailed together and found he was able to relax as Granger scooped out the last of his cocoa butter and went to work again on his legs. Bob had been giving massages to all the Canadian runners and had quickly run through his supply. When he sensed that Percy was starting to get restless he gave him a book to read.

The competition in the final would be stiff. At twenty-nine McAllister should have been past it by the standards of the day, but he had been running like a man possessed and judging from his powerful build would still have a lot of energy left. Frank Wykoff was not living up to all the advance billing, but he had made it this far and had to be considered a threat, particularly in light of his phenomenal performance at the Boston trials a few weeks before. Anyone who could win four one-hundred-metre races in a single afternoon, all in Olympic-record time, had serious talent and guts. The South African Wilfred Legg was fast, but not unbeatable. Word had it, moreover, that he had an injured thigh. George Lammers had emerged as the strongest of the feared German quartet. He had finished second in his semi, ahead of Wykoff.

Finally, Jack London looked to be perhaps the most dangerous opponent of all. A native of British Guiana attending medical school in England, Jack trained under the legendary Sam Mussabini, who had coached Harold Abrahams to his gold medal victory at the 1924 Paris Olympics. No one, not even the British, had been very optimistic about Jack's chances in the lead-up to the Games, but he had proved himself, tying the Olympic record twice in winning his second-round heat and his semifinal. Like McAllister, he was intimidatingly big and strong and he likely still had plenty of drive left.

∽

Four o'clock. An official with a clipboard stepped into the change room. One-hundred-metre final, gentlemen, he announced, striding between the benches and tables. One-hundred-metre final, if you please.

Bob pulled back the blankets he had been using to warm Percy, releasing him from the massage table, his body smelling of cocoa. Well, it's time for another race, he said, trying to keep his voice calm. You've been here before, boy. It's just another Brockton Point race.

Percy slid off the table and began shaking his legs, testing them, and rotating his arms. His muscles felt good — warm and supple. He wasn't smiling. His face had a hard-set look. Bob, watching him closely, could sense the determination and the inner struggle. Deep breaths now, he said. Deep breaths, boy.

Percy filled his lungs, pushing against the tightness in his solar plexus. He kept at it as he put on his baggy sweatsuit and the rubber-soled canvas sneakers he would wear out onto the track. Then, for added warmth, he slipped on his black sweater.

The other competitors were heading for the door. Percy exchanged nods with London, Legg and Lammers, grim looks like those between soldiers waiting to scramble out of their trenches and go over the top. US coach Lawson Robertson shepherded his two athletes past, Wykoff and McAllister. McAllister as usual was talking. Percy glowered.

Bob accompanied Percy down the tunnel, dark and quiet with a stab of light at the end, and came to the stairs that led up to the track. Robertson was trying to bluff his way past the guard stationed by the top step but was having no luck. Only athletes and officials were allowed past this point. Granger desperately wanted to stay with his runner as well but there was no getting by the guard. He gave Percy a final pat on the back. Remember, it's just another race, he said. And then Percy was gone. Bob returned to the dressing room and silently folded his blankets and towels and packed up his bag with his liniments and tape and wraps and the empty can of cocoa butter. Then he followed Robertson up the long flight of stairs that led to the stands, "trembling like a leaf as I went."[10]

∽

Stepping out of the quiet of the tunnel and into the middle of a packed stadium reverberating with noise was disconcerting. The contrast struck Percy almost like a physical blow. He made his way to the head of the hundred-metre course and found a spot on the grass. The semi-finals of the women's dash were underway, the Canadians doing well.

Percy removed his sneakers and put on his "toe pushers," low-cut socks made of soft chamois. Next he slipped into his spikes. The fit when he had the laces done up was not very snug, so he wound two turns of white tape around the instep to ensure that there would be no slippage. He stood to test them, bouncing and taking a few slow starts. They felt good, moulded to his feet. He kept on his sweater and sweat-suit.

The women's semis had ended and the Canadians had aced it. Three of them would be going into the final. Stadium workers began raking the track, removing the spike marks. They didn't use a roller, so the surface would be soft. Down at the finish line officials in dark blazers and white boaters were milling about.

A start-line official in a beret said something in Dutch and motioned

Percy and the other finalists to the chalk line. Percy had lane three. Lammers and Legg were to his left, on the inside. London, McAllister and Wykoff were on the outside to his right. Percy kneeled at the head of his lane and went to work with his trowel, excavating his holes in the cinders. From his seat in the stands down by the finish, Bob Granger noted approvingly that his boy was switching from one knee to another. The announcement of the event began over the loudspeakers.

The stadium was now pulsing with noise, a steady hum punctuated by shouts and cheers. On the far side of the field a German contingent had begun waving a large tricolour and was shouting out the name of their hero, Lammers. In another section a large body of Americans let loose with organized cheers of "Wy-koff! Mc-All-i-ster! U.S.A.!" There weren't enough Canadians present to do much cheering for Percy but a few isolated calls of "Will-yams! Will-yams!" drifted up from the Dutch fans. Percy looked so slight between McAllister and London that he had taken their fancy.[11]

Percy concentrated on his holes, gauging the depth with his fingers, getting the back angle just right. Then he stripped off his sweater and sweatsuit and laid them on the grass by his sneakers. Unlike the other finalists, he had not pinned his number, 667, to his jersey, but across the front of his shorts so as not to obscure the red maple leaf on his chest.

The runners began to gravitate back to their lanes. In a wordless ballet they crouched in their holes, took two or three starts, ran a few paces at three-quarter speed to loosen their legs and bring on a sweat. Then they were directed to the start line. McAllister, towering over Percy and outweighing him by seventy pounds, drifted past, grinning as he looked the delicate Canadian up and down. You sure you're up for this, kid? he said. It was the Bowery cop's usual pre-race malarkey.[12] To Percy it was just bad manners. He didn't say a word.

The shrill blast of a whistle alerted the officials at the far end of the track to get ready. The timekeepers took their seats on the five-step stand in line with the finish and reset their stopwatches. Canadian team captain Bobby Kerr was among them. The finish judges clustered on either side. On the inside and slightly behind the runners, Franz Miller took his place with his pistol.

"*Auf der platz!*"

On your marks. Percy gave his legs a final shake, gazing down the length of his lane, breathing deeply, repeating Granger's soothing mantra: *You've been here before, boy. It's just another race.* He held back a moment, letting the others get down first.

He inserted his left foot in the forward hole and positioned his hands tight against the white of the start line, gave his right leg a final kick and placed his other toe in the hole to the rear. Right knee down, touching the brick dust, in line with the instep of his left foot. Head down. Breathing deeply. Relax. Relax.

"*Fertig!*"

Percy raised his hips until his back was parallel with the track. Head up, eyes cast down the track. Knees off the ground, red dust clinging to the skin. Spikes pressing back into the holes, tension building, his entire body coiled like a spring. A final deep breath. Hold it. Hold it.

A movement off to his left. Wilfred Legg in lane one had started early. Herr Miller ordered them up and issued the South African a warning. Percy rose from his holes and began pacing back and forth, focusing on the sound of Granger's voice: *It's just another race, boy. Just another high school race.*

"*Auf der platz!*"

A few final bounces and arm flaps. Percy settled again at the chalk line, careful not to damage his holes with his spikes. If the back angle of either hole were broken down, it would rob him of a good start.

"*Fertig!*"

Body up and poised. Tension building. Deep breath. Heartbeat thundering in his ears.

Again a flash of movement, this time on the right, followed an instant later by the gun and a fleeting whiff of powder. Frank Wykoff in lane five had bolted. Up they came a second time. Percy jogged a few paces down the track before returning to the start for a bit more pacing. Herr Miller served up Wykoff's warning. There had been wild talk that the Americans might try something sneaky like the false-starting trick Paddock had mentioned. Seeing the young Californian now, that didn't seem likely. He was tense and jumpy. One more false start and he would be out.

"Auf der platz!"
This is just another race . . .
"Fertig!"
. . . just another high school race . . .
The gun.

༄

The practice in the hotel room with Granger tells. Percy gets away fast, exploding out of his holes, torso rising quickly to the vertical as he accelerates and lengthens his stride. McAllister in lane six is keeping pace, off to one of his best starts ever. The others are just a fraction behind.

From up in the stands it looks like the entire field is breaking together. Bob Granger, the blood drained from his face, is on his feet, hanging on to the wire fence running in front of his seat. Come on boy, he says softly. Come on boy.

Twenty metres. Percy's legs are cycling beautifully, smooth, vicious downward stabs, feet driving into the track and bouncing back. He has his stride. He's loose and relaxed, exhibiting that style that makes what he does look so deceptively easy. The pre-race nervous tension is gone and forgotten. All the pent-up energy, all the fear, is being funnelled direct to his legs.

Thirty-five metres. Percy and Jack London are in the lead. Legg, on the inside lane, is a fraction behind. His troublesome thigh is holding together. A tic behind him, in a tight bunch, is the rest of the field. It is still anyone's race.

Fifty metres. Percy pulls ahead of London and into the lead. He has now reached his maximum speed, 10.4 metres per second, 23.3 miles per hour.[13] Legg is fighting with Lammers for third. Wykoff, the American hope, is fading. The softness of the track, the upset in training, the extra weight — something is throwing him off. McAllister in lane five is still a threat. This is his destiny he's fighting for. This is his last chance. He bears down and pushes himself to the limit.

Sixty metres. London challenges, coming up beside Percy. Percy remains in stride, torso erect, legs pedalling with complete relaxation. The two briefly run even. London drives harder.

Seventy metres. London can't pull ahead of Percy. He's having difficulty sustaining the effort. Legg is falling back. Lammers in lane two moves up to claim third.

Eighty metres. Percy's head is down, chin pressed into his chest. He's in the lead, clearly this time, the rest of the field angling back on either side, forming an arrow with Percy at the tip. London and Lammers are battling for second, followed by Legg and MacAllister for third. Wykoff, his face contorted, is last.

Eighty-five metres. McAllister staggers, a hot needle of pain searing through his thigh. Something has torn. He starts to fade. Wykoff, still struggling, comes even with him.

Ninety metres. The finish line is there. Beside it are clustered more than a dozen officials, five clutching stopwatches, necks craned forward. The look of controlled determination suddenly vanishes from Percy's face. Arms outstretched, head back, mouth agape, features strained in the final throes of agonized effort, he throws himself through the tape in one almighty leap, ahead of London by a metre, Lammers a further few inches behind. Legg, Wykoff and McAllister follow.[14]

Percy slows to a trot, then a walk. Well, he's done it. He turns to start back up the track. He always does that afterward, usually at a jog, heading back to the start line to pick up his gear. London and Lammers stop to shake his hand. So do the others, murmuring their congratulations as they struggle to catch their breath. McAllister offers his hand, a pained look on his face, then bends to rub his thigh. Destiny has just passed him by and all he has to show for it is a torn muscle.

Frank Wykoff is the most visibly upset. Just three weeks before he had been in the peak of condition, ready to conquer the world, praised to the skies. The emotional roller coaster of the past two days, culminating with a loss, is too much. He starts weeping.[15]

And then here is Bobby Kerr, running over from the finish line, forgetting the impartiality expected of a judge in all the excitement. He throws his arm around Percy's shoulder and is laughing as he congratulates him, he's so tickled. Percy, chest still heaving, utters his first words: "Won't Granger be pleased?"[16] For a moment they are two

Olympic champions together, the old and the new. Percy had been two months old when Kerr won his gold medal in the two hundred metres at the London Games in 1908.

And with that the noise comes washing over Percy, the thunderous cheering sweeping down from the stands, a wave of exhilaration at his unexpected victory, casting aside the last of his focus, the tunnel vision. And he realizes that this is not just another race after all. Asked later to describe his emotions at that moment, all he would say was, "I just felt queer. It struck me funny for a while."[17]

Up in the press box Bobby Robinson is picking his typewriter up from the floor and placing it back on the table. He had leaped to his feet during the race and sent it flying. Vancouver reporter Robert Elson, still a bit stunned, looks over to the small Canadian section of the grandstand on the other side of the press enclosure and sees Bob Granger standing there, staring at the field. His hand is bleeding, he had beaten it so hard on the fence in the final seconds as he urged his boy on. Granger doesn't seem to notice. Tears are streaming down his face.[18]

Down on the track Percy's teammates Brant Little and Phil Edwards bound over from the athletes' enclosure, hooting and hurrahing like a couple of kids. They hoist Percy onto their shoulders and parade him the length of the grandstand to the applause of the crowd as he awkwardly hangs on. Then it is over to the winner's podium where they set him down for the flag raising and anthem. The official results have by this time been announced over the stadium loudspeakers and are up on the giant board: the gold medal to Percy Williams, first in 10 4/5 seconds, silver to Jack London, bronze to George Lammers. Wykoff is listed as having placed fourth, Legg fifth, McAllister last. Percy climbs onto the top step, where he is flanked by London and Lammers. A long pause follows as a scramble takes place to find the Canadian flag but eventually it is located — an undersized one, the Canadian officials sourly note. They will lodge a protest. As it is run up the pole the Dutch band feels its way through "The Maple Leaf Forever," which it evidently hasn't practised. The anthem starts just as Percy is trying to pull his sweatpants back on over his spikes and his shorts. He yanks them up quickly and stands at attention.[19]

∽

Back in the dressing room afterward, Bob McAllister, no longer cocky, came up to explain why he hadn't won. Percy and Granger listened but were unsympathetic, doubly unimpressed now with the Flying Cop as he demonstrated that he was also a bad loser. After he left, a herd of reporters corralled Percy and began firing questions at him. Bob Granger overheard a correspondent from Sweden trying to set up a time in the evening when he could drop by the hotel for an interview. "I'll see you at ten minutes to eight," Percy said. Then: "No, make it nine minutes to eight." That's when Bob knew just how excited he was. "He would never believe me afterwards," he chuckled later, "but those were his words."[20]

Suddenly the name of Percy Williams was known all over the city and was being flashed round the world. Few people, though, knew what he actually looked like. As he left the exit from the stadium dressing rooms, bundled in his sweater and looking slight and boyish and decidedly unathletic, he was able to pass right through the crowd that had gathered outside to see him and boarded the team bus without anyone realizing who he was. "Why, he simply doesn't look like a champion," one of the American coaches would say. "He looked too much like a kid," observed another.

The same thing happened back at the Holland Hotel. After dinner Percy and Doral noticed a throng outside the entrance and strolled out to see what was going on. "We joined the mob, looking over shoulders," Percy recalled with relish many years later. "I asked a person in front of me why they were there and he said: 'We're waiting for the Canadian runner, Williams, to come out of the hotel.' I didn't tell him who I was. I stood around, waiting for him too, and talking to people. It was more fun."[21]

The evening was now well advanced and Bob was anxious to get Percy rested. His next event, the two hundred, began the following day. He asked Doral and Harry Warren to take him out for a walk to settle him down, then sent him to bed. The tearing excitement of his victory had now eased and Percy was able to at least pretend that he was unaffected. "Well, well, well," he recorded in his diary. "So I'm supposed to be the World's 100 M Champion. (Crushed apples.) No more fun in running now."[22]

With Percy safely tucked up in his room, the upper floors of the Holland were placed off limits, reporters who continued to show up asking for interviews not getting past the lobby. Our champion needs his sleep, Pat Mulqueen told them. The three Bobbys, Robinson, Kerr and Granger, headed out early to try to quiet the street. When things had settled down Bob Granger stationed himself in the hall outside Percy's door to guard against disturbances. His anxiety had returned with a vengeance. He remembered Percy's tendency to pull the sheet over his head in his sleep and slipped a note under the door to Harry Warren, keeping watch over Percy on the inside, asking him to make sure that their boy was all right. Percy was sleeping soundly, came the jotted reply.[23]

CHAPTER 10

Canada Euphoric

EIGHT TIME ZONES TO the west, the attention of Vancouver was focused on the scalp of Mayor L.D. Taylor. It had received a gash and the skull beneath it was cracked. The damage had been done as poor L.D. was stepping off the inaugural flight of BC Airways' new triangular service linking Vancouver with Victoria and Seattle. He had just climbed out of the fourteen-passenger monoplane and was stepping forward, smiling and waving — when he walked straight into one of the propellers. Thankfully it was on its last rotation and had almost stopped moving. Otherwise it would have clipped his head right off.[1]

Then came the news, the marvellous, magnificent, spectacular news: Percy Williams had won the Olympic gold medal. It arrived in the morning, in time to make the city's two evening dailies. "Local Boy Wins Sprint Crown" cried the *Vancouver Sun* in an eight-column banner headline, with stories below titled "Percy Williams 100 Per Cent Vancouverite" and "Crowds Acclaim Williams" and "New Champion

Thanks Coach for Victory." The *Daily Province* splashed a photo of Percy in his Commerce High togs across the entire height of the front page under the words "Percy Williams Puts City on Map" and beside the subtitle "City Is Agog with Pride."[2]

It certainly was. Vancouverites were tripping over themselves in their delight, for Percy was one of them. He was *theirs*. "There is no other town or city," crowed the *Sun*, "that can lay claim to even the tiniest share of the honour which this fleet-footed, clean-living young athlete has brought to his own home town. Williams . . . was born, raised, schooled and trained here — has lived all his life in Vancouver."[3]

Down at 196 Twelfth Avenue West reporters were already at the door, wanting to interview Percy's family. When the man from the *Morning Star* arrived, Grandpa Harry showed him in and soon had a photo album in his lap and a drink in his hand and was rattling away about Percy. Here he is when he was three, Harry was saying, as the mascot of the East End Lacrosse team . . . And did you know he was a prize baby? Well there's your proof . . . Oh Lord, and here he is with those old dogs . . . And — oh, that's us Rhodes men, "The Four Domes." We're bald and proud of it, eh? Eh? Percy, now, he has his father's hair . . . And now look at this. Four-leaf clovers! The lad collects them, you know, must have twenty in here. Oh, and there's quite a story that goes with that . . .

They looked up as Dot bustled in, followed by Percy's grandmother Selina. The reporter tried to ask Selina a few questions but she wasn't quite so easy to talk to as Harry. She did admit, however, to having been very anxious about Percy and not sleeping for the past two nights.

"Did you expect him to win?"

"Of course I did," she snapped.

The conversation turned to Dot. She spoke of how important Bob Granger was to her Percy's running success and went on to talk about how Percy was a very private person, that he didn't like attention and talking about himself.

"Why," piped up Selina, "when they asked Percy in Hamilton if he thought he was going to be seasick going across, he said 'I'm not there yet,' and that's typical of him."

"Have you any of Percy's trophies?"

"Well," Dot said hesitantly, "I'm not sure where they are, and perhaps he would not like me to show them to you." But she was soon rummaging about upstairs and reappeared with two silver cups.

"Is that all?"

"Oh no." She tipped over one of the cups. It was brimming with medals. "He has a few more." They weren't just for running, she noted, but also for tennis and shooting and what have you. "And he plays golf quite a bit."

"And he draws nice cartoons," added Harry.

"I suppose he plays the piano too?" said the reporter.

"Well, he is not so good on the piano," Harry replied, missing the humour. "But I'll say that boy handles a darn fine Uke."[4]

Elsewhere in the country the excitement was every bit as intense. Percy's victory was trumpeted in banner headlines from the East Coast to the West, articles gave glowing accounts of the race, editorials and sports columns were filled with praise and emotion. There were even poems.

The Toronto *Globe* kicked things off with something in the traditional line: "The thrill of victory sweeps o'er the seas / Canada's flag floats proudly in the breeze / Proud are we of this youthful native son / Who the one-hundred-metre race has won . . ." and so on for another twenty-eight lines.[5] The *Daily Province* came out with a four-stanza piece entitled "Son of the West" which included the lines: "We longed, you know / To see you on your mark, get set, and dart like arrow from the bow / Speeding upon the wind / Strong-winged of heel and palm / While England, Germany, Africa and Uncle Sam / Trailed hopelessly behind."[6]

Others went with the earthy argot that was popular with readers in the 1920s, such as the offering from the *Hamilton Spectator*'s sporting pundit "Ezra Reckles," replete with misspellings and unabashed Canadian resentment. The Americans "boasted for days be4 the race," it read, "but they were put back in there place, these disciples of Smith and Hoover, by a young lad from Vancouver. Even Wykoff, the Yanks best man, was made to look like an also ran, by the lad from the Pacific coast, the lad who listened to their boast, the little speed merchant so modest, crushed there hopes down in the sawdust. . . ."[7] And in another paper, one "C.M.K." assumed verbal blackface to spin a tale of getting into a fight over Percy in a bootleg gin joint, taking on an American who said that the States would snatch up Canada's hero as soon as he got back from Europe:

> I'm not fight so moche, so dat's maybe w'y
> I'm not lose so many fight.
> But I'm ready for get plenty more black eye,
> For see Williams treated right!
>
> Too many our boys pass on U.S.A. —
> Dey're goin' dere every year.
> De place I am t'inkin' for have dem stay,
> Is where dey are born — right here![8]

∾

In the United States the news of Percy's victory was greeted with bewilderment. "What's the matter with the American Olympic team?" began the page one story in the *New York Times*. It had been assumed that US athletes would dominate track and field; as Douglas MacArthur had put it a few days before, they had "nine firsts sewed up."[9] Now, in one awful afternoon, they had lost the hammer throw to an Irishman, the four-hundred-metre hurdles to an Englishman and, worst of all, the hundred-metre dash to an unknown Canadian schoolboy. Since the first Olympic Games in 1896 Americans had won a total of five golds and six silvers in the hundred and had never done worse than second. And yet here they were, shut out entirely from the medals after sending to Amsterdam what everyone had thought was their best crop of sprinters ever. The American papers gave Percy his due. He had earned his accolades. But what people really wanted to know wasn't why he had won but why the Americans had lost. Bob McAllister had torn a muscle. Fair enough. But what happened to Frank Wykoff? And why had Claude Bracey and Henry Russell not even made it into the final?

All sorts of reasons were suggested: the Americans had been overworked going into the Games, with many leaving their best performances at the trials in Boston; the sprinters were used to top-notch tracks back home and got bogged down on the mushy Amsterdam surface; the US team had too many coaches and trainers, resulting in the athletes getting conflicting advice; the athletes themselves were staying up late and carousing and breaking training, not like in the good old days, when rule-breakers risked getting tossed off the team.

And then there was the matter of all that food aboard the *Roosevelt*, tempting the athletes to overindulge. Frank Wykoff fell in for particular criticism on this score. It was reported that "he had been stuffing himself on double portions of beef-steak on the voyage and since his arrival until he became ten pounds over-weight."[10] One disgruntled American coach anonymously stated: "I've never seen anything like it. Why, go up in the smoking room at 11 o'clock and you'll see those fellows tearing into bologna sausage like a pack of hounds."[11]

The thought of porcine Americans losing due to overeating delighted the foreign press and they ran with the story. A writer in London's *Evening Standard* stated that the American sprinters had failed due to "lavish feeding," adding, "I have been rubbing my eyes in wonder with the statistics of ice cream consumed by the American team."[12] Another critic said that the team had "dug its grave with its own teeth." A reporter for the *Toronto Star* recalled dining with the abstemious British and South African teams and coming away hungry, but noted that when the Americans invited him aboard the *Roosevelt* they treated him to "thick soup, salmon with mayonnaise, roast Long Island gosling, baked potatoes and ice cream."[13] With American extravagance — gluttony! — as the back story, it was perhaps inevitable that the Canadian public would read a few days later of how their own Percy Williams had dined on "a light repast of tomato salad, cucumbers and mineral water" and gone straight to bed.[14]

For the American team and their supporters it was a bit hard to take.

It wasn't that Americans were bad losers. After David Lord Burghley of Great Britain won the four-hundred-metre hurdles, his US rivals congratulated him so effusively that he gushed: "What splendid losers those Americans are! They were awfully sporting about it."[15] What was really annoying was that, off the track, other nations were sometimes not very good winners — not the athletes per se, certainly not fellows like Percy Williams and Lord Burghley, but the officials and journalists and fans. They took delight in seeing the States beaten. They seemed to have a deep-seated resentment of the USA, a scarcely disguised jealousy of the American team's size and talent, its self-confidence and influence, and in particular its generous financial backing, epitomized by the *President Roosevelt* anchored out in the harbour. It seemed to *bother* other nations that the United States had spent a great deal of money to send a large and talented team to the Olympics, adding lustre to the Games. It seemed to *annoy* them that the Americans took excellent care of their athletes, housing them in comfortable quarters and providing them with good food and plenty of coaches and trainers. When Percy Williams won the hundred, the rejoicing that ensued therefore wasn't just over the fact that a Canadian or a member of the British Empire had won, but that he had beaten the Americans — that an American had lost. That was what was so galling. That was what was so hard to take.

"The greatest trouble about losing to the foreigners," wrote US lacrosse player Louis Nixdorff that evening, "is seeing the thrill they get out of beating an American. They are very enthusiastic about anybody who can trim an American. That is their great objective. It is really quite nauseating and infuriating to see the ardor with which they beat us. However we [may] make them take a back seat yet."[16]

CHAPTER 11

"I Just Ran"

PERCY, STILL IN HIS pyjamas, sat on the bed in his room at the Holland Hotel the next morning, surrounded by his roommates Harry, Doral and Stan. Jimmy Ball had come in too to join in the fun. They were going through the congratulatory cables that had been pouring in for Percy since the previous evening, having a whale of a time opening and passing them around. Bob Granger stood quietly in the doorway. He liked to see Percy like this. Reading the telegrams was keeping him relaxed, his mind diverted from what was coming later that day.

There was a message from Percy's mother, just two economical words: "Congratulations. Delighted." The University of Washington had cabled with fresh assurances of a scholarship in the fall, promising that a room would be saved for Percy. There were telegrams from Coach Bruce at Commerce and Coach Yeo at King Edward, from some of Percy's other teachers and from a score of well-wishers back home. There was one from an ancient Vancouver saddle maker named Charles

Quick whom Percy had known since he was a boy, a teller of tall tales who signed himself "Dad Quick, 107 years of age." There was one from Bobby Gaul and Percy's Hexamis friends, from the acting mayor of Vancouver, from prominent leaders in sport, from business leaders, some accompanied by job offers, from the premier of British Columbia and other politicians — even from Canada's prime minister, Mackenzie King. "Gee, that's nice," said Percy as he passed it along.

The boys started having fun with an enigmatic cable from someone named Spuddie that read only: "Atta boy." Perce, they said, you never told us you had a girl. That's who Spuddie is, right? A girl? Percy didn't answer at first and just sat there grinning as Doral and Jimmy kept up the ribbing. Finally he shot out his hand to waist height. "Why, Spuddie is only a boy that high," he said. It was from the four-year-old son of Verna Felton and Lee Millar back home, actor friends of his mother's who performed at the Empress Theatre. To Spuddie, Perce was like a big brother.

Percy turned to Bob in the doorway, holding out another of the little typed papers. "Bob, you'll have to get somebody to write you a speech or two. Here's a telegram from the Canadian Club inviting us to dinner, and you'll have to do the talking."

Bob just smiled. He was still glowing. But he also had a lot on his mind.[1]

∽

"Sure he got the 100 okay," said Charlie Paddock. "But another win? That boy can't possibly take the 200 metres."[2]

Charlie was a great one for talking, for stirring things up with what his detractors considered were sometimes ill-judged pronouncements. But on this point it was hard to fault him. The odds of Percy striking gold again were very long. The elusive Olympic sprint "double" had been won only once before, by the American Ralph Craig at the Stockholm Games in 1912, competing against a smaller field, running fewer heats. It was a rare accomplishment not just because it was so physically demanding. Equally important was the mental strain involved.

In winning his two gold medals in 1912, Craig had had to prevail in three rounds of competition in the hundred and three in the two hundred, a total of six races. Percy had already run four races to win his gold medal and was now faced with four more in the two hundred — assuming he got into the final — making for a total of eight. That was a lot of physical work, a punishing grind that left tendons sore and muscles aching. Even worse than the physical toll, however, was the mental wear and tear. Competing in an Olympic sprint race wasn't just a matter of running down a straightaway or doing a half turn of the track. There were the hours of tension leading up to the race, the anxiety, the pumping adrenalin, the pounding heart — what one magazine summed up as "the terrible 'keying up' process that track champions must go through."[3] Going through it just once, for a single race, was hard on a runner. Going through it four times and then starting all over again for a second event was more than even the greatest champions could sometimes endure. Charlie Paddock admitted that his "fine edge" was lost after winning the hundred-metre gold medal at the Antwerp Games in 1920, and that he had great difficulty working himself up for the two hundred, which suddenly seemed anti-climactic. He ultimately placed second. Jackson Scholz in those same Games dropped out of the two hundred altogether, saying that the mental strain of the hundred had left him undone.[4]

Percy was therefore faced with an extreme test of physical and mental endurance as he prepared to enter the two hundred metres. And the challenge facing him was about to increase further. The Americans had decided not to have any of their sprinters compete in both dash events for the very reason that the strain was considered too killing. To maximize their medal prospects, they were sending a completely new squad of runners into the two hundred: Charlie Borah, Henry Cumming, Jackson Scholz and Charlie Paddock. The German entries would be fresh as well: Helmut Koernig, Jacob Schuller and Herman Schlosske replacing Lammers, Corts and Houben. In fact, of the six men who had made it into the hundred-metre final, only two, Percy Williams and Wilfred Legg, would now be contesting the two hundred.

∽

The first round of heats was scheduled to begin at 2:50 that afternoon, Tuesday, July 31. It was chilly and intermittently raining. The track would be wet — again. The seventy-eight entrants would compete in fifteen heats, the first two finishers in each advancing. All four members of the Canadian sprint squad would be in contention, with Harry Warren still held in reserve.

Johnny Fitzpatrick won his heat without much trouble. Ralph Adams qualified as well, running second to Jackson Scholz. So did Percy in the second last heat, an easy victory in 22 3/5 seconds, two yards ahead of Hambridge of Great Britain. He immediately got back into his warm-up clothes and returned to the dressing room for rest and massage. Now more than ever the game was about conserving his strength.[5]

Buck Hester was sitting on a bench, looking distraught. He hadn't made it, once again because of bad luck. He had finished his heat in second place, good enough to advance, but was then disqualified for running outside his lane. An examination of the track verified the charge, spike marks from three steps veering an inch over the chalk line.[6] It was a small error that had not interfered with any other runner and the Canadians raised a protest, arguing that the German Helmut Koernig had not been disqualified for doing the same thing. It didn't do any good. Buck was out and he was hurting. For him it wasn't just a personal failing. There was also the overwhelming sense that he had let down the team. In the time trials run before the start of competition, Harry Warren had convincingly outraced him and there were those who felt that Harry should take his place on the team. In the end Buck stayed, only to be eliminated twice, in the hundred and now the two hundred, because of stupid mistakes. The recriminations would soon start. The papers were already calling him "the hard-luck boy of the Canadian team."[7]

Harry burst into the dressing room. The line-up for the second round had just been posted and it hadn't worked out well for Percy. In fact it looked like a looming disaster. He would be facing German speed ace Helmut Koernig and Charlie Borah of the University of Southern California. With only the top two finishers advancing, Percy would have to beat at least one of them to survive. Both were world-class, widely viewed as almost certain to get into the final — and both were fresh, not having competed in the hundred. "I can still remember my horror," Harry later recalled. "It meant that one of these three great runners was to be eliminated even before the semifinals."

It also meant that Percy was going to have to run his heart out. Even if he survived, the effort would likely undo him. Bob tried to sound optimistic but it was obvious from the way he was pacing that he was frantic with worry. "Don't try to win," he urged. "Run to beat whoever is running second, Borah or Koernig." He got one more blanket and placed it over Percy, then was pacing again, then was back to pile yet another blanket on top.[8]

∽

Back on the track a drama was unfolding in the women's hundred-metre-dash final. The Canadians were quietly confident of another gold medal, for three of the finalists were Canadian women, among them Myrtle Cook, their ace. But the tension of starter Miller's long holds was too much for Myrtle. Incredibly high-strung by nature, she bolted from her holes early and was issued a warning. One more false break and she would be out. The six contestants settled in again, and again Myrtle couldn't hold back, taking with her this time one of the two German runners, Helene Schmidt. Herr Miller motioned the Canadian off to the side and issued Schmidt a warning.

Myrtle, stunned at her disqualification, slumped down on the track behind the runners and started to cry. Miller paused the proceedings and got her off to the side, where she continued to bawl loudly, only to have to disqualify Schmidt for breaking early at the next failed start. The German runner wasn't the teary type and left the track swearing. The next start was deemed fair. The remaining two Canadians and the German, however, were now rattled and so afraid of jumping the gun that they got away poorly. It ended in a contentiously close finish be-tween Elizabeth Robinson of the USA and Fanny Rosenfeld of Canada, Ethel Smith, also Canadian, clearly in third. There was disagreement among the judges but the decision eventually went to the American. Rosenfeld got silver. The Canadian officials angrily objected, claiming Rosenfeld had won it, and when their formal protest was disallowed they got even madder.[9] It was, some of them felt, another example of undue favour being given to American athletes. Fresh threats ensued that Canada would *definitely* not send a team to the 1932 Los Angeles Olympics, team manager Bobby Robinson fuming that "Canadian officials are being treated like a lot of monkeys."

At the far end of the track the Canadian runners had trotted back to where Myrtle Cook was still uncontrollably crying. They gathered around and tried to console her.[10]

∽

It was six o'clock in the evening now, minutes to go before Percy's second-round heat. He still lay immobile on the massage table, additional blankets and coats piled on top for a final few minutes of intensive warming. Bob wanted to spare Percy the energy-consuming work of a traditional warm-up out on the track, where it was chilly and windy. Better to bring on a passive sweat by heaping on blankets. As he lay there Percy reread a long letter from Bobby Gaul, little anecdotes from home interspersed with soaring predictions of how Percy would slip past the competition and leave them gnashing their teeth in his wake. Granger liked to have Percy read these letters from home before his races, particularly the ones from Bobby. He felt they acted as a stimulant, boosting his determination to win.

Percy was in the sixth and final heat. Out on the track he recognized Borah and Koernig from the national insignias on their jerseys. The other runners were from Italy and Australia. As in his previous races he didn't know any of them; he scarcely knew what they looked like.[11] In the press box overlooking the finish, Bob McAllister, the Flying Cop, was overheard to say: "Here's where we win. Nobody in the world can beat Borah at this distance."[12]

They got away cleanly and headed into the first turn — and up in the stands Granger thought: My boy is going to lose. Percy didn't have much experience running on an oval and now seemed to be taking it too easy going around the curve, lagging too far behind to challenge Borah and Koernig when they hit the stretch. They came out of the turn and Percy remained well back in third, five metres behind Koernig, four behind Borah. There was little chance he could make up that much ground in the distance remaining, not against champions like this. Granger was already resigning himself to disappointment. "It's too bad," he was thinking. "but he's out of it now."

With sixty metres left Percy started closing the gap with the two frontrunners. Borah surged as well, moving almost even to Koernig. Percy kept gaining, slowly gaining, but the finish was now getting awfully close. Twenty metres to go and it was still Koernig first and Borah second, with Percy now a metre back in third.

And then Percy's chin dropped into his chest and he unleashed that final burst, that animal surge, that eruption of red-eyed competitive fury that was such a key part of his race. Where other runners at this point were struggling simply to manage their deceleration, Percy had what seemed to be the rare ability to rip some sort of hidden reserve from his tissues and actually *accelerate* back to top speed. In an explosion of energy, analogous to an entire day's work compressed into the space of two seconds, he willed himself past Borah and across the finish in second place, inches behind Koernig.[13]

He had survived. He would go into the semis. He would later call it one of the toughest races he had ever run in his life. Back at the Holland Hotel he wrote in his diary that evening: "Miracles still happen. I'm in the semifinals. Eliminated Borah. One of the nicest fellows I have ever met."[14]

∾

It was raining again in the morning. Again the track would be soaked. Percy got out of bed feeling stiff and sore. The previous day's race, coming on top of the hundred-metre competition, had taken a heavy toll. He was really into it now, the long hard grind, the reality of Olympic sprint competition, the game that was as much about endurance as speed. At least his nerves weren't quite so jumpy. The work of daily competition was keeping them in check.

The smart money now was squarely on Helmut Koernig. Backing Percy to win the double had undeniable emotional appeal but by any sober estimation he had to be regarded as finished. Harold Abrahams expressed the majority opinion when he said that Percy was unlikely to get much further — not after what he had gone through to edge out Borah.[15]

Charlie Paddock thought so too. "Williams is a wonderful track man," he said, "but I do not think he can withstand the hard going in the semifinal or final race. It took a lot out of him to make second place. He is only a boy and needs more experience in the two hundred metres."[16] Charlie was in fact optimistic about his own chances. There were those who thought both he and Jackson Scholz were "ancient hacks,"[17] even though they had both won their preliminary races, and in respectable times. Privately, Charlie was feeling pretty good, almost as he had in his prime, and the US coaches and trainers intimated that he had been keeping something in reserve and would now "spring a great surprise" in the semis and final.[18]

Even the Canadian camp was pessimistic about Percy. They had heard the prognostications that he couldn't win and it was hard to refute them. Robert Elson, who was staying with the team at the Holland Hotel, observed that an "air of gloom" hung over the place. "Yes, yesterday's race was pretty tough," was all that Bob Granger would concede. But you could see it in his face, the doubt, the strain, the worry. What could his boy have left, physically and mentally, after winning gold in the hundred and then conquering Borah? All Bob could do was try to keep Percy rested and hope for the best.[19]

The semifinals began at two o'clock. Percy was in the first heat. He was facing South African Wilfred Legg, the German Jacob Schuller, Walter Rangeley of Great Britain and Gomez Gaza from Mexico. And there, over in lane six, was Charlie Paddock. Two years before Percy had pointed out to his mother a picture on the wall of a Vancouver gas station and solemnly told her: "That is the world's fastest human."[20] Now he was standing alongside him. He was going to race him. Charlie looked rather heavy but then he always had. He was an inch taller than Percy and outweighed him by fifty pounds. He was obviously tense but was smiling and friendly; none of those pre-race cracks that McAllister favoured. Before going to his marks he walked over to a wooden hurdle alongside the track and touched it for luck. Percy knew he would do that. It was part of the legend.

After the drama of the second round, the semifinal was anti-climactic. Percy showed no signs of the incipient exhaustion that everyone predicted. To Bob's great satisfaction, he maintained a good clip going into the curve, staying with the front-runners while Paddock struggled behind. They came into the stretch and Percy's strength still hadn't deserted him. They neared the finish and he shifted into overdrive and moved into the lead, reaching the tape first with no sign of strain on his face. From start to finish it had been a relaxed, fluid, almost easy performance.[21]

Charlie Paddock had finished fourth behind Rangeley and Schuller. He was out. He walked dejectedly off the field, feeling exhausted and hugely disappointed. "I didn't have a thing left," he said afterward. "It must be age; my old kick isn't there." The spectators were still roaring for Percy and didn't seem to notice, unaware that they had just seen the last important race of the World's Fastest Human. Charlie was through with track. He would make it official with an announcement when he returned to the States.[22] He changed into his street clothes and went up to the press box to begin his write-up of the day's events for the papers back home, including an account of his own elimination. It was one of those controversial things he did: earning a living. As he was pecking away at his typewriter, Coach Lawson Robertson came by and touched him gently on the shoulder. "Come on," he said, and led Charlie to a drink stand outside the stadium where champagne was sold by the glass. "Robbie" was an old track-and-field man himself, having represented the US at the 1904 and 1908 Games. He knew all about the highs and the lows — and particularly about that final indignity when a champion walks away for the last time, licked and forgotten. He bought them both a glass and they drank it in silence.[23]

As soon as Percy got back to the dressing room Bob Granger covered him with blankets and had him lie perfectly still. Not an ounce of energy, not a calorie, was to be wasted. Now, more than ever in the past two years, preserving Percy's strength was Bob's foremost concern.

Ninety minutes crept by slowly. Percy seemed remarkably calm. It was nearing ten minutes to four, time for the final. One by one the other athletes started making their way down the tunnel under the stands and onto the field to begin warming up. Johnny Fitzpatrick was among them. He had just barely survived his semi in what the team was hailing as a real display of guts, the exertion so great that it had left him light-headed.[24] Cap Cornelius hovered by his side. Cap had trained Johnny all through high school, had brought him along from when he was a scrawny ninth grader. Now his boy was in an Olympic final. Cap reappeared a few moments later, looking anxious. Percy stayed immobile on the massage table. Jimmy Ball, who was in the dressing room with him, commented that he should take off his heavy training socks and put on his chamois toe-pushers. Percy, Jimmy later recalled, replied that "he didn't have a chance to win, but at least he was going to keep his feet warm."[25]

Out on the field the other competitors had their spikes on and had commenced their jogging and practice starts and high knee raises. It was surprisingly chilly for the beginning of August. They would need quite a bit of warming up. In the stands the forty thousand spectators were bundled in coats and sweaters.

Still no Percy. Back in the dressing room Bob now had him under the full blanket-and-coat pile, bringing on a sweat, warming him up. It wasn't until the last possible moment that he finally released him and walked him down the tunnel leading out to the track. Percy stepped into the daylight bundled in his white team sweatsuit with his now familiar black sweater. He hadn't been kidding with Jimmy about the thick woollen training socks. He still had them on. He was actually going to wear them racing. He did what to observers seemed a ridiculously truncated warm up, the barest minimum of trotting and one or two starts.

The race was called. The runners moved to their lanes and went to work on their holes. The track was soaked. Percy remembered again to switch from one knee to the other as he dug. He kept well bundled.

A delay. Something was happening down the track that had officials coagulating into a knot. The other runners, now stripped to their shorts and jerseys, stood off to one side, bouncing up and down, twisting about, jogging on the spot trying to stay warm. Percy, still in his warm-up gear, just stood still. He was really feeling the tension again, that rubbery sensation in his legs, the pounding heart, the fluttering stomach. A little jogging would have helped ease the strain. But he just stood there, letting it build. He was saving everything — *everything* — for what lay ahead.

The race would be called at any moment now and some of the Canadians in the stands were getting nervous. Why was Percy still in his sweatsuit and sweater? Whatever had caused the delay had been cleared up and the runners were instructed to move into their lanes. Only now did Percy, with exasperating slowness, start to strip down to his racing outfit, the T-shirt with the red maple leaf on the front, his number pinned to his shorts. "He'll be rushed at the mark," someone nervously hissed, watching Percy undressing as the other runners were already preparing to settle into their holes.[26]

The two hundred would consist of a half-circuit round the track, the lanes staggered to make up for the curve. Percy was in lane two, near the inside. That suited him well. Only Jacob Schuller in lane one would be starting out of sight behind him. All the others were ahead. Johnny Fitzpatrick was in lane six, on the outside and furthest in front. Beside him in lane five was the defending champion, Jackson Scholz, winner of the two hundred at the Paris Games four years before. He was the oldest man in the race, at thirty-one a veritable granddad. But he had a tremendous amount of experience and could not be discounted.

"Koernig is your man to beat," Granger had told Percy in the dressing room an hour before. "He is a front runner — an inspirational runner — and if you come out of the curve even with him, or just ahead of him, you will kill his inspiration and win." The German was settling into his holes in front of Percy in lane four, number 722 pinned to his jersey. He didn't look physically imposing, not like Jack London or Bob McAllister in the hundred. But he was fast. His record-tying 21 3/5 seconds in the second round was better than anything Percy had run at this distance or in the furlong.

Percy got away to a mediocre start at the gun but managed to maintain his position. They kept roughly in their places as they thundered down the opening stretch, Fitzpatrick in the outside lane in front, Scholz in lane five on his heels, then Koernig and Rangeley and Percy and Schuller. So far so good. As they went into the turn Percy closed the gap with Koernig and parked on his heels. Sticking to the German would ensure that he kept up his speed in the turn. Koernig, an aggressive runner, strayed a bit out of his lane, cutting a corner on Percy. The officials didn't notice. Percy's okay.

As they come out of the turn it's Koernig and Percy and Rangeley and Scholz all running together in a pack out in front. Johnny Fitzpatrick is fading. So is Schuller. Percy is in excellent position for changing gears and unleashing his finishing burst, just a foot behind Koernig. The real question now is: does he have enough left? As they come down the straightaway he bears down and there it is, that sweet, sweet surge. "It was his wonderful finish that did it," exulted the *Toronto Star*'s Lou Marsh, watching from the press box. "Hot mama!" With the tape thirty metres away Percy is moving into the lead, leaving Koernig to fight it out with the other two in a knot behind. The stadium is on its feet, everyone is cheering, Canadians and Britons and even the Dutch caught up in a delirium of excitement and shouting. The reedy Vancouver schoolboy just might pull it off. "Hot mama again!" writes Lou. They're almost at the tape now and Percy's chest comes out and his head goes back and his mouth opens wide in a silent shriek of agony or ecstasy or *something* and boy oh boy he's across the line in first by a yard and everyone's roaring and howling and falling all over themselves.

A mob of spectators is racing across the field. They have climbed over the railing, slid down the bike track embankment and shoved past the guards to join the athletes and photographers clustered round Percy. A Canadian flag is produced and draped over his shoulders, then he is hoisted aloft and now he's looking embarrassed. When they finally set him down to take his place atop the winner's dais, Canadian

Olympic president Pat Mulqueen is seen bolting from the judges' table, raincoat flapping, lumbering across the field to seize Percy in his arms and plant a big wet kiss on his cheek. The crowd loves it. The cheers crescendo again.[27]

Percy had won his second gold medal. His time was 21 4/5 seconds, a fifth off the Olympic mark but good considering the wet condition of the track, followed by Helmut Koernig, Walter Rangeley and Jackson Scholz all in a bunch. It took a while to sort them out but eventually the silver went to Rangeley and the bronze to Koernig. Scholz was fourth. Once again the Americans were shut out.

The Canadian red ensign was once more raised to the top of the flag pole and once more the band struck up "The Maple Leaf Forever" as the scattering of Canadians present gamely mumbled their way through the half-remembered lyrics until they got to the more familiar chorus.

> At mm-mm Heights and dum-dee-dum,
> Our brave fathers dum-da-dum,
> For freedom, mm-mm-mm-mm dear . . .
> THE MAPLE LEAF, OUR EMBLEM DEAR,
> THE MAPLE LEAF FOREVER!
> GOD SAVE OUR QUEEN, AND HEAVEN BLESS,
> THE MAPLE LEAF FOREVER!

Percy stood there at attention, trying to look solemn, but a smile kept creeping onto his face. He was feeling giddy. When the music stopped and he stepped to the ground for another round of backslapping from his teammates and the Canadian officials he said, "And four years ago a doctor man in Vancouver told me I had a leaky heart. Look at me today!"[28]

CHAPTER 12

The Deluge

PRAISE FOR PERCY WAS coming thick and fast. "You're a great kid," Jackson Scholz told him in the dressing room after he won the two hundred metres. "That boy doesn't run," Charlie Paddock enthused. "He flies." Douglas MacArthur proclaimed that Percy was "the greatest sprinter the world has ever seen and he will be even greater." Toronto sportswriter J.P. Fitzgerald wrote that "there is every reason to believe that Percy Williams will in the next year set records at these sprinting distances that will stand perhaps forever."[1]

Even Bob McAllister got in on the act. "There goes the greatest sprinter in the world today," he blurted out in the excitement that erupted when Percy breasted the tape. "Now I can say that I have beaten the world's best — once anyway!" And it was true: he would certainly say it.[2]

After winning the two hundred, Percy went back to the hotel, had a light supper — the aforementioned salad and water — and went straight up to bed. He needed to rest. "Well, it's done," he wrote in his diary that evening. "Won the 200 M. Not so bad. Telegrams galore. The girls' team sent flowers to me. Hot dog! McAllister, Paddock, Scholz, Borah and Wykoff all congratulated me."[3] Members of the English team showed up around nine o'clock to offer their congratulations and reporters continued clamouring for interviews, but Percy was unavailable. "He is sleeping like a baby," Pat Mulqueen told them. "Don't disturb him. He must run in the relays next Saturday." Team officials had offered to let Percy drop out of the relay and take a well-deserved rest but he had declined. "My work isn't finished yet," he said. "I'll see it through. Keep me on the relay team."[4]

∽

Dear Mother:

Everything here is just great. I guess there isn't any use in telling you about the 100 and 200 sprints because you can read all about it in the write-ups. To-day is the last day we have to run or maybe we will have to run tomorrow too, we aren't sure yet.

We leave here Monday morning for London, and take part in the Empire Games in which there were fifteen of our team chosen to take part. This is the most that has ever been chosen from Canada before. After that I think they want some of us to go to Scotland or Ireland and then I think that a few of us are wanted to go to Paris to make a showing in some meet. If we go, it will be by plane. That should be quite an experience. I have had offers from nearly everyone to go and run in their country, Sweden, Scotland, Ireland, England, Australia and New Zealand.

I have an awful slew of telegrams and cables from everybody. Everybody on the team has decided that I must go to the best university now without fail. They tell me that all I have to do is choose my own school and then let that school know. All the officials here have decided also that I must go to school. This morning I got a telegram from some firm in Vancouver that if I hadn't decided to go to school that I would be given a good position as soon as I returned home. Not so bad. I don't know what I have to do for the committee here but they have decided that they won't let me run any more flat races. They are only going to let me run in relay races.[5]

∞

In Vancouver reporters were back knocking on the door of Percy's home on Twelfth Avenue, wanting to speak to his family. A writer from the *Sun* was invited in and started scribbling as Dot gushed about her Percy. She was "wildly overjoyed" at her son's two gold medals and was bursting with pride as she read out the letter she had just received from Percy, written on board the *Albertic*, describing little happenings on the voyage and how he had managed to stave off seasickness. "It is just characteristic of Percy," she said fondly, "just like some of his dry humor."[6]

She and Grandma Selina then started on about what an exceptionally thoughtful son Percy was, always remembering Dot's birthday on July 2. He had not been at home the previous month to congratulate his mother in person, but had sent a letter from Hamilton wishing her happy birthday, and asking her to go up to his room and look in a special place where he had hidden some money just for the purpose. Dot got that letter out too and started reading aloud. "I guess by the time you receive this letter it will be your birthday," Percy had written. "I want you to take the money I left and spend *all* of it for a present."

"Tell how much it was, Dot dear," prompted Grandma Selina.

"Well, I suppose I don't need to be ashamed of it. There was $20 hidden away just where Percy said. Wasn't that splendid of him? But he has been just like that all along."[7]

∞

Down at the *Daily Province* a fund was already being raised to bring Bob Granger home in style. The story of his travails in getting to Hamilton and then Amsterdam had been widely reported and it was revealed that he was now "financially down to bedrock," with no way to get home. Soon five hundred dollars had been collected and was on its way. There would be no scrounging for third-class passage this time for Bob. He would accompany the Canadian track team and travel in comfort.[8]

What to do for Percy was more problematic. The city couldn't just heap riches on him, as that would jeopardize his amateur status. Everyone agreed, however, that something really impressive had to be done, for fears were widespread that an American college would snatch him away. Scholarship offers had already been cabled to Amsterdam and rumours were circulating about how the Americans were scheming to lure him south of the border, just like so many other Canadian athletes before. On the very day when the news broke of Percy's second gold medal, Canadian anxiety over possibly losing him was already coalescing into suspicion of an American plot. "Williams World's 200-Metre Champion" read the *Vancouver Sun*'s headline, and right beneath it: "US Colleges Want Percy; City Urged to Keep Him Here."[9]

It was therefore with a great sense of relief that Vancouverites read the next day of Percy's assertions that he had no intention of leaving Canada. "When we start home," he told reporters, "I want to get back to Vancouver as soon as possible and stay there. My friends are there, and I want to stay there." He was unequivocal about the American scholarship offers as well. "I don't want to appear ungracious, but I just want to say that I have no intention of going to the United States to live." Even better was a story Cap Cornelius told of how Percy had come to him asking what to do with a cabled scholarship offer from the University of Washington. "I said tear it up," Cap said, "and he did so."[10]

Percy was a good Canadian boy, loyal and true, there was no denying it. But wiser heads in Vancouver noted that he was still young. As he experienced more of the world and outgrew his innocence, those American offers would become more attractive and eventually, inevitably, he would go where opportunity beckoned. The city therefore had to come up with incentives equally attractive to encourage him to stay. As one editorialist put it, the city would have to "bid high."[11]

So what could be done for Percy? That was the question. A committee of leading citizens was appointed and a general meeting called where all interested parties could make their suggestions. In the meantime Vancouver's acting mayor got in touch with Dot Williams, offering to include a message from her in a second congratulatory telegram he was about to send off to Percy. "Vancouver and Canada rejoice your wonderful achievements," began the mayor's cable. "Your mother sends following message: 'My dear Percy boy, words fail to express my great joy. Mother and all mothers in Vancouver awaiting your return. Don't tie yourself up with any promises until you hear the great things Vancouver has in store for you.'"[12]

∞

Of course, everyone now wanted to know Percy's secret. Why was he so fast? What made him win? One reason that was suggested was that Percy, unlike the Americans and Germans, never raced the clock, only other runners. Even in training his focus had always been squarely on beat-the-other-guy competition, often in handicap races in which he started several yards back. This constant practice in overtaking and passing had given Percy a ferociously competitive spirit that came as a surprise to those who didn't know him, those who saw only the slightly built, mild-mannered young man.[13]

In his own analysis of Percy, Charlie Paddock came up with something else, what he saw as Percy's unique ability to use two different styles of running in a single race. "He starts a race as a pull runner," wrote Charlie, "with his leg action in front of him and his knees high. But in the closing metres of a race he's not a pull runner, but a driver. In all my years of running and watching runners, I've never seen a sprinter who could employ two methods in one race."[14]

Bob Granger, tackling the subject in a 1929 newspaper piece subtitled "Percy's Secret," wrote in much the same vein. His boy, he asserted, was an "absolute master" of two styles of running, an easy flowing style which he used to conserve energy through most of a race and a driving style he unleashed near the finish as needed to destroy the competition. "He starts the 100-yard dash with the flowing style, uses it as far as his competition tells him he can use it, then shifts into a driving finish that fairly eats up the ground. He starts the 220-yard or 200-metres with a short drive, shifts to the flowing style, will run with that style all the way unless pushed too hard; if he is pushed he can shift again into that driving style.

"He can run all day with that flowing style. It is natural speed, delivered from the hips with the least possible exertion. He is loose, natural, enjoying himself when he is using it. His driving style is a package of dynamite when it is unloosed. I have seen it bring Koernig, Borah, Wykoff, McAllister, Paddock, Wildermuth, Bowman, Bracey and Tolan back to him as though an immense rubber band was suddenly contracting, pulling him up, them back."[15]

Percy himself never had much to say on the subject. When reporter Robert Elson asked after his two-hundred-metre victory how he had done it, Percy shrugged and repeated what he had said after the Canadian national trials: "I just ran."[16] He would elaborate in the following weeks but only a little. "I don't know exactly how to describe what I strive for," he stated upon his return home. "I guess, most of all, it's for balanced arm and leg action. Bob Granger has been improving my style. He sees a flaw and picks it to pieces, and I correct it. Running nowadays is not so much a matter of strength as a combination of many things, although you use everything possible to develop strength. I take stretching exercises every day when I get up and before retiring. I don't diet, except by not eating candies and pastry. I don't see, either, how an athlete can use cigarettes and tobacco and hope to equal the men of ability who don't. I've seen the English athletes smoke all the cigarettes they want, and train on beer, but it's my opinion that they put a certain amount of poison into the blood."[17]

∽

The inaugural meeting to plan Percy's future got underway in the dining lounge of the Hotel Vancouver on August 3 at eight o'clock in the evening. Two hundred leading citizens were in attendance, Acting Mayor F.E. Woodside presiding. After ovations for Percy's mother and his grandfather Harry Rhodes — his father Fred was staying completely out of the spotlight — the assembly got down to business.

Everyone agreed that the city had to lay on a terrific homecoming celebration for Percy, "Vancouver's Lindbergh." It was announced that every band and piper in the city had already volunteered to take part in a mammoth reception. What was more contentious was how to honour Percy after that. There was talk of paying his way through university, of erecting a bronze statue, of giving him a leg up in a career, but none of these seemed adequate. A lot of people present wanted Percy to receive something more personally enriching, something that would induce him to remain in Vancouver.

The idea of a fundraising drive had already been broached at the start of the meeting. George Goulding, gold-medal winner in the ten-kilometre walk at the 1912 Olympics, now suggested the target of ten thousand dollars, to be held in trust until Percy turned thirty. That way his amateur status would not be imperilled and he could perhaps use the money to set himself up in business. The next speaker seconded the idea but urged that the fund be bigger, at least twenty-five thousand. "Why not make it a hundred thousand?" exclaimed someone else.

A vocal minority disagreed. Raise the money, they said, but use it to build a new stadium, named after Percy, that would benefit the youth of the city. UBC professor J.G. Davidson emerged as the leading spokesman of the dissenters, reminding everyone that Olympic victors in ancient Greece received only a laurel wreath. A trust fund, he said, smacked of how things were done in "another nation," by which he meant the United States. "If we raise a fund for this boy and give it to him in an indirect way, the action will contain a world of suggestion. We would be sending him into veiled professionalism. . . . How about a 'Percy Williams Gymnasium' at the University of BC?"

Commerce High vice principal and coach Graham Bruce chipped in with the proposal that doing something to support Percy's mother rather than Percy directly might be the way to proceed, adding that it wouldn't be right to capitalize on Percy's success by collecting money for a project that Vancouver or UBC should build anyway with their own funds. Dr. Davidson responded with more ominous warnings against creeping professional, quoting an unnamed authority who had confided to him that the offering of financial inducements to athletes was one of the greatest dangers threatening American university life.[18]

The meeting ended and the matter was passed to a committee. At their first gathering two days later it was decided to establish a trust fund for Percy to the tune of twenty-five thousand dollars and a scholarship to UBC should he decide to further his education. Dot Williams also would be sent east, all expenses paid, to meet her famous son and accompany him home. To raise the necessary money a drive was launched, appeals being published in the local papers, the *Vancouver Sun* taking the lead by printing a daily list of donors and a thermometer illustrating how the collection was progressing. In the days that followed, donations were received from car dealers and lumber yards and banks and hotels and clubs and organizations and the wealthy denizens of the West End. Schools held fundraisers and sent along five or ten dollars. Paper boys for the *Daily Province* collected thirteen dollars and fifty cents in pennies and nickels and dimes. One hundred dollars came from the employees of BC Electric, where Fred Williams worked. Johnnie Dedrick and his Rainbow Orchestra held a benefit dance and raised seventeen dollars and fifty cents. Chalmers United Church added another five dollars, the Empire Café and Grill another ten, the staff of the Hudson's Bay Company another forty.

And then there were all the people who sent along the minimum donation of a dollar, the thousands of envelopes addressed to the "Percy Williams Memorial Fund" from "A Friend" and "An Admirer" and "Kenny Boy" and "Jiggs"; from "Tom" and "Willie" and "Well Wisher" and "Skeezle"; from "Ruth" and "Sophie" and "Anonymous" and "Joe." The total soon approached ten thousand dollars but that was still far short of the target. The *Sun* turned up the pressure in articles with headlines like: "Will Your Conscience Be Clear?"[19]

∞

The letter was anonymous. It appeared to be in a man's hand and was signed "Fair Play."

"Dear madam," Dot read. "I would respectfully remind you that you owe to your boy more than the high flown oratory which the so-called business man of Vancouver is so apt to give you. The meeting which was held at the Vancouver Hotel bears out what I have in mind. The shallowness of their talk and the sentimental tenor of deceit was clearly visible to a deep thinker. What is the underlying motive of all this open handedness? It means that they are going to boost the City of Vancouver at the expense and prowess of your boy.

"I say, Mrs. Williams, do not be a party to such action. . . . I ask you not to let your boy's mind be led away by sentiment. This is your opportunity and I advise you to make the most of it. I say with my best wishes make the Vancouver orators pay through the nose for his services. Let your boy get the full benefit for his splendid work and it will help him when I and you are no more."

Not much new here. Dot had been receiving quite a bit of this sort of advice. She set the letter aside and picked up another.

"Dear Mrs. Williams. Let me congratulate you on your brilliant son. I am one of the oldest women in Vancouver, have known the Granger family since 1892, am also a friend and admirer of Mrs. Granger, a WCTU woman since 1888 who *abhors liquor* with her whole heart and would beseech you, his mother, to keep your son away from strong drink, it is and has been the ruin of thousands. Let us women do all we can to save the young from its power, if we can."[20]

∞

Back in Amsterdam, the legion of journalists besieging the Holland Hotel were finding Percy a difficult subject. When they did get a chance to interview him, he would be uncomfortable and mumble short answers, and revealed a touch of irascibility by brushing aside some of their questions as "foolish." The interviewer would flounder about, trying to get Percy to say something, and gradually Percy's roommates and his other teammates would start answering for him and Percy would lapse into silence.

On one occasion Percy was distractedly fumbling through a sheaf of newspaper clippings as the assembled journalists listened to Doral, Jimmy and Harry give their thoughts. Suddenly he cried out, "I found it." The room fell silent. "Reporters always get things wrong," Percy continued. "Listen to this," and he read from a clipping: "'Percy Williams is expected to run for Canada in the 1,500 meters and do well.'" When the interview was over and the reporters were out of the room, Percy indignantly said to the others, "Why do they ask me how I feel before a race, and how I run? How does anybody feel — scared as blazes."[21]

Percy didn't want to talk, to reveal himself. And he became even more reticent to do so following his first experience of the trouble that candour could cause. After allowing reporters into his room at the Holland, descriptions of the humble, crowded little space were widely circulated in the press. The reports deeply embarrassed team officials. "You're not going to send this to Canada," one of them anxiously asked a reporter after Percy innocently admitted that his cot had a tendency to collapse. Yes, the reporter replied, he was. What came out was an overblown exposé detailing the conditions under which the Canadian athletes were housed, "conditions of which few housing sanitary authorities would approve."[22] Percy himself had never uttered a public word of complaint — he thought spending a lot on a hotel in Europe was a "waste" and "plain foolish"[23] — but because of his burgeoning celebrity status it fell to him to join with team officials in trying to undo the damage. The reputations of Pat Mulqueen and the rest of the badgers had already been sullied by accounts of their infighting, and here they were now being accused of keeping the athletes in a Dickensian hell.

"Kindly say for me," Percy later obligingly repeated, "that the Canadian officials at Amsterdam were wonderful; that they couldn't do enough for the welfare of the Canadian team; and that every member of the team feels deeply grateful to them for their many acts of kindness and their constant thoughtfulness. Everybody from Mr. Mulqueen down was out there all the time doing their best for Canada and there was perfect harmony at all times. Our housing was comfortable and we could not possibly have received better treatment."[24]

But back to the sprint relay. Winning it wouldn't be just a matter of running the fastest. Equally important was mastery of the skill of baton

passing. It had to go from one runner to the next without any diminu-
tion of speed, the runner in front reaching back as he accelerated and,
relying solely on feel, getting a secure grip on the stick. It took a lot of
practice to get the transfer done safely and smoothly, all within the
twenty-metre transfer zone.

On the Canadian squad Johnny Fitzpatrick, Ralph Adams and Buck
Hester were all experienced relay runners. Percy was not. He therefore
had been initially given the position of lead-off runner. It was the logi-
cal place for him, requiring only a forward hand-off and no blind receiving. In the wake of his double gold-medal performances, however,
the perhaps inevitable decision was made to switch him to the finishing
anchor leg, the position of honour, with Johnny taking the lead-off. It
meant that the relatively simple forward transfer to Ralph that Percy
had been practicing suddenly went out the window. Now he would
have to reach behind him, feeling for the hand-off from Buck. The
team had two days to practice before the relays started. But very little
was done involving Percy. The star of the Canadian team needed to rest
after his four days of individual sprint competition.[25]

Thirteen national teams were entered in the 4 x 100-metre relay.
There would be two rounds: elimination heats on Saturday, August 4,
with the final to be run the next day. The team that won the gold would
logically be the one with the greatest breadth of talent, four top-notch
runners rather than just one or two aces. That described the American
squad of Frank Wykoff, Charlie Borah, Henry Russell and Jimmy
Quinn best, assuming they were back in form, with the German team
of Lammers, Koernig, Corts and Houben the most likely contender for
second. The Canadians had Percy and Johnny Fitzpatrick, but Ralph
Adams and Buck Hester were considered not quite up to the mark. The
sober assessment was that the quartet had a shot at third and the bronze
medal.

The qualifying heats came off much as expected. The American
team won theirs in the fastest time of the day, the Germans coasted to
an easy second behind the French, and the Canadians edged past the
British.

It was in the final that things fell to pieces. Johnny ran a solid first leg, keeping the team in contention, and Ralph didn't let things slip by much. The baton went to Buck and he lost a fair bit of ground in the turn, the Americans and Germans now well out in the lead. As he neared the transfer zone Percy was anxiously hopping about, seeing that he would be starting his leg a full ten metres behind the frontrunners. The British were still within striking distance, however. There was a chance that Percy could overtake their anchor man, Jack London, to claim the bronze. He lit out like a greyhound when Buck hit the warning mark scratched in the track, accelerating so fast in his impatience to get going that Buck, running on empty, couldn't reach him for the hand-off. As Percy neared the end of the transfer zone and Buck realized that he wasn't going to catch him, he made a desperate lunge to get the baton into Percy's outstretched left hand. The stick almost found its mark — but not quite. It bounced off Percy's wrist and fell to the track. Percy stopped and turned and picked it up and shot back up to speed but then slowed to a stop as the realization sunk in that they had been disqualified the moment the baton touched the ground. The Americans went on to win it in forty-one seconds, tying the world record their compatriots had set at the Paris Olympics four years before. The Germans took silver, the British the bronze.[26]

Although Percy was at least partially responsible for the fumbled baton pass, it was Buck who received all the blame. In daily summaries of Olympic happenings, newspaper editors across the country sub-headed the sprint relay results with titles like "Poor Running by Hester" and "Hester is Weak Link" and "Hester Loses Ground." Most cutting of all was the *Hamilton Spectator*'s sports columnist, Walter McMullen. He headed his piece on Buck's rotten luck with "Jonah of the Team."[27]

The Olympic relay final on August 5, 1928, marked the end of the track career of George "Buck" Hester. He had gone from the greatest sprinter in Michigan and an Olympic hopeful to being openly scorned. He would do no more serious running. He found a job as a salesman, had two daughters with the wife he had recently married and eventually moved to Indianapolis where he worked for a firm selling paper products. He died there in 1951 at the age of forty-nine.[28]

For Percy and the rest of the Canadian track and field team the Olympics were over. They had done surprisingly well — so well that team officials were radiant with delight. In addition to Percy's two gold medals, Jimmy Ball had won silver in the four hundred and had joined with Phil Edwards, Stanley Glover and Alex Wilson to take bronze in the 4 x 400-metre relay. The women's team, meanwhile, had won gold in the relay and both silver and bronze in the hundred, and Ethel Catherwood had taken the high jump and attracted all sorts of attention with her movie star looks. There would be no lazing about in Amsterdam for Canada's newest heroes, however, no watching other sports now that their running and heaving and jumping was done. The Olympic Committee didn't have enough money for that. To squeeze the most out of the costly trans-Atlantic expedition, the bulk of the athletes set off under Cap Cornelius and Bobby Robinson on a tour of UK and continental meets, the expenses for which were being covered by local organizers and clubs.

Percy was at the top of the list of those to make the circuit. He had been invited while the team was still aboard the *Albertic* and had expressed guarded interest, explaining in a letter to his mother that he welcomed the chance to do a little more sightseeing at someone else's expense.[29] Now, after his double sprint wins, his presence on the tour was essential. People wanted to see the Olympic champion and were willing to pay, and meet organizers were consequently insisting that he be included.

The tour would be an interesting experience and on the whole pleasant, like being part of a travelling road show. The racing itself wouldn't be too gruelling, for Percy and the track squad were largely restricted to relay running. "I don't mind relays," said Cap Cornelius, "but no solo events. We want Williams and the others to go back home with undimmed honours and not to give anyone the chance of beating them after they have tired themselves at the Olympiad."[30]

Buck Hester wouldn't be going along. His spot on the sprint squad had finally been given to Harry Warren.

The Canadian team travelled first to London for a British Empire vs. the United States meet. Percy wasn't overly impressed with the city.

"You can go along the street," he wrote, "and inquire for some place on the opposite side of the street and anybody you ask will first give you a blank stare and then shake their head, say they never heard of the place, and then go quietly back to their day-dreaming."[31] The Americans came out on top at the meet, winning eight of the fourteen events. In the sprint relay Percy and the Empire team lost by inches to Frank Wykoff and the Americans, an unpopular outcome with the fans and a decision that Bobby Robinson said was proved wrong by photographs of the finish.[32]

Percy and a few others then made a quick hop back across the Channel to Paris for a hastily arranged appearance in what was being billed as a mini Olympics. The journey — by plane, Percy's first experience of air travel — was an ordeal of engine failures and forced landings and the alarming experience of being buffeted about in the air. By the time they reached Paris, everyone was limp from vomiting and ashen-faced with terror, Johnny Fitzpatrick was lying in the aisle and the women's team chaperone had to be carried off the plane. "Sea-sickness is nothing compared to this," Percy wrote to his mother gaily when they were safely at the hotel. "I wouldn't have cared if the plane went down in a tail-spin. . . . Every once in awhile the plane would hit a pocket and then it would roll like a ship in a storm. They supply us all with nice paper bags for any excess baggage we wish to dispose of during the trip. I still have mine for a souvenir, along with one other fellow."[33]

The Paris meet itself turned out to be a flop. A number of athletes who had promised to attend and who had been duly advertised failed to show up, some of the airsick Canadians included, having taken to their beds, prompting an ugly display from the spectators who had paid good money to see the show. Seat cushions rained down on the field, windows were broken and the stadium reverberated with cries of "Robbers!" and "Thieves!" Percy, pressed to make his only individual sprint appearance on the post-Olympic tour, won a special hundred-metre dash for Canadians only, competing against his teammates. Jackson Scholz won a separate dash against a mostly American field. Charlie Paddock, who announced beforehand that this was his farewell appearance, placed third.[34]

Back in London, Bob Granger was thoroughly enjoying himself. He had lost his money and his train ticket and watch — a pickpocket, he figured — and a Dutch barber had left him with practically a bald head but none of it seemed to dampen his spirits. He was on the go all day, having a ball, so caught up in taking in the sights that he was seen only for fleeting moments at breakfast. "Granger," observed Robert Elson, "has two great weaknesses — a failure to realize that track and field is not the principal business of this world, and an absolute passion for sightseeing."[35]

In a letter written more than a year later, Bob's enthusiasm over the Olympic experience still bubbled up from the page. "The stay in Amsterdam was wonderful, Cyril," he raved, "so many wonderful things I couldn't possibly write about them unless I took a week's holiday. As a matter of fact, when in London some time later I wrote a 160-page letter telling all about my adventures or rather all the things that happened on the trip, the games, the sights, etc. It was keen, boy. . . . Westminster Abbey, the Tower of London, Kew Gardens, Oxford, the Thames . . . the green hills of Ireland, the fairy golf links of Scotland, the rolling hills and dales of Scotland, the yokels of merry England, the knaves of Ireland, the quaint people of Vollendam, Amsterdam, Rotterdam and boy, did they have good nut bars there, you and Pilot Fish Jack would have returned as fat and sleek as seals if you had been on the trip — it was all wonderful, very wonderful, just like a great fairy dream land — boy, would I like to go again and take all the boys. . . ."[36]

It wasn't just the opportunity to see Europe that had Bob in tearing high spirits. Things suddenly were going very well for him. His dreams were finally coming true. Percy had done even better than he had hoped, winning not one gold medal but two, and Bob himself was at last getting recognition, praise as the wonder coach, the creator of the phenomenon, the unheralded trainer who people were at last saying deserved much better. He had already received a coaching job offer from Oxford University, the sporting officials there considering him "the finest coach available," and there was talk that additional offers would soon be forthcoming for big schools in the States. It was hugely gratifying but Bob would turn them all down. "I wouldn't go to the

States if they gave me New York," he wrote to Dot Williams, "nor to Oxford if they gave me London, nor to France if they gave me Paris. I want Vancouver, the most wonderful place in the world to me. Always has been and always will be." Newspaper editors, meanwhile, were clamouring for him to write up a story on Percy for serialization, a potentially lucrative deal if he could get it done fast, while Olympic fever was high. Bob considered himself a poor writer but was eager to try because "I knead the dough very badly." He hoped to get it written by the time he got back to Vancouver, he said.[37]

"I guess I'm a terrible person when all is said and done," he concluded toward the end of his rambling letter to Dot. "However, I won't lose my head as my neck is still connecting it to my shoulders. And I keep my boots tied into my berth and I sleep with my socks under the pillow. My hand bag is now split open but the contents are still there. And I haven't quite lost my mind yet. That's why I left the East before I did and to save you from hitting me with a rolling pin. They say they are expensive.

"However, if you do think that I am terrible I will perhaps (and hope) to make up for it in the course of time. They say time mends everything. Well, it had better (but I wouldn't take a chance on it mending a rolling pin). I sure have learnt some very valuable things on this trip which should stand me in good stead, even if you think I am hopeless. I don't. While there is life there is hope."[38]

∞

From London, Percy and Bob and the rest of the team headed off to participate in a series of meets in Ireland, England and Scotland. First stop was the Tailteann Games in Dublin, Percy marvelling at the bullet marks that could be seen on the buildings, reminders of the 1916 Easter uprising.[39] Still confined to competing in the relay, he teamed up with Johnny, Ralph Adams and Jimmy Ball to beat US and Irish squads over twelve hundred metres. Harry Warren, by this time at the peak of condition, made a stir when he won the hundred metres in 10 3/5 seconds, tying the Olympic record. "To make this more outstanding," Percy wrote later that year in an article on Harry for the UBC student newspaper, "this race was on a grass track. Later I heard that a rather odd thing happened regarding this. As I understand it, the newspapers came to the conclusion that to have run the race that Warren ran would be next to impossible so they published the result as 10 4/5 seconds."[40]

Then it was on to Woolwich for the Army, Navy and Air Force Games and Edinburgh and Glasgow for some friendly competition against the best athletes in Scotland. For Percy it was more relay races, all of them wins. The Scots were generous hosts but sometimes the fans could be a little too enthusiastic in their quest for souvenirs, one of them making off with Percy's coat. Then there was the sign posted on the back of the seats at one of the stadiums in Scotland. "Absolutely no money refunded under any circumstances," it read. Percy and the boys thought that was a hoot.[41]

And with that the grand Olympic adventure was over. On August 24 the team boarded the White Star steamer *Doric* in Glasgow and embarked on the return voyage across the Atlantic. The shipboard chefs were already planning a special banquet to honour the Canadian athletes, a meal that would begin with "Consommé Fitzpatrick" and "Salade Glover" and include a main course of "Supreme of Chicken à la Williams" with "Granger Potatoes."[42] Percy was anxious to get home, to step away from the fuss and enjoy some peace and quiet, maybe head up to Lytton for a week of horseback riding and hunting. The season would just be starting by the time he reached Vancouver. He was thinking now that he didn't want to enter university in the fall, either in Canada or in the States. "I don't know what I want to do," he mused. "Probably I'll go into business. University doesn't appeal much, and this is sure — I'm done with track for this season."[43]

∞

The quarter-page ad for Vancouver's Pantages Theatre showed Percy, clad in his Commerce High togs, down in his starting crouch, tensely waiting to sprint off the edge of the page. "Scoop!" read the headline.

"First in West! Via Air Mail! Moving Pictures of Percy Williams Winning 100 Metres Championship at Amsterdam."[44] The show contained lots of other footage as well, Lord Burghley winning the hurdles, Paavo Nurmi, the opening ceremony, the sights of Amsterdam and more. But for those few seconds when Percy was flying down the track, the darkened theatre erupted in cheers and whistles unlike anything that had ever greeted Buster Keaton or Douglas Fairbanks, Clara Bow or Charlie Chaplin.

At the *Vancouver Sun* the Percy Williams Fund continued to grow, but slowly. It still had a long way to go. "Fund Needs Your Cash, Send Now!" the paper urged its readers.[45] Some continued to grumble about the taint of professionalism, others about how slowly contributions were trickling in. Andy Lytle, the *Sun*'s sportswriter, was particularly incensed both by the naysayers and the city's stinginess. In one column he slapped down the tale of Olympic victors in ancient Greece contenting themselves with olive-leaf crowns. They got gifts too, Andy pointed out, and likely plenty of them, everything from a bottle of booze to a well-stocked wine shop. In another piece he tried to prime the gift-giving pump by raising that most primal Vancouver fear: American poaching. "Send Percy down to Seattle for a day," he quoted a visitor from Washington State as saying, "and we'll raise that twenty-five grand in twenty-four hours. Give us any assurance that he will locate at the University of Washington and we'll raise double that figure in half the time." Andy headed the piece with "It Would Be Just Too Bad."[46]

Down on Twelfth Avenue Dot Williams was getting tired of allaying public fears that her son would be lured across the border. She had been doing it for the past two weeks. No, she told reporters, Percy wasn't going to the States. Yes, universities in Washington and Oregon and elsewhere had been trying to recruit him. No, he hadn't accepted their offers. Yes, he was planning to remain in Vancouver. No, he hadn't signed anything yet. No, he wouldn't be attending the Oregon Agricultural College. Reports to that effect in the Seattle press were mistaken.

And no, she wasn't going to give up her job as cashier at the Capitol Theatre. Yes, she had received several flattering offers, but preferred to stay where she was.[47]

Finally it was time for Dot to make her trip east to greet Percy on his return. It was first class all the way. Resplendent in her best dress and two-tone pumps, her white fox stole and feather hat, she arrived in Montreal at the end of August to more questions about Percy, more fears that he would be lost to the States. Percy, she began again, would *not* go to an American university in the fall. "He will attend the University of British Columbia and will complete his education there. He will decide for himself, but I am sure he will stay in Vancouver and Canada."

"Vancouver is so anxious to greet him," she flustered. "You would think he belonged to them, and not to me."[48]

CHAPTER 13

Homecoming

⁓

To
Percy Williams
on His Return to Vancouver, Sept. 14th
— 1928 —

Hail to you Percy, our own city's son,
Triumphantly returning to your town.
Smiling and gay as flowers in spring you come,
Wearing so modestly the victor's crown.

Wondrous indeed but gloriously true
The news came thrilling your familiar friends
And now we long to catch a glimpse of you,
To greet you as your splendid journey ends. . . .[1]

HE WAS COMING. There was his train. It was rounding the final bend in the track and easing into Vancouver Station, coming to a stop with a screech and jolt right on time at a quarter past nine in the morning. The platform was packed with people, photographers pushing and shoving, movie men making final adjustments to their tripods and lenses. Passengers could be seen moving about inside. Was that him? That one there? Then the door to car number 133 opened and out he stepped, "Vancouver's Lindbergh," "The Canadian Cheetah," "The BC Bullet," "The New Dutch Cleanser," slim and delicate and pale and not the least bit larger than life, and yet the biggest thing to have ever hit town. He stood at the top of the steps while the police cleared a space in the crowd below, licking his lips nervously, looking embarrassed, fumbling with the knobby end of his cane. The sky had been overcast all morning, but at this very moment, so the papers asserted, the clouds majestically parted and the sun started shining.[2]

∽

So began the final paroxysm of adulation for Percy on his triumphal homeward journey. It had started an exhausting two weeks before, when the *Doric* docked in Montreal and he was whisked through customs to a procession and a banquet and speeches and gifts and crowds. The attention hit Percy like a tidal wave. On board ship one of the *Doric*'s officers stated that he had been "a very quiet lad . . . and did not seem to realize that he had done something really great. He was so unassuming about the whole thing that it was practically impossible to get him to talk." The other passengers similarly learned that Percy did not like being fawned over and praised. "The only way to enjoy his company," observed one writer, "is to shut up. Otherwise he would hole up somewhere where he could not be found."[3]

Percy by this point was eager to see his mother. He was playing quoits on deck when word arrived that Dot would be coming aboard at Quebec City, the vessel's penultimate stop, rather than meeting him at Montreal as planned. Percy instantly abandoned the game, tossing the rubber rings onto the roof and dashing down to his cabin to straighten it up for his mother's arrival. As the *Doric* neared Quebec City he stood anxiously at the starboard rail, trying to catch the first glimpse of Dot. A reporter who had managed to get on board downstream tried to interview him but all he got was "Ask mother."

"American universities have reserved rooms for you this fall."

"It will be the University of British Columbia, I am sure," replied Percy. "But ask mother."

"What is your program in Canada before Vancouver?"

"Ask mother. Whatever she has agreed to will be my program."[4]

The questions kept coming but Percy didn't want to talk about himself. When he did have something to say, it was usually about others. "If I have accomplished anything as a runner," he told a gaggle of Quebec City newsmen, "you can justly give the credit to Bob Granger, and to the desire to justify the confidence which was placed in me. I owe everything to Bob. He took hold of me when I started to run three years ago and he taught me how. I wish I could say it the way I mean it, but anyhow, it was Bob who won the 100 and 200 metre races at Amsterdam."[5]

It was in Montreal that homecoming celebrations for Percy kicked into high gear. With his petite "sweetheart-like mother" at his side, Canada's greatest sporting hero descended the gangway into the arms of Mayor Houde and the assembled city fathers and the speeches began. "The name of Percy Williams is known all over the world," proclaimed the Francophone mayor in his functional English, "and wherever the English she is spoken." And turning to Percy: "Don't take it away from us." He then presented Percy with a fine gold combination timepiece and stopwatch. "Just a little chronometer with which to register your future deeds for Canada, because at twenty, you're not burnt out yet."[6] Percy stammered a few words of thanks into the microphone and quickly stepped back. He was so clean-cut and well-groomed, so humble and unaffected, and so obviously uncomfortable in the glare of the spotlight that it was impossible not to like him. "Percy Williams," wrote one of the reporters present, "sprints into the affection of people as easily as he sprints down the cinder track. . . . The first reaction you get is the wedded fragility and manfulness of this surprisingly youthful world champion. He was twenty years old last May, he said. Hair is almost black, trimly brushed down and shining. Eyes are dark, too. The actions are quick and nervous. Great willpower shows itself from the usual tense expansion of the chest; arm muscles apparently consciously flexed."[7]

"How fast had you been running at home?" a reporter barked.

"I don't know," Percy replied. "I never have run against a watch."

"How do you run then?"

"Well, I just try to beat the other fellows and run as fast as I can to do it."[8]

∽

There was a long letter waiting for him from Bobby Gaul, just back from seeing the Olympic newsreels at one of the downtown theatres and almost frantic with joy. "Oh fung but they were great," Bobby had written. "Hot dog, holy doodle, but how you tore. Gosh, but you sure made Paddock, Borah, Wykoff and all those beginners look like 'Oscar.' Gee whiz, but when you opened out on that crew of world beaters in the last 15 metres of the 200, I thought that they were running backwards. And then when they all made a rush for you when you won the 200, and carried you on their shoulders, and wrapped that flag around you, oh gosh I guess you know what I mean. All I can say is that we felt pretty darn good. We can't realize it yet, boy. I know that you will be so very busy when you get this letter that you won't have time to read it. But nevertheless I have so much to say to you that I just have to go on. You will have to excuse me for writing like this to you, but I can't help it, I feel so darn happy I just have to.

"Why don't you tell us all about your races, Percy. We are all dying to hear what you say about them. How did you feel? But it's no use, you wouldn't say a word about yourself in a hundred years. . . .

"Win, I think, expects you to go to UBC next year, and join his Frat. 'Ain't that nize.' What would all those classy Frats in the States say. But to be serious, Percy, you ought to consider such universities as McGill, Toronto and Oxford. They might offer you good positions in

154 / I Just Ran

business, but you are still very young, and you certainly would enjoy a varsity education. They can never take that from you, and you can get the best the world can give you, all for nothing. That's not to be sneezed at Percy. You're only young once, and believe me, it will be plenty soon enough to go into business 5 or 6 years from now. Besides there is $25,000 waiting for you when you are 30.

"So why don't you talk it over with some of your many friends and see what they think. I know that your future is your one thought now. I guess this is none of my business and I hope you will excuse me, but I, as well as all the rest, want to see you get the best out of your achievement that you can. Listen to Bob, Perce, on this subject, because he has plenty of brains, believe me, and as you know, he would be overjoyed to see you get the best that they can give you. He would not try to favour your taking a position just to keep you in a certain place for your famous name, like so many will. Remember Percy these business firms want you solely for your name, same as the States want you solely for your running. . . .

"How has Bob been behaving himself? I haven't heard from him for some time so I guess he has been pretty busy. I hope to gosh that he takes that Oxford job. It is the best in the world, thanks to Percy Williams and his trainer, the now famous pair. Don't let Bob slip up any jobs like that Perce, or I will never forgive you. I know how he likes Vancouver, but he wants to strike while the iron is hot. He won't ever get a chance like that again, tell him."⁹

∽

From Montreal it was on by train to Toronto. More speeches. More gifts. More banqueting and attention and photos and cheering. Mayor McBride presented Percy with a cabinet of silver, and to Dot, "who might be mistaken for his sweetheart," a silver plate and an enormous bouquet of flowers. As the mayor went on with his speech, Percy stood with his hands behind his back, fingers nervously twitching. He managed to say a few words when called on, and Dot, with a little less coaxing, stepped to the microphone as well. "Having such a wonderful time," she cabled her mother in Vancouver at the end of the day. "Am afraid I will wake up and find it a dream."[10]

After that it was down to Hamilton for what was being billed as a "monster reception," an outpouring of adulation from the Ambitious City that would surely put Toronto's effort to shame. Despite a downpour, Percy, Dot and Bob and the rest of the athletes were intercepted on the road outside the city by a procession of beribboned automobiles for a parade that snaked up and down Hamilton's thronged streets, prizes to go to the best decorated car. More speeches. More gifts. Another dinner. More soaring pronouncements of Percy's greatness. More urgings that he must stay in Canada where he so clearly belonged. At one point in the program Brant Little and Phil Edwards obligingly hoisted him onto their shoulders in front of the assembly in a re-enactment of the now-famous moment following his hundred-metre victory. Percy had to remain perched there, profoundly embarrassed, while the audience sang "The Maple Leaf Forever." He was their champion, their hero, their own "wonderful little gentleman," and they wanted him to know just how much they valued his presence. When it was all over and Percy was led out to the cars for the return trip to Toronto, he made a point of stepping over to thank the police officers who had led the parade on their motorcycles. That touched them deeply. "No wonder everybody loves him," they gushed.[11]

Another gathering at Toronto's Canadian National Exhibition followed, where Percy's presence left the midway's star attraction, Big Jim the World's Tallest Captive Gorilla, hugely eclipsed. Then finally — finally! — Percy and the other Western Olympians were allowed to board the Trans-Canada Limited and begin the long journey home — or at least travel as far as Winnipeg, where another reception awaited. This time hometown heroes Jimmy Ball and Brant Little were lionized alongside Percy. Brant hadn't made it past the eight-hundred-metre semifinals at Amsterdam, but Jimmy had gone almost all the way, winning silver in the four hundred metres, second to American Ray Barbuti by a bare inch due to a fateful sideways glance right at the tape. "You shouldn't have glanced!" Jimmy's hometown well-wishers told him, and he wagged his head sheepishly as if he hadn't already heard that dozens of times. Doral Pilling soon bid the party farewell, telegrams having been received urging him to hurry home to Calgary where a reception awaited, and then Stanley Glover was off as well to Edmonton's welcoming arms.[12]

When Percy got back on the train with Dot on September 12, he was all that remained of the westward-bound Olympic party, the last one yet to make his triumphal entry into his hometown. According to what was being reported in the papers, Vancouver was planning something big.

∞

And so, on September 14, 1928, Percy stepped off the train in Vancouver Station and the sun came out. There was the reception committee at the bottom of the steps, smiling, gesturing broadly, waiting to embrace him, BC premier S.F. Tolmie and Vancouver mayor Louis D. Taylor at the forefront, L.D. on the road to a miraculous recovery from the propeller blow to the head. He had just commenced his re-election campaign under the slogan "Taylor at His Worst is Better than Malkin's Best," and a few photos with Percy wouldn't hurt his chances one bit.[13]

There behind them was Percy's father Fred Williams, shy just like his son, holding back in all the commotion. He eventually managed to get close for a few awkward words of welcome. Then, with Premier Tolmie leading Percy by the arm and Mayor Taylor offering his arm to Dot, the party headed to the cars lined up outside the station and drove down to the CPR docks where floats and cars and bands and marchers were assembled and waiting to begin the mile-long parade through the heart of downtown. It would be unlike anything that had ever happened before in the city, so special that arrangements had been made to cover the spectacle live over the airways by reporters with microphones stationed along the route, a first in Canadian history.

Percy was seated in the first car, wedged between Premier Tolmie and Mayor Taylor, police officers on motorcycles and a military band and an RCMP honour guard leading the way. Bob Granger was squeezed in as well. He had arrived in Vancouver a few days before and had slipped aboard Percy's train at the station to share in the welcome. They proceeded up Granville Street, the sidewalks thronged, people hanging out windows, tossing confetti improvised from torn-up sheets of paper. Dot was in the car behind, the roof down like Percy's, Fred a few more vehicles back with four city aldermen, Grandpa Harry and Grandma Selina beaming further back in car number nine. Then came another band, playing "See the Conquering Hero Comes," then another, interspersed with formations of athletes in their team regalia representing every local sport, baseball and basketball and cricket teams, tennis and cycling and swimming and track clubs, soccer and lacrosse and rugby players. They were singing now, bellowing out: "How d'ye do, Mister Williams? How d'ye do? How d'ye do, Mister Williams? How d'ye do? We are with you to a man, We'll do everything we can. How d'ye do, Mister Williams? How d'ye do, do, do." Then they started into another: "When Percy comes marching home again, Hurrah, hurrah, We'll give him a hearty welcome then, Hurrah, hurrah. . . ."[14]

And here were the school children, thousands of them, released from their classrooms by a publicly declared holiday, excited and shouting and waving, marching along in loose formations with banners at the fore proclaiming the name of their school and messages of welcome to Percy. "Hundred metres and two hundred metres. Oh Boy!" read one, and "Percy, you're a wonder," and "Your old school, King Edward, is proud of you." The High School of Commerce had an enormous banner proclaiming that Percy had just graduated from *their* school. The King Ed contingent, wanting to demonstrate their own particular familiarity with the champ, interspersed their cries of "Atta boy, Percy!" with "Atta boy, Luke!"

And they just kept on coming, a thousand school kids, then another, and then another, stretching back over a mile, pushing floats and carrying banners and shouting and waving. The owner of an Italian restaurant along the route was heard to say, "If I had a dollar for each keed is here, I would be wort' twent' fi' tousan' dollar."

The parade turned right on Georgia Street and was now approaching the Hotel Vancouver where Charles Defleux, reporting for CNRV, stood at the mike. He didn't quite know how to go about a live radio broadcast out on the street, so he just started talking, describing the huge crowd around him. Then: "There is Percy himself! Standing up to take the cheers! Listen to the band, folks! Listen to the cheers! Here's Percy! They are crowding round him. They are pouring confetti on him. Percy does not know how to take it. He is turning around in bewilderment. Vancouver's hero is home.

"Here's another band — ! If it was a goosestep they couldn't lift their feet any higher. There's a red-headed boy with a grin a yard wide. There is not a school in Vancouver today which is not proud that Percy Williams is a Vancouver school boy. . . .

"Here come more school kiddies. There are three thousand of them in this parade. It's wonderful. What an enthusiastic bunch of youngsters — jumping around and cheering! How many of these boys will be secretly planning next year to come out and emulate Percy Williams? That's one of the fine things about this."

The parade continued down Georgia as Percy shrank into the back seat. Shouts started to be heard of "Stand up, Percy! Come on Percy, stand up and let us see you!" He self-consciously hoisted himself to his feet to a resurgence of cheering, then sat back down again. A boy darted out from the sidewalk and jumped onto the running board and shouted in his face: "Say, Percy! Aren't you going to say hello to me?" "Hello," said Percy, not particularly pleased. He didn't like all this shouting, people bellowing at him as if they knew him, using his first name. Other kids started doing the same, breaking from the crowd, grinning wildly, yelling into his face.

Out at the Stanley Park grandstand, CNRV station director George Wright could now hear the music approaching and see the lead cars and took up the commentary for the "shut-ins" back home.

"Here they come! The band is too far away to reach the microphone, but you'll hear it presently. . . .

"See the crowds of people jamming the park now. Oh, boy! See the people coming down here. What a crowd when they all get here! There's the band coming. . . . Now you'll begin to hear the noise of the crowd. Here's two little girls quarrelling as to who is to get up on a bench. There, that trouble's all over.

"Hear the cheering? Hear the drums? Don't mind all that noise and laughing, folks. Everybody's happy here and congratulating Percy.

"All the school children are arriving up in the enclosure here, all carrying banners, signifying what school they belong to. Too bad some of you folks outside of Vancouver are not here to see this fine sight. Hear them cheering!

"The noise is everybody calling for Percy now. More cheers! Everybody is taking their places now. Roars of cheers! My voice is drowned!"[15]

The procession came to a halt in front of the grandstand where twenty thousand spectators were already seated and Vancouver's Olympic hero and the guests of honour were led from the cars and up onto the stage to be presented. After a huge ovation for Percy, Dot and Bob, Graham Bruce from Commerce and Emslie Yeo from King Ed were brought forward and introduced as Percy's old coaches, then some of Percy's high school track buddies, then "Dad" Quick as Percy's oldest friend (he claimed to be 108 but was in fact 92), and four-year-old "Spuddie" Millar as his youngest. The call went out at some point for Fred Williams but he had slipped away in the transfer from the cars to the stage and was keeping his head down somewhere in the crowd.

And on it went. "Oh, what a homecoming!" began Premier Tolmie when he at last got his chance to make a speech. "He is our Percy," added Mayor Taylor when his turn came, "and we have him with us now." Percy as usual didn't have much to say in response, perched unsteadily atop a chair on the stage, but he did offer the assurance everyone was dying to hear. "I have seen a lot of Europe," he said, "but if you put it all beside Vancouver, I would choose Vancouver." The thunderous cheers ascended to the heavens, up to the sky that was now clear and brilliant with sunlight that was streaming down on Vancouver's very own golden boy.

As uncomfortable as all the public adulation made him, there was no denying that Percy liked receiving gifts and prizes. He in fact kept a careful list of everything he received, the medals and cups and watches, the books, the gold key from Hamilton, the statuette from Winnipeg, the gun, the travelling bags, the golf clubs, the multiple silver tea sets, the plates.[16] But Vancouver was now going to outdo all that.

His countenance beaming beneath his stitched-up scalp, Mayor Taylor stepped forward to present Percy with a special gift from the city, a brand-new Graham-Paige Model Six-Ten coupe, painted a sporty blue — something Percy could use to drive himself back and forth to UBC, Taylor noted, where he would surely continue his studies. Buying him the car had prompted more grumbling of professionalism, and of how city ratepayers wouldn't appreciate seeing their tax dollars squandered, but the objections were quickly slapped down. As the *Sun*'s Andy Lytle later quoted a local sporting official as saying, "That doesn't make him a professional — if you keep quiet about it!"[17] The majority wanted to honour Percy, and they wanted to do it up right.

With the formal side of the program now complete, everyone repaired to nearby Brockton Point and crammed themselves onto the bleachers and gathered round the track, for their Percy had agreed to run an exhibition race. It would be the perfect end to the festivities, a chance for all his hometown admirers to see the blazing speed that had conquered the world. Percy's old Commerce High teammates, Wally Scott and Dave Hendry, had been called out to give him a challenge. Hec Urquhart was suited up as well. As the excitement built all around the track, Percy got into his now-famous Olympic outfit with the red maple leaf on the chest and took a few practice starts to breathy explosions of "oohs" and "aahs" from the crowd. Then the boys settled into their holes. It took a couple of false starts but finally they got away cleanly, Percy contenting himself with an easy loping stride, staying just ahead of Dave and Hec, letting Wally lead but keeping him well in his sights. That gave the audience a jolt, some gasping, "Why, Wally is beating him!" But then came the surge — not an all-out effort, just enough to get the job done. The gap between the champ and Wally shrank to nothing and Percy kept on going, on through the tape to win with ease by a yard.[18]

CHAPTER 14

"If I Had Any Brains
I Would Skip the Country"

ℭℴ

THE PERCY WILLIAMS Memorial Fund was officially closed on September 29, the total sum collected amounting to $15,893.25 — almost ten grand shy of the target, but a small fortune nonetheless in 1928.[1] Just what to do with it would remain a source of debate and confusion, but everyone agreed on the initial outlay: providing Percy with a scholarship to UBC, Class of '32. Percy didn't want a general arts degree. He was more interested in business administration, which UBC did not offer. But everyone seemed to want him at the hometown university, so he went along. "Frankly," it was anonymously revealed, "he is remaining in Vancouver for the year because he feels that it would be unfair to those who welcomed him so wonderfully and who have been so good to him."[2]

By the end of September, Percy's plan was to remain at UBC for a preparatory year of general studies, then to transfer into a business program, either one that UBC itself was talking about starting, or more likely at the University of Washington, where one actually existed. Before finalizing his first-year classes, he accordingly took a trip down to Seattle to see what credits the American university would accept should he decide to make the move. He returned saying he would definitely be transferring to the U of W the following year. The news of Percy's visit was reported in the papers in Seattle, and when it hit Vancouver it made the front page.[3]

The University of British Columbia. The Blue and Gold. It was fun for the first few weeks, the welcoming ceremonies and meet-and-greets, orientation, joining the Phi Gamma Delta fraternity, even the initiation "ordeal" where all the frosh were ordered to show up at the Horseshow Building downtown — in their pyjamas.[4] And Percy got to do it all in style, setting out each morning in his brand-new car, picking up a couple of his fellow freshmen for the drive out to the Point Grey campus at fifteen miles an hour.[5] When it came time to actually hit the books, however, Percy found himself struggling to fit it all in. Since his return home there had been almost no let-up in the whirl of engagements and calls on his time. There was always someone who wanted something, another club requesting his presence, another school beseeching him to hand out awards to the kids. After the generosity Vancouver had shown him in raising the fund, Percy could hardly refuse the requests. So he gamely tried to keep everyone happy, enduring the attention and hero worship that he found so unpleasant, giving away his time, allowing his studies to slide.

It went without saying that with Percy attending UBC he would be on the track team. With him anchoring the squad and moulder-of-champions Bob Granger coaching, everyone was predicting a hugely successful season. But Percy, tied up with all his other obligations, wasn't seen much around campus. And, a month into the term, neither was Bob.

Bob by this point was in extremely high spirits, trying to bring his dreams to fruition. He had not finished writing his story on Percy and the serialization deal was dead, but he didn't care much. He had other irons in the fire. Upon returning to Vancouver he had been invited to join the committee overseeing the collection of the Percy Williams Fund and had spoken out in the press urging the city to put it over the top. He was doing it not just for Percy. Like most of the rest of the committee, Bob was coming to view the fund as more generally intended to advance the cause of athletics in Vancouver, seed money for a sporting renaissance that would transform the city into a Western version of Hamilton, a Pacific Coast Ambitious City.

A key first step was to build a new stadium with a proper cinder track to replace Brockton Point with its ruts and pebbles and humps. Brockton Point, Bob pointed out, had nearly cost Percy his chance at the Olympics when he stepped in one of its many holes at the trials and twisted his knee. The city and its young athletes deserved better than that. They deserved a grand new stadium similar to what Hamilton possessed. Why let other cities take the lead? Why let other countries lure away Canada's best athletes? "I have heard many people say," said Bob in a speech, reaching out to poke that oh-so-tender spot, "that Percy Williams should go to the United States; that Vancouver would not do anything for him. I'd like to see these young fellows change that opinion. . . . Let us show them that we have got wonderful spirit in Vancouver, so that our young men will not have to go over the border for their opportunities. If we all get behind the idea of building a stadium here, we can do it."[6]

In the meantime, Bob was trying to set himself up with a job — not another menial position sweeping out classrooms, but something in coaching that paid. He had proven himself with his success with Percy, both as a world-class coach and as an asset to Vancouver, and now it seemed only fair that Vancouver do the right thing by him. There had been private assurances from various Percy Williams Fund committee members, promises even, that money from the fund would be made available to him to support him in his athletic endeavours.[7] That was gratifying, but nothing had yet been forthcoming. For a time an offer seemed to be in the works over at Vancouver College, a bona fide salaried coaching position, but nothing came of that either.

There was still UBC, however. Bob had devoted countless hours of his time coaching at the university since 1926, all of it for free, in any sport where his talents were needed. It owed him something for that, and for the part he had played in encouraging Percy to enrol as a freshman, with all the publicity and prestige that would bring. All he wanted was to be paid to continue his coaching; not a large sum, just something on which he could live. It didn't seem like so much to expect. He was now a recognized track expert, after all, and his protegé Percy . . . well, Percy's reputation spoke for itself. Together they would put UBC athletics on the map, a force to be reckoned with all across Canada and down into the States. Wasn't that worth a small salary?

In the fall of 1928 a movement was launched at the university to pay salaries to coaches, with Bob's name being the most often mentioned. It was "presumptuous," asserted an editorial in the student paper, the *Ubyssey*, "to expect these services for free."[8] The university itself wasn't about to come up with the necessary funds, the prevailing view being that paying coaches would be the first step in the commercialization of campus sports, of professionalism. But there was one other source of funding, the coffers of the student Alma Mater Society, and it was here that the battle lines were drawn. Letters and editorials in the *Ubyssey* were supportive of the idea of salaries for coaches, one referring to Bob as a "martyr."[9] "If paid coaches commercialize sport," thundered another, "then paid professors will . . . commercialize education."[10] When the Alma Mater Society finally met in late October, however, the motion was turned down without debate or discussion. Bob, who it had already been announced would be coaching the swimming, basketball and track teams that year,[11] was understandably upset. It wasn't just the prospect of continuing financial hardship that was so distressing. Worse was the insult, the implication that the university didn't value what he did. He had achieved the greatest thing that a track coach could do, and UBC was in effect saying it wasn't worth a nickel. In a fiery letter to the *Ubyssey* editor, one of his supporters reminded readers that Bob had declined an offer of employment from Oxford to return to UBC. "His services were very thankfully accepted and then, when it was too late for him to accept a position with any other club, he was informed that there will be no pay for coaches. Council is very sorry, but he is out of a job. If this be justice — !"[12]

Bob Granger withdrew his services from the university in late October. He would not be seen any more around campus that year.

∽

Things at UBC were not going much better for Percy. Faced with an endless succession of functions and public obligations, he was missing classes and falling so far behind in his studies that by mid-fall he knew he couldn't pass the December exams. He was also caught uncomfortably between the university and Bob Granger in Bob's dispute over salary. In a later letter Bob would in fact privately complain that "I lost my Varsity job over him."[13] It's hard to imagine how this could have been true, Bob having quit of his own volition over the salary issue. Perhaps it was that Bob had been expecting Percy to use his fame and influence to help him, and that his not doing so felt like a betrayal.

In any event Percy wasn't happy. Bob had left UBC in a huff, there were sore feelings, and it was looking as though he himself was going to flunk out at Christmas. Even running with the track team and his friend Bobby Gaul, a fellow freshman, wasn't much fun. In Percy's handful of appearances for the Blue and Gold, mainly as anchor in relay races, the baton was handed off to him with a lead and he had only to jog it home, unleashing a finishing burst solely for the entertainment of the spectators.

Percy was also starting to chafe under the weight of his celebrity status. He hated the open staring and intrusive curiosity he encountered in public, the familiarity of complete strangers, the advice everyone felt so free to dish out — and the endless stream of people who *wanted* something. Most admittedly were decent folks. But quite a few were shameless hustlers. Even the letters from kids, autograph requests mostly, included the odd con. "Dear Uncle Percy," read one from a lad in the States claiming to be his nephew. "Well I heard that you are married. How are you. What are your wife name. What her people name? . . . Listen uncle Percy would you mind sending me a little money if you don't mind it. . . ."[14]

And then there were Vancouver's expectations. The city had been very generous to Percy but seemed intent on controlling him in return

— the businessmen, the city fathers, the athletic officials, the trustees of the Percy Williams Fund holding the purse strings to his trust money. It had been easy for Percy to overlook the strictures in those heady days surrounding his homecoming. But as the weeks passed it became harder to feel fully content. American universities with real business programs and fat scholarships still wanted him as a student and star runner. Athletic organizations across North America and Europe and as far away as Australia and South Africa were begging him to compete, dangling the lure of all-expenses-paid world travel. Companies were urging him to endorse their products. Even Hollywood was after him, a representative from a little-known outfit called Consolidated Sound Pictures coming up from LA with a movie deal that "would place Percy in the lists of wealthy men." Percy, after consulting with his mother, turned it down.[15] Becoming a movie star was about the last thing he wanted to do. But still — it was gratifying to see the breadth of opportunity out there.

It was around this time that an interesting proposition arrived in the mail. It was a letter from Bobby Robinson, manager of the Olympic team and all-round sporting impresario, conveying an invitation to compete in the Millrose Games at New York's Madison Square Gardens, the premier event in the upcoming indoor track season in the eastern USA. Johnny Fitzpatrick, Phil Edwards, and Myrtle Cook and the rest of the women's relay team would be appearing, so Percy wouldn't be alone. There were a number of other big meets Percy could enter as well, making the trip east into a tour, a road show, a "US invasion."

Robinson had been trying to set something up for Percy and his teammates since Amsterdam the previous summer, a tour of the US indoor circuit that would add further lustre to Canada's growing track reputation. Percy, eager to get home, had at the time been lukewarm to the idea. Now it started to have some appeal. It would be a chance to break away from the endless round of commitments in Vancouver, doing some running and some sightseeing with the Millrose people paying the bills.

And there was more. It was an open secret that promoters commonly offered under-the-table payments to get top amateurs to compete in their meets. As sportswriter Robert Edgren put it in March 1929, "Why, everybody connected with athletics knows that many of the athletes most favoured in AAU circles, the lads who go anywhere and compete where their appearance is most useful to the gate receipts, don't have to work for a living."[16] The discreetly passed envelopes were usually quite light, typically containing just a few hundred dollars, pocket change alongside the six- and seven-figure deals openly offered to today's amateur stars. In the 1920s, however, when anabolic steroids were unknown and terms like "performance-enhancing drugs" would have drawn a blank stare, those thin envelopes were the number-one scandal haunting the track world, the barely hidden reality that amateur stars had to deal with.

Percy, beneath his public persona of clean-cut innocence, knew all about it. Hearing of illicit payments to big-name track stars would have been part of his education as an athlete, picking up the inside dope from other runners and especially from Bob Granger, who made it his business to know about every aspect of track. If there had been any gaps in Percy's understanding, they likely were filled in by the time he returned home from the Olympics, and certainly by the end of February 1929. Was he shocked? It doesn't appear so. He considered himself savvy, and he was as keen as the next guy to make money.[17] The choice, after all, wasn't so hard. You accepted how things worked and took the money and headed home with a nice little something that everyone seemed to want you to have. Or you turned it down and left with nothing and the thanks of no one, maybe just a slap on the back from the meet promoter, grinning because he'd be keeping your dough.

Percy would take the money. It wouldn't amount to all that much, certainly not enough to make him rich, and sometimes wouldn't even be paid in cash but rather as his choice of "souvenir" of a specified value, a common method for allaying AAU suspicion. It was all done off the books, of course, but the evidence is still there, in letters and diary entries.[18] By today's standards it might seem a small thing, hardly worth notice. But in Percy's world it was a serious matter. It was the secret he had to keep.

While Percy himself would scrupulously maintain a veil over all his financial dealings and his personal thoughts on the system, his supporters were often vocal in asserting his right to make the most of his stardom, with *Vancouver Sun* sports columnist Andy Lytle leading the way. "There are those," Andy wrote in early 1929, "who will say that it would be terrifically sinful for Williams to capitalize his undoubted talents to his own good . . . and run only when the gate receipts may be surrounded and taken great care of by amateur overlords. It sounds awfully well, that sort of balderdash, but how many times, for instance, is it necessary for an athlete to win Olympic contests for his country, before giving him a chance to do something for himself while he is still a world figure?"[19]

Andy's idea — and he wasn't alone in his thinking — was that amateur track and field stars should get an open, fair cut of the gate receipts according to their drawing power; the "big wigs of a hypocritical cult," as he called the axis of the AAU and meet promoters, had no right "to take all the gravy." You had to be pretty naïve, however, Andy went on, to believe that promoters didn't offer stars something under the table to get them to enter their meets in order to sell tickets. And you had to be doubly naïve to expect the stars to turn down those offers, choosing instead to compete for free and leave every drop of the "gravy" to the delighted promoter. What would be the point of that? To uphold the rules governing amateur sport, the rules that the athletes themselves saw being bent and stretched and ignored all around them, the rules that Andy summed up with the tongue-in-cheek definition, "Yes and No"? "One of these days," Andy concluded, "it will all come out, and our holy amateur bosses will express great horror and indignation."[20]

That day came sooner than Andy expected, following the suspension just two weeks later of Olympic four-hundred-metre gold-medal-winner Ray Barbuti for failing to appear at a track meet. Ray felt this was unfair, having not signed an entry, and responded with a public outburst against the AAU and the hypocrisy of amateur track. After cooling down, he denied some of his more inflammatory comments, such as "I and other athletes have been lining the pockets of the AAU and its affiliate clubs for years." But he stood by his contention that stars often received money over and above their meet expenses and that this was widely known among athletes, coaches and journalists — and even top AAU officials.

That earned Ray an even deeper suspension. He struck back with a three-thousand-word exposé in the April issue of *Sportsmanship* magazine entitled "Our Athletes Are Paid." "As a rule," he wrote, "only star athletes are approached, and an intermediary, generally a 'good fellow,' well-known and a constant attendant at track meets, is chosen as the man to secure entry of the stars and to pay them." This intermediary sometimes played a role similar to a boxer's manager, Barbuti explained, haggling over appearance fees on the athlete's behalf and at times keeping a portion of the sum for himself. The appearance fee typically was passed to the athlete through him, tucked discreetly in an envelope and always in cash, the sum ranging as high as five hundred dollars. Ray admitted that he himself had received offers of this nature totalling thousands of dollars following his return from the Olympics. The whole system, he concluded, was rotten, strict amateur rules being enforced in public while money flowed freely just under the surface. What was needed was a "new deal in amateur athletics." Things had to change.[21]

Of course they didn't. The AAU's amateur rules, which Barbuti called "fanatical," remained in place, and no attempt was made to identify the athletes and officials he alluded to but refused to name. The Union simply kept Ray's suspension in place and let him sweat for nearly a year, ostensibly for defaming the AAU, but in reality, at least as some people saw it, for violating that most important rule of amateur athletics: *Keep your mouth shut.* Finally, in January 1930, he retracted his statements in a publicly released letter of apology and was allowed back into the fold.[22]

∞

On December 7, 1928, an announcement by Bobby Robinson came out in the papers that a select few of Canada's top Olympic runners would be competing the following February in the Millrose Games in New York. The list of athletes included sprinter Johnny Fitzpatrick, middle-distance runners Jimmy Ball and Phil Edwards, the gold-medal-winning women's relay team — and Percy Williams.[23]

This raised eyebrows in Vancouver. They rose still higher the following day when it was revealed that Percy would be leaving UBC and making a whole slate of meet appearances in the East, not just at the Millrose Games but also in Toronto, Boston and Detroit and possibly other cities as well.[24] For some Vancouverites, these two nuggets of information taken together could mean only one thing: our Percy was turning pro.

The storm broke on December 9. In a front-page story in the *Daily Province* the custodian of the Percy Williams Fund launched a broadside against Percy. "He's got to come clean and say what he is going to do," declared George Harrison. "There's no reason why he can't say what he is going to do. He's got to show down. If he is going East to turn professional, the fund will cease. He will have to suit the trustees. They have absolute power with the fund. They won't object to him finding that he can not be a student. . . . But he will have to take up something worthy. If he won't do that, then he won't get a cent."[25]

The insinuations of bad conduct left Percy boiling. In a front-page response the next day he stated that he had not definitely accepted any invitation to the Millrose Games or any other meet, and in any event they were all amateur affairs. "How could I turn professional," he pointed out hotly, "at a strictly amateur meet?" And: "Is it any crime if I should wish to compete at what is recognized as one of the largest indoor amateur athletic meets in the world?

"The whole thing is just another of those miserable misunderstandings to which I have been subjected ever since I won the first race at Amsterdam. Before I left for the Olympic trials at Hamilton to qualify, I could scarcely borrow two cents from my best friends. After I came back, every rumor in the category from turning professional and booking for vaudeville has been credited to me. Any games promoter that has nerve enough to wire me an invitation to run at a meet and then announces to the press that I am going to compete gets me into a fresh lot of trouble."[26]

Percy, the *Vancouver Sun* observed, was clearly upset, indignant at the implication that he was out to cash in on his Olympic success. And he wasn't finished. "If I am going to turn professional," he went on, "are Pat Mulqueen and Robert Robinson, two of the leading Amateur Athletic Union officials, likely to coax me to do that? . . . As far as I am concerned I have not promised or agreed in any way to run at the Millrose games. The announcement that I was to do so was entirely unauthorized — like a lot of other announcements about my actions — and it has got me into a lot of trouble." Percy continued on at length in what for him was an extraordinary outburst of volubility, then he went down to personally confront George Harrison about what exactly he meant when he said that Percy had to "come clean." Harrison, realizing that he had overreacted, retracted his statement but the damage was done. For Percy, the sense of obligation and loyalty to Vancouver, already teetering, now started to crumble; his distrust in others and his desire for secrecy grew — and his cynicism increased.

It was hard not to notice, for example, that while he was expected to adhere to a draconian amateur code, companies were freely cashing in on his name and his image. The Northwest Biscuit Company in Edmonton had been one of the first to jump on the bandwagon with "Our Percy" chocolate bars. The Biltmore Hat Company was hawking a new model, "The Olympic," in quarter-page newspaper ads showing Percy breaking the tape at Amsterdam to win the gold medal. Birks came out with a coat and hat ornament commemorating his Olympic success at $1.25 a pop. Vancouver's Bingham-Tyrwhitt Motors used a shot of Percy posing beside his new roadster to advertise their Graham-Paige line. And then there were all those events he was hauled to where his presence was used to sell tickets.[27]

And what about the way things worked in amateur track? Although ostensibly devoted to the principles of amateurism, the AAU controlling the show was in effect a business.[28] It ran on the money the public paid to see the athletes in action — money earned directly at Union-run meets or as a percentage charged to promoters of meets the Union sanctioned — and its officials spent the proceeds freely on themselves. Percy would never forget how he and Bob had been left to pay their own way to the nationals in 1927 while the local AAU representative travelled to Toronto at Union expense in first class. The athletes, meanwhile, the very stars generating this income, were supposed to abide by a raft of rules restricting their compensation to travel and living expenses, and to not make a fuss. And if they did, if they stepped out of line or otherwise caused trouble, the AAU would use its powers to sanction and disbar to turn their world upside down, as Charlie Paddock and Paavo Nurmi and others had already found out, and as Ray Barbuti was very soon about to. It was as if the rules of amateurism were really intended to keep the athletes in line and working for cheap, locked in a state of indentured servitude.

If Percy had had any reservations about the trip east, the "come clean" brouhaha blew them away. He was going, all right. And Bob Granger was going with him.

Bob was keen for the trip. It would be another chance for an adventure. He also wanted to see Percy silence the naysayers south of the border who were claiming that his boy at Amsterdam had just got lucky, catching America's top sprinters when they were out of condition and slowed by a soft track. "Doesn't it make you boil?" seethed the *Toronto Star*'s Lou Marsh.[29] The point about the soft track seemed a stretch considering that the condition of the cinders had equally affected all the Olympic runners. Dean Cromwell, however, the coach at USC where Frank Wykoff had now joined Charlie Borah on the varsity track team, revealed a "secret" to explain how the Americans had been disadvantaged. In preparing the track before the Games, he said, the Dutch had lightly steamrolled only the inside four lanes, leaving numbers five and six softer and thereby handicapping the runners who drew them — runners like Wykoff and McAllister in the hundred-metre final.[30] With the initial disappointment and recriminations of the Olympics behind them and with several months to think about it, certain American writers had come to the conclusion that Percy perhaps wasn't really so great, and that Wykoff could probably beat him "nine times out of ten."[31]

Percy made his last appearance with the UBC track team on January 5, a relay followed by an exhibition century race — for Percy little more than a jog.[32] The expense money from the Millrose Games promoters arrived a week later. "Received the cash," he confided in his diary for 1929, this one a private record for himself and not for his mother. "Not yet proven a professional. If I had any brains I would skip the country."[33]

Two days later he boarded the train for the East.

CHAPTER 15

Hurricane Out of the West

⌒

PERCY WOULD LATER say that his 1929 tour of the indoor track circuit was the most fun he ever had as a runner. Going from city to city and meet to meet with his friends Johnny Fitzpatrick, Phil Edwards and Jimmy Ball — for Jimmy was now going — was like being part of a carnival, a travelling show. "I was enjoying myself," he recalled years later. "I was running so often I didn't need to train. I liked the indoor circuit better than the outdoors. It had a real circus atmosphere. It was more fun."[1]

It began on the train just three hours east of Vancouver, when the Trans-Canada Limited rammed into a slow-moving freight and five cars were derailed. Fortunately no one was hurt. There were plenty of people in his car to talk to, everyone tickled to death to be travelling with the one and only Percy Williams and overflowing with questions and advice. "All I get from people who should know," Percy confided in his diary, "is that my wisest move would be the one where cash predominates. In other words, exchange cheques for cheers." No, that didn't sound right. He added "vice versa." People were really beginning to annoy him, though, and so he tried to keep to himself, retreating into his copy of *Trader Horn*. "Why is it," he wrote between dips into the African safari adventure, "everyone insists on telling me all about their younger lives as sprinters? Even the big fat conductor used to be one."[2]

First stop was Winnipeg to hook up with Jimmy Ball. The local sporting crowd put Percy up and showed him a good time: dinners, entertainment, seeing the sights, a training session on the YMCA's indoor track with Jimmy. When it was learned that Percy liked shooting, the boys treated him to a boozy session in someone's basement firing range, trying out various pistols and rifles, and promised to send him a gun as a gift. At dinner one evening one of the guests suggested that he go into the haberdashery business. Percy liked the idea.[3]

Next stop was Toronto, where Alexandrine Gibb, manager of the women's Olympic team and now a sportswriter with the *Star*, was waiting to hustle Percy and Jimmy off the train one stop short of Union Station. Photos were taken and exclusive comments secured and then they were taken into town and put up at the paper's expense. The first meet of their tour, in Boston on February 2, was now getting close and both runners were starting to feel anxious. On the calendar in his diary Percy had the date circled and "Waterloo!" written above it. With just a week to go they decided that they really had to get down to work, and resolved to set aside 4:00 to 5:30 "to do earnest training. Nothing can interrupt us." It was hard, though, to find the time, and their training remained intermittent. There was just so much to do, dinners, shopping, sightseeing, a show in the evening, and so many things to think about in between. Now that they were on the scene in the East, promoters were imploring them to appear in their meets and the reimbursements they were offering were very attractive, more than just a train ticket, meals and a room. "Big deal with Doc about Buffalo," Percy penned in his diary after he and Jimmy added a February 22 meet to their trip. After getting that settled they went out to dinner and then a movie, the African safari documentary *Simba: The King of Beasts*. Percy loved it.[4]

∽

On January 29 Percy and Jimmy took the night train to Boston and were put up at the Boston Athletic Association's clubhouse downtown. They were now in the American heartland of running, the BAA being one of the oldest clubs in the country and its annual indoor meet among the most venerable, an institution since 1890. Percy was expecting to meet up here with Bob Granger for two or three days of fine-tuning in the BAA gym, but when he arrived at the clubhouse there was no sign of his coach. Percy wasn't worried. He had no idea how Bob was going to get east but he knew he would manage it somehow, just as he had done getting to Amsterdam the previous year. When asked as he was leaving Vancouver if Granger would be accompanying him, Percy had replied simply, "Bob will be there."[5]

Boston reporters found Percy and Jimmy looking and acting like a couple of tourists, keen to take in the sights and giving little thought to training. One sportswriter wanted to know if they played much hockey up there in Canada. "Did I ever play hockey!" exclaimed Jimmy. Then, tapping his chin: "Look at those scars." Percy as usual was a tough interview subject — "the sober, staid, dignified, keep-your-distance-please Percy" as one paper put it — clamming up whenever reporters started probing too deeply. Tell us, one of them urged, about the welcome Vancouver laid on for you after the Olympics. Percy wouldn't say much.

Do you like that sort of thing?

"No."

Why not?

"Oh, you have to try to be so nice to people — nice enough — that you never saw before."

They kept at him and Percy kept bobbing and weaving, determined not to reveal too much. Finally, when they started pressing him on the matter of girlfriends, he got a bit testy.

"Girls? I haven't thought much about them, seriously. I like to meet them at parties. But I've never been engaged to one. I think — yes, I'm quite sure — I might like an American girl. Or I might like a Canadian girl. I can't very well tell just now, can I?"[6]

Bob finally showed up on February 2, the very day of the Boston meet. He came with the exciting news that he would be working as correspondent for the *Daily Province*, sending reports back to Vancouver on Percy's races. He also had hopes of reviving his half-finished newspaper serial on "The Life of Percy Williams," begun the previous August. If he could land a syndication deal, it would be published in papers all across North America and be worth thousands of dollars. He just had to get it finished. Maybe Percy could help.

They went out for a dinner of steak, peas and onions, with ice cream for dessert. If there was anything Bob loved as much as coaching and travel, it was a good feed. Then they headed over to Boston Arena to see if Percy would sink or swim in his first US indoor appearance.[7]

⁊

Ever since returning from the Olympics, Bob had been predicting that Percy would run even faster. Over one hundred metres he was sure that his boy could lop at least a fifth of a second off his best Amsterdam time, posted on a wet, slow track, and tie the world record. "I look for him to make ten and two-fifths seconds on some favorable day," Bob announced. "I'm certain that if he gets a fine balmy day on a fast track like they have in the southern States, or even like the last day at Hamilton, with good competition, he will do it."[8]

Bob was just as confident of Percy's chances on the indoor circuit. No one in fact was more optimistic. "Never has a visiting runner been able to vanquish American indoor sprint stars on their home paths," he stated in the *Daily Province* before departing Vancouver, "but I have great hopes for Percy's ability to do so." In another piece he stated that Percy was going to "clean up."[9]

Percy himself didn't see his prospects as nearly so rosy. When corralled by reporters, both he and Jimmy Ball repeatedly stated that their indoor tour shouldn't be taken too seriously; that they were just doing it for the experience and had a lot to learn about running on the boards.[10] They seemed to mean it too, judging from the way they were doing no training and spending all their time prior to the Boston meet sightseeing. In one of his lighter moments Percy even made a pun of it. "You never can tell," he told a Toronto reporter. "Boston is famous for its beans, but I guess perhaps we'll be its 'has beens.'"[11]

Percy wasn't just being modest. Indoor racing was an altogether different game in which more than a few famous outdoor champions had gone down to ignominious defeat. Charlie Paddock, for example, learned early in his career that indoor meets weren't for him and thereafter limited his appearances to outdoors. German sprinting sensation Hubert Houben was similarly thwarted when he tried his hand at the US indoor circuit. After beating both Paddock and Loren Murchison twice at outdoor meets in Germany, he had come to the States in 1926 confident of doing just as well inside. Instead he was repeatedly beaten. The blow to German prestige was such that the German Athletic Federation barred its athletes from further competition in the USA.[12]

The first challenge of indoor sprinting was that the distances were shorter. With meets held in armouries, arenas and gymnasiums offering limited space, sprint races were typically fifty or sixty yards, not the one hundred yards that Percy knew well. This meant that a key element in his outdoor game was no longer valid, the fluid striding he used to conserve energy before kicking into high gear for the finishing drive to the tape. Indoors, it was all about start and acceleration, an all-out scramble from the gun, high gear all the way.

Such short distances also meant that it was nearly impossible for even a great runner to consistently win, as any small error, particularly a bad start, was apt to be fatal, there being so little time to recover. For this reason there was a large degree of luck involved when top-level sprinters got together to compete indoors. Pit them against each other in a string of meets and in all likelihood they would end up splitting the wins, one runner winning tonight, another guy on the weekend and yet another next week, all depending on who got the best start or who was in the best condition on any particular day.

Then there were the indoor tracks themselves, often temporary constructions of boards. They could be disconcertingly loud to run on, and the more poorly built ones were none too solid, making it hard for a runner to really open up. The turns were also extremely sharp and had to be banked steeply so that runners could maintain their speed rounding the corners. This took a good deal of getting used to, powering full bore into a turn, body aslant, trusting to centrifugal force to keep you from tumbling over. Percy, sprinting down straightaways, fortunately would not have to contend much with banks, but they would be hell for Jimmy Ball in his middle-distance races. For sprinters, though, indoor racing frequently reserved a special peril: an alarming lack of space to slow down. When an arena was particularly cramped, mattresses would be placed against the far wall so the athletes wouldn't injure themselves, and in extreme cases a gang of men would brace themselves just past the finish line, holding a rope across the track as a brake. These precautions usually prevented runners from braining themselves or otherwise incurring serious injuries, but it still took nerve to face that kind of finish. Percy in effect would have to race straight at a barrier with all the strength he could muster and not think about how hard those bricks or that iron railing looming beyond the tape might be.

For sprinting on boards, outdoor track shoes with their big spikes were out of the question. Runners instead wore a special type of indoor shoe with short pin spikes affixed to the sole. They had a different feel to them, and the pair the Millrose organizers had sent to Percy had only just arrived for him to try out. Finally, there were the starting blocks. These were almost entirely new to Percy, who in all his racing had only ever started outdoors from holes dug in the track. Indoors, the practice was to push off from angled blocks of wood tacked into the board track surface. Bob had cobbled up a pair back in December for Percy to use in his training for the eastern tour, sessions on the basketball court at the Vancouver Athletic Club gym where all he did was practise his starting, kicking off and accelerating to maximum speed and then immediately slowing down out of respect for the wall.[13]

That was it. That was the extent of Percy's experience with indoor running prior to the Boston meet: two or three Vancouver exhibition races and some indoor sessions practising his starting. Bob Granger may have been confident, but not many others were. In the American press the consensus was that Percy was heading for a fall.[14]

Some were looking forward to it. As one American correspondent put it in a letter to the *Daily Province* on the eve of Percy's departure east, "Williams was lucky to win at Amsterdam, always in the last few yards. . . . But Yankee supremacy will be upheld when your alleged 'world's champion' toes the mark on the eastern tracks . . . and your Vancouver people need not be shocked when he receives the licking of his young life."[15]

∞

Some of the best indoor sprinters in the USA had been called out to the Fortieth Annual Boston Athletic Association Games to give Percy a run for his money. The big names included Jimmy Daley of Holy Cross, inter-collegiate champion and winner of the Boston dash the two previous years; Chester Bowman of the Newark Athletic Club, joint holder of the indoor sixty-yard record, former hundred-yard indoor champ and fourth-place finisher in the 1924 Olympic sprint final; and Georgetown University's Karl Wildermuth, national indoor sprint champion for two years running and a sure bet for the 1928 Olympic team had he not taken sick. All were known as exceptionally fast starters. And with tonight's race over just forty yards, starting was the name of the game.

The venue was the hockey rink in Boston Arena, a track of boards laid on the ice. The building was unheated and it was cold, the athletes warming up in bulky sweatsuits, the eight thousand fans bundled in coats. Percy had been battling a cold for the past two days, but Jimmy Ball, a pharmacist back home, had given him a concoction and he seemed to have it under control. The brand-new indoor spikes on his feet were awfully tight. Bob had insisted that he train in rubber-soled sneakers as the spikes would stiffen his legs, so this was his first real chance to wear them.

His preliminary heat was called. "Well, here goes," he said, stripping down to his Vancouver Athletic Club togs with the winged "V" on the chest. The track looked very short. There wouldn't be much room down at the far end for stopping. Bob, seated in the press box, worried about the effect of the cold air on his boy. Seated beside him was Arthur Duffy, the Boston track legend who had invented the dip finish, the "Duffy lunge," three decades before. He said something cautionary about these American sprinters being awfully fast off the mark. Bob replied stiffly that his Percy didn't exactly hibernate either.

The evening had been a bust for Jimmy Ball. The track wasn't banked but the tight turns had thrown off his stride, as had all the flying elbows and shoving. "A bit rough, isn't it?" Percy commented after, amazed at how much indoor running resembled a fist fight.[16] The best Jimmy could manage in his race was fourth. He retired to the stands and watched Paavo Nurmi, the old pro sharing top billing with Percy, make it look oh-so-easy, flying around the corners in his two-miler and lapping the competition before breasting the tape.

Percy made it look pretty easy as well in his first heat of the forty-yard dash, winning by more than a yard in 4 3/5 seconds, a fifth off the world indoor record set back in 1905. It was true: it *was* all about starting. He had gotten away beautifully and the rest was a cinch. His semifinal proved it again, this time a bad start almost causing his elimination. By giving it everything, he managed to place a qualifying second, behind local favourite Linwood Pattee, but was pushing so hard at the finish that he crashed into the wall at the end of the track, giving his right toe a hard knock. He had injured it earlier in the winter in exactly the same manner, colliding with a wall in a fundraiser exhibition race on the ice of a hockey rink. The blackened nail of his big toe was already about to fall off, and now was throbbing as well.[17]

It took three tries in the final before they got going, the starter calling them back twice and charging Percy with jumping the gun. Fortunately the two-false-starts-and-you're-out Olympic rule was not used at these indoor meets. On the third report of the pistol Percy was away well, remaining even with the field for twenty yards before pulling into the lead to be first through the tape, beating Wildermuth by two feet and Daley and the rest by a yard. Up in the press box one of the American scribes was heard to mutter: "That skinny shrimp musta been sired by a kangaroo and dammed by a gazelle."[18] Down on the track an incredulous meet official said to one of the Canadians congratulating

Percy, "Do you *know* who he beat?" and proceeded to reel off the accomplishments of Wildermuth and the rest of the vanquished.[19]

In his diary all Percy had to say was, "Boy, what a surprise to all."[20]

∞

"Yip!

"Yip-ee!!

"And likewise Whoop-ee!!!"[21]

So began Lou Marsh's *Toronto Star* report on Percy's Boston win, and it pretty well described how all Canada felt. And the eastern US papers were only slightly less enthusiastic. Percy's victory against America's best in his very first indoor appearance was an irresistible story and they ran with it, the *New York World* splashing the news in banner headlines across all eight columns: "Williams of Canada, Olympic Sprint Champion, Shines in Boston."[22]

Offers to appear in other meets suddenly started pouring in for Percy. "Now see what I have let myself in for by winning that race," he joked, adding a February 7 meet in Newark to his schedule. Pat Mulqueen advised him to turn it down, pointing out that the Millrose people, whose meet would be held just two days later, were paying his expenses and had first claim on his time.[23] Percy accepted anyway. The Newark promoter had promised that he would have to run only a single dash, so it wouldn't interfere with the Millrose Games. It would just sharpen him up.[24]

From Boston, Percy, Bob and Jimmy took the train to New York and the New York Athletic Club's exclusive twenty-four-storey "clubhouse" overlooking Central Park, where guest rooms awaited. Bob immediately fell in love with the city and was off to see the sights. He was having a great time, constantly on the go, soaking it all in. "New York was wonderful, boy," he enthused in a letter. "I used to see the great buildings looming up in the dawn, boy — it was great. Wall Street, the White Lights of Broadway, life, life, life and then some more life. Six people were killed in one night by taxis but I only found an account of it in one paper, and then in the advertising section."[25]

Percy was less enamoured. The staff at the New York AC at first wouldn't let them in, he was cheated out of fifty cents at a discount eatery where they stopped for dinner, and everyone generally seemed "so crooked they could hide behind a corkscrew." After two days he wrote in his diary that he was sick of the Big Apple and wouldn't live there "if you gave me the Woolworth Building as a club house and the Statue of Liberty as a radiator ornament for my Jesabelle," Percy's name for his Graham-Paige coupe. And as he added in a letter home, "I think there are more Jews here than any place I ever saw in my life."[26]

It was now Tuesday, February 5, and the Millrose Games were looming large ahead on Saturday night. It was the premier event of Percy's Eastern tour and he was getting anxious. In his diary he wrote: "Really scared of Saturday nite."[27]

The Newark meet on Thursday evening, meanwhile, wasn't causing him much worry. He and Bob in fact almost missed it, three subway rides and two elevated trains landing them out in the cold somewhere in Jersey City. After some frantic asking around they found their way to Newark and the 113th Regiment Armory just in time for Percy to toe the line in the evening's main attraction. It was a sixty-yard race, against a lesser field than he had faced in Boston. To make it more interesting it would be a handicap match, the other runners starting a yard out in front. They wore tennis shoes, pin spikes being useless on the armoury's concrete floor, and would start flat, without blocks. The starter was an old-timer named Johnny McHugh, a minor track celebrity who had been wielding the pistol at meets going on thirty years.

Percy got away fast and fairly at the first report of the pistol, but McHugh called them back and accused him of jumping the gun. "Leave him alone, I'm the one to blame," shouted one of the other runners as McHugh proceeded to lecture Percy on fairness. To Bobby Robinson, covering the meet for the *Hamilton Spectator*, it was clear that McHugh was purposefully trying to unnerve Percy.

They tried again. It was another fast, fair getaway by Percy, but again McHugh called them back, declaring he had false started. That got Percy annoyed and he argued about it. He had already conceded a yard to the others. Did he have to put up with tricks from the starter as well? For Pete's sake, in these short indoor sprints the start was *everything*.

They got down and tried a third time. Bob, looking on from the press box, was fast developing an intense dislike for McHugh. He seemed to think he was the star of the show rather than just a badger, strutting around with his pistol and glaring at Percy. He started into the commands, again with the theatrical drawl he affected.

"On your ma-a-a-r-k. . . .

"Get se-e-e-t. . . ."

And then he just waited. Percy, whose starting crouch included an extreme forward lean, struggled to hold it, started to fall forward and finally had to go back. That's when McHugh fired his pistol. The field was off and Percy, back on his haunches, was facing a disadvantage of not one yard, but two. With his competitive juices now positively boiling, he gave it everything he had to race down the others. The boys were no slouches and sixty yards didn't give him much space. The brick wall at the end of the track was hard not to notice as well. But Percy wasn't going to lose this one. Not tonight. Not to McHugh. He pushed with everything he had and caught the leader five yards shy of the tape and went on to win by inches in 6 2/5 seconds, a fifth off the world record that had been set with starting blocks and spikes. Bob Wiese of the New York AC was second.[28]

Percy's record on his US invasion was now two wins and zero defeats. Next up was the Millrose Games. "Lordy," he wrote in his diary, "but tomorrow night is close and what's going to happen?"[29]

∽

It was like an Olympic reunion at Madison Square Garden, with a whole slate of Percy's former Amsterdam teammates on hand for the Millrose Games on February 9. Johnny Fitzpatrick had come down from Hamilton and joined Percy and Jimmy Ball in the guest suites at the New York AC. Their noisy fooling around, racing up and down the halls in their pyjamas, had already led to complaints.[30] Phil Edwards was there as well, and Alex Wilson, and the entire women's sprint team of Myrtle Cook, Fanny Rosenfeld, Florence Bell and Ethel Smith, and manager Bobby Robinson and president Pat Mulqueen.

Bob Granger as usual was bursting with confidence in Percy, predicting in his *Daily Province* dispatch that "America's greatest sprinters will be chewing perfectly good splinters which the flying hoofs of the western gazelle will send shooting out into the cool Garden air." The only thing that could beat his boy, Bob proclaimed, was the starter McHugh. "He has reached the stage where he thinks it clever to make the runners break, and he generally holds them on the mark so long that they feel like stopping there for the winter instead of running."[31]

Percy wasn't so sanguine, but he no longer saw himself as such a long shot and he wanted to win. The toughest competition again would be from Karl Wildermuth, Jimmy Daley, and Chet Bowman, all of whom he had beaten at Boston. Olympic sprint relay gold-medal winner Jimmy Quinn, known as a particularly fast starter, would also be there. So would Johnny Fitzpatrick, now generally regarded as the fastest man in Canada after Percy.

Bob McAllister reportedly was entered as well. Ever since returning from Amsterdam, the Flying Cop had made much of his defeat of Percy in the hundred-metre semifinals, claiming that he would have won the final had he not torn a muscle. His trainer, McAllister said, had neglected to warm his legs before the final in the electrical warming machine he had come to rely on. That's what did it. Finally, in January 1929, after five months of talk, McAllister had announced that he was coming out of retirement to take on Percy indoors, and that he would beat him at any distance between sixty and a hundred metres.[32]

There was no venue on the indoor track circuit like Madison Square Garden for twanging the nerves of an athlete. The recently completed sports entertainment palace was enormous compared to Boston Arena and the armoury in Newark, fifteen thousand spectators crowding the seats that encircled the track and extended up into the rafters, their cumulative clamour echoing off the walls and ceiling in a way that exceeded anything in a stadium outdoors. And it wasn't just the noise. The fans were so *close*. The ones in the front row were practically shouting right in your face.

In the dressing room Percy had difficulty putting on his spikes. His big toenail had just fallen off and the tight leather bit into the tender skin underneath. It wasn't too bad at first, but the longer he had the shoes on, the more his toe hurt. He tried to be careful with it in private, walking with a limp, but out on the arena floor he made a point of not showing any signs of discomfort. He hated excuses. The prohibition against them was number two in the "Ten Commandments of Sport" that he kept in his desk back home, right after "Thou shalt not quit" and before "Thou shalt not gloat over winning" and "Thou shalt not be a bad loser." "Thou shalt not alibi," it read. He had it marked with a big "X."[33]

No sign of Bob McAllister. He was reportedly laid up in bed with the flu. Percy didn't much care. But the starter was Johnny McHugh. That got him worried. He would first have to survive a sixty-yard preliminary dash to qualify, then a fifty-yard final. Against Wildermuth and the rest it would be hard enough. With McHugh handling the gun, it promised to be even harder.

Bob Granger was covering the meet again from up in the press box, this time with a telegraph operator at his side to transmit his comments instantaneously back to Vancouver. "And now a hush falls over the throng," he dictated to the telegraph man, "for the starter is calling them to their marks." It was Percy's preliminary race, the sixty-yard qualifier for the final, run on a sprint track laid up the centre of the arena. McHugh had already called them back once and had made a show of lecturing Percy on false starting.

"The stage is set. 'Get on your marks — ' BANG! and away go the world's greatest sprinters, tearing for all they are worth for a little white string just 60 yards away. . . . There goes champion Daley, running for Holy Cross. There goes Chet Bowman with the world record in his shoes, and there, running as if possessed, is the mighty giant Ed Hamm, champion of the South. . . . A mighty roar goes up, for the runners are rushing towards the tape. But where is the Western Gazelle?"

The telegraph transmission ended while the telegraph operator started scribbling down Bob's next instalment. Three thousand miles away, the *Daily Province* staff sweated. Then the dots and dashes started again and they learned that Percy was trailing Daley by a yard at the halfway mark, having gotten away poorly after another long hold by McHugh.

"And then the Hurricane came out of the West. SWISH BANG, and the tape parted on the nifty Williams, the Vancouver Athletic Club marvel. Time 6 2/5 seconds. Wonderful time for such a start. . . . Percy was just too fast for them when he opened up. Please phone Fairmont 2102R now and tell them result." That was the phone number of Percy's house, where Dot and his family were anxiously awaiting the news.[34]

In the final it was Wildermuth, Daley, Jimmy Quinn and Percy. Johnny Fitzpatrick hadn't qualified. Percy broke early the first time, unable to maintain his forward lean through McHugh's excruciatingly long holds and unwilling to go back. "McHugh is very stagey in action," observed the *Toronto Star*'s Lou Marsh, sharing Bob Granger's distaste for the man, "and he likes to hold the boys on the mark, drag a couple of them off and then hand them a lecture. It's great stuff for the movies, but it is danged hard on nervous, high strung sprinters like Williams."[35] The runners got set and once more McHugh held them, until Percy was unable to hold it any longer and this time eased his weight back.

That's when McHugh pulled the trigger. Once again Percy was caught flat-footed, all his practice perfecting his starts rendered useless. Once again he lowered his head and charged down the track after the leaders, digging his spikes viciously into the boards, working his way through the field and coming even with the leader, Wildermuth, in the final few yards. And once again he won it, this time by inches, in 5 3/5 seconds.

Percy's indoor record was now three final victories and zero defeats. And he wasn't done for the evening. After a rest he teamed up with Alex Wilson, Jimmy Ball and Phil Edwards for the international medley relay, racing on a banked oval for the first time in his life and doing amazingly well. The turns were tricky, just as Jimmy was saying, and he took them cautiously in his lead-off 220-yard leg. On the straightaways, however, he opened up and shot ahead like a bullet, handing his teammates a lead of ten yards.[36]

The Canadians went on to win it and Percy walked away with "two dandy medals. Both have a diamond in them. Not very large diamonds but not bad."[37] His record was now four and oh.

❧

On February 12 Percy extended his streak to five and oh in Philadelphia at the Meadowbrook Games. He was no longer doing any training at all. The regular competition, he explained to incredulous reporters, was enough to keep him in shape. He spent most of the day napping, then headed out to Philadelphia Arena with Bob and Jimmy to face once again the likes of Karl Wildermuth and Chester Bowman, setting a new world record of 4 9/10 seconds in the process, smacking hard into the padded wall at the end of the track after breaking the tape. His toe still hurt, he was running in flat shoes, he had started without blocks, but none of it mattered. Toronto's *Evening Telegram* exulted that Percy "could probably run in his bare feet and beat them." The *New York Times* called him "the king of speed." In the *Hamilton Spectator* he was "the sprint marvel of the age." Arthur Duffy wrote in the *Boston Post* that "I do not know any one who can beat him." A *Herald-Tribune* sportswriter declared him "invincible," and in casting about for superlatives came up with a new nickname, "Loup-Garou," the werewolf-like apparition that flitted through the woods of Quebec, too fast to be seen. Lou Marsh liked it so much he appropriated it in his next day's headline in the *Toronto Star*: "Loup-Garou Adds Another to His String of Victories."[38]

Next it was back to New York for the Crescent Athletic Club meet in the Brooklyn Armory on the sixteenth. "Run tonight," Percy jotted in his diary that day after sleeping till noon. "Wonder how it will turn out. Don't care?"[39] Competing with the honourary number "1" pinned to his jersey — meet organizers were reserving it for him now; even the great Paavo Nurmi was having to settle for a "2" or a "3" — Percy won an exhibition sixty-metre dash in 6 4/5 seconds, breaking Bob McAllister's record by two-fifths of a second and devastating the competition with his finishing burst. Afterward a disappointed Jimmy Quinn was heard to mutter, "He comes up at the 35-yard mark and makes you look like a dub . . ."[40] McAllister himself had made noises again about appearing to face Percy, but again he failed to show up on account of the flu. In his newspaper dispatches Bob Granger began to openly deride the Flying Cop, claiming that he was dodging his boy.[41]

Percy's record was now six victories, zero defeats.

∽

Amid all the soaring adulation for Percy and his perfect indoor record, no one remained more blasé than Percy himself. Even in the privacy of his diary he expressed no pleasure in taking McAllister's sixty-metre title, brushing his headline-making performance aside as "one of the records anyone can make if they find enough odd distances."[42] He had come east for adventure and to work the indoor track circuit, and that's what he still intended to do, regardless of the outcome. He continued adding meets to his schedule until he was racing almost every evening and the papers were calling him an "iron man." Percy probably liked that, proving to the world and maybe to himself that he wasn't so delicate after all. He knew he was likely heading for a fall, but didn't seem to care. The only qualms came on the eve of his February 18 appearance at the New York AC meet at Madison Square Garden. He had given tickets to an old family friend, the actress Edythe Elliott, from Dot's days at the Empress Theatre. She was now in New York appearing on Broadway and had invited Percy to visit, and he wanted to look good when she watched him run. "Guess it will be the time to lose, just when I'd like to win," he philosophically noted, "but I've played Lady Luck so long now that we're old friends."[43]

It was all causing Bob Granger a lot of concern. Percy, he felt, was becoming reckless in competing so often. It was tiring him out and taking a toll on his legs, particularly his bad knee, which Bob was carefully nursing. Bob himself was a great one for burning the candle at both ends, running around seeing the sights all day and staying up most of the night, stopping by the telegraph office at dawn to get the cheaper rate for sending his newspaper stories off to Vancouver.[44] But he didn't have a perfect indoor record to protect. Bob's words of caution, however, fell on deaf ears. After the Madison Square Garden meet on the eighteenth, Percy agreed to appear in Detroit on the twentieth for an exhibition race, in Toronto on the twenty-first to headline the first ever Canadian Indoor National Championships, in Buffalo on the twenty-second for the meet he had previously entered, and then again in Madison Square Garden for the US Indoor Championships on the twenty-third. And after that he was talking about travelling all the way out to Los Angeles for a "Paavo Nurmi-Percy Williams Invitational Meet" on March 23, where he would go head to head against Frank Wykoff. It was all too much for Bob and he couldn't help revealing his anxiety to *Province* readers back home. Percy, he wrote on February 18, "is booked up too heavily and didn't even rest today, going for a 250-mile auto trip. He started in early morning, despite the fact he was at a banquet till 2 a.m."[45]

Vancouver was revelling in Percy's successes and didn't take immediate notice. That would come the next day, with the news that he had suffered his first loss. It was at the February 18 meet, the one Percy had had premonitions of losing — premonitions that became stronger when he saw that McHugh would be doing the starting. "If I am defeated on this tour," Percy had confided to Bobby Robinson earlier that week, "it will be in some race in which Johnny McHugh is the starter."[46] McHugh was down on the track now, just below where Bob Granger was sitting, scribbling out his latest dispatch. Bob jotted down that he looked "just like Hoot Gibson toting a cap pistol at a cattle roundup."

The event was a sixty-yard dash. There would be only one race, Karl Wildermuth and Jimmy Daley having withdrawn and the planned two rounds of competition being condensed into a final. Percy lined up against Jimmy Quinn, Johnny Fitzpatrick, Bob Wiese and Jack Elder. Quinn and Johnny were the ones to watch. Wiese, who had placed second in the Newark handicap race, didn't seem to pose much of a threat. Neither did Elder, a stocky Notre Dame running back, one of Knute Rockne's boys, who had been eliminated in the first round at the Philadelphia meet.

McHugh called them to their marks, set them, and then, true to form, left them hanging until Percy could no longer hold his forward leaning crouch and was forced to go back. When the gun finally sounded it caught him hopelessly flat-footed, last off the mark and badly trailing Elder, whose early break McHugh flagrantly overlooked. Percy managed to get past Wiese and Quinn, and then Johnny Fitzpatrick in the last few yards, coming on with a closing burst and Paddock-style leap and hitting the arresting rope so hard that he was sent sprawling onto to the floor, rope burns and bruises across his arms and his chest, Fitzpatrick landing on top. He had almost pulled it off, but not quite. Jack Elder was declared the winner and the stunned crowd came alive with cheering. "Nice place," Percy wryly noted in his diary. "Elder beat me. Jumped the gun and with the aid of the wonder starter McCue [sic] I was left flat."[47]

∞

Percy's first loss came as a blow to the folks back home. In an instant the cry of "Go get 'em, Percy!" was forgotten. Now everyone was convinced that he was overdoing it. The *Sun* laid the case out clearly, in a cartoon showing Uncle Sam milking "Loup-Garou" and an editorial entitled "Burning up Percy." "If Vancouver is interested in his fortunes," it read, "somebody in Vancouver who has influence with him should advise him to take it easy before he ruins himself and his fine prospects."[48]

And so the telegrams started flying. "Will endeavor to have Williams curtail engagements," Vancouver's new mayor, William Malkin, responded to an entreaty from a concerned Ontario sportsman.[49] "Teachers all worried about length of programme," Commerce High coach Graham Bruce cabled direct to Percy. "All ask me to suggest that as you have won everything you cancel everything possible and avoid possible nervous exhaustion with possible disastrous results or losses." "Billy and I are delighted at your success," read another cable, this one from family friends. "But don't overdo yourself. Good people are scared." "Great," dashed off Dot when Percy again started winning. "So why run after Saturday. Come home and rest."[50]

It seemed that everyone in Vancouver — in *Canada* — wanted Percy to stop running. But would he? Knowing that Dot was urging restraint was a comfort. Those intimate with the Williams family, however, knew that for all Percy's much-publicized affection and esteem for his mother, the best way to influence him was to go through his father. A contingent of concerned citizens therefore went down to see Fred Williams in his room at the Stratford Hotel.[51]

CHAPTER 16

Break Up

ॐ

"I HAVE RECEIVED a telegram from Dad," Percy announced to the press, "asking me to cut out running for a while and return home. When a fellow knows his parents' wishes he should obey."

What did he plan to do next? reporters wanted to know. Well, he wasn't sure. He definitely didn't want to return to university. He was more interested in business. Maybe he would open a haberdashery shop.[1]

The fact was that Percy had already decided to wind up his indoor tour and head home, and had written as much to his mother in a letter she had not yet received. While he was rather enjoying working the indoor circuit, indoor racing was itself a strain, the short distances placing too much importance on the starts and the unyielding wood and concrete track surfaces hard on his joints and his feet. He was also "doggone tired" from all the competition and excitement, the night trains and going without sleep.[2]

That being said, Percy didn't regret a single appearance he had made, and chided his hometown supporters for their well-intentioned interfering, pointing out that every race he had added to his schedule had been carefully considered and had served a purpose. Accepting the Newark invitation, for example, "was the luckiest thing I did on the entire trip. It was at Newark I first ran up against Johnny McHugh, the New York starter. My experience taught me what to expect at New York. Had I not learned his ways at Newark I would have been beaten in the Millrose Games." As for his loss to Jack Elder, Percy claimed that it had nothing to do with fatigue, but rather to McHugh's "deliberate effort to leave me flat-footed." A number of others had already come forward to back him up. Johnny Fitzpatrick, competing in the same race, stated that Elder beat the gun by two yards. Pole vaulter Vic Pickard, watching from the sidelines near the finish, said the same thing. So did Phil Edwards, adding that, with a fair start, Elder would have placed third behind Percy and Fitzpatrick.[3]

Before heading home, Percy had to fulfill his remaining obligations, three meets in three days in three different towns, a crescendo of competition. First there was an easy sixty-yard exhibition race he had agreed to run in Detroit against some second-rate talent. That, anyway, had been the understanding. When he arrived at Detroit Arena with Bob Granger on the evening of February 20, Percy found that the race had instead been set at forty yards, a crapshoot of a distance, and that some special talent had been called out in an obvious effort to beat him, including University of Michigan sophomore Eddie Tolan and Percy's former Olympic teammate George "Buck" Hester. "They stacked all their slickers in a 40 against me," Percy groused in his diary. He was tired out from the night train from New York, unable to sleep because of another passenger's snoring, and was in no mood to put up with what looked like tricks and bad faith. He therefore refused to compete. After some frantic pleading to think of the fans, he relented, allowing himself, as he put it, to be "rooked" into the race.[4]

Poor George Hester, rousted out of retirement, had hardly run a step since Amsterdam and it showed. He was eliminated in the qualifying heats. Not so Eddie Tolan, Buck's successor as Michigan's top track man and emerging as one of the best sprinters in the country, gifted with a particularly fast start. As expected, he got away brilliantly while Percy, looking visibly tired, was forced to play catch-up. Percy outran the others but Eddie was tough. It was only by making a Herculean effort that Percy managed to edge past the Wolverine star in the closing yards and win by six inches, equalling the indoor record for the distance of 4 2/5 seconds set back in 1905.[5]

Percy didn't know it yet but it was the start of a rivalry. He would be seeing more of Eddie.

From Detroit Percy and Bob hopped on the train to Toronto for the first ever Canadian National Indoor Championships scheduled for the very next evening. Percy made the trip expecting finally to come up against Bob McAllister and put an end to his talking, for the Flying Cop had actually submitted a signed entry this time and was on hand in the city. And sure enough, when Percy arrived at the CNE Coliseum, shivering in his overcoat in an evening snow flurry, there was McAllister's name on the program and there he was in the flesh.

But he never got out of his street clothes. His official reason for not running was the change that had been made in the program, the special open event in which he was to have faced Percy having been cancelled and all the sprinters lumped into the Canadian championship dash instead, which would entail three rounds of racing. McAllister said he had only just recovered from the flu and wasn't up for that. He had come to Toronto to give his all in a single race against Percy — the Bowery cop called him "Poicy" — and refused to run in anything else.[6]

That was the official story. Unofficially, McAllister stated that he *would* run in Toronto, but only if Percy returned with him to New York for the AAU national championships at Madison Square Garden, where Johnny McHugh incidentally would do the starting.[7] Percy had initially expressed interest in the meet, but had not signed an entry despite the best efforts of the promoters. A clumsy attempt had even been made to trick him into signing, an entry form being slipped under his pen when he was besieged by autograph seekers at a Philadelphia banquet. "What's this?" Percy had asked. "It's just for autograph purposes, isn't it?" He was assured that it was and so scrawled his name across the top of the paper, well away from the dotted line at the bottom. The document was waved about a few days later as a binding entry but the ruse was easily proved. Percy, disgusted, pulled out of the meet altogether.[8]

McAllister, representing the New York meet organizers, now wanted Percy back in. When his quid pro quo offer was brushed aside, he tried to lure Percy into a Knights of Columbus meet scheduled for the Garden on March 16, laying out what Percy in his diary called a "big business deal" whereby Percy would throw the Toronto race and let McAllister win, thereby stoking interest in a rematch at the K of C meet where they would both get a handsome cut of the profits. The deal smelled. Percy didn't touch it.[9]

Percy went on to win the Toronto sixty-yard dash, beating Johnny Fitzpatrick to the tape to equal the world record in 6 1/5 seconds, the sound of their spikes on the wooden track reportedly echoing through the drafty Coliseum like gunshots. Afterward he ran back up the length of the track as was his practice, grinning broadly and acknowledging the cheers of the sold-out crowd with bows as he went. "Nobody'll trim that kid," announced a stout gentleman with a cigar in his mouth. "They're all fast till Percy lets loose. Then they're just runnin'."[10]

In the autograph scrum that followed, one young woman coming away with Percy's prized signature was overheard to say: "He's not a bit high hat, is he?"

"Oh-h-h! I just love him," gushed her companion.

McAllister never did run against Percy. He returned to New York without his rematch, his career as a sprinter effectively over.[11]

∽

Percy wound up his US invasion with an appearance in Buffalo the following evening, February 23, racking up another victory, an easy one this time, over the familiar distance of a hundred yards. His biggest challenge was to avoid trampling the spectators seated on the armoury floor just past the finish.[12] He had now competed in ten meet finals and had won nine of them, running a total of seventeen races for a record of fourteen victories and three second-place finishes. It was an unprecedented record for indoor sprinting, where so much depended on quick starts and luck. "Ordinarily," observed the *New York Times* in assessing Percy's performance, "the sprinters take turns beating each other in the short dashes on the boards. It might almost be classed as a gambling game."[13] But somehow Percy had done it. He had done it despite having had almost no prior experience of indoor racing. He had done it without imposing conditions, as other big-name sprinters often did, as to what distances he would run and who he would face. He had done it even though he often got away to bad starts that left him trailing at the outset.

There would be no more talk of Percy having been lucky in Amsterdam. With a spectacular indoor record now added to his two Olympic gold medals, the list of his detractors shrank almost to nothing and few chose to contest that he was, as the *Hamilton Spectator* put it, "the greatest sprinter of the age." The question now was: How long would he keep the title?

✏

Dear Mother:

Things have been going so fast lately that I didn't get a chance to write. Don't pay any attention to these newspaper reports. I ran fairly steady for about three days, but I am all thru now. If I come home now it will be a case of a second Olympics in the case of receptions etc. The best thing for me to do is stay here and rest for a week or two.

The city of Hamilton want me to stay there until the 20th of March and then run in their meet. Then I will come home. While in Hamilton they will put me up and I can get a job *working*???? for the Graham Paige motor cars. It will be a case more or less of having one to drive around instead of selling them. . . . I've been out all day with Mr. Armstrong of Winnipeg. He insists on buying me a gun.

Love, Percy

P.S. I'll be coming home with watches, diamond medals, silver trays (presented by Toronto with one the other night) and what have you.[14]

∽

It had been Percy's original plan to return home directly following the Buffalo meet and take a long break from sprinting. The invitations to run continued to arrive, however, and now they were coming from Canadian cities. Montreal, Ottawa, Hamilton, Winnipeg, Edmonton — they all wanted to host an indoor meet of their own, with Percy headlining to ensure it would turn a handsome profit. Some sent along straightforward invitations. Others opted for a pushier approach. "Everything is in readiness for Williams' arrival," read an Edmonton cable, "to hold meet Easter Monday night April first. Meet cannot be run without him. . . . Heavy expense already incurred. Will treat him liberally. Cannot break up arrangements at this date as people of Edmonton would be too much disappointed and would cause too much reflection on Mr. Williams."[15]

Percy didn't like his accommodating nature being presumed upon. He turned that one down. He also changed his mind about making an appearance at the Los Angeles Coliseum. There seemed to be too many strings attached.[16] He opted instead to spend a month in Hamilton to headline the upcoming indoor track meet the Ambitious City was organizing for March 20, tickets to range from fifty cents to a dollar and a half. Bobby Robinson talked him into staying, sweetening the deal with a lucrative job selling cars for a local Packard dealer named Roy Reynolds: fifty dollars a week plus commissions and a free room at the Royal Connaught Hotel. Percy was keen to start working and figured he would be inundated with attention if he returned right away to Vancouver. And so he accepted. It would be "a cinch of a job," he figured, "no work, just driving around in a car most of the time."[17] Jimmy Ball, who had finally mastered the art of indoor running to win his last several races, agreed to stick around as well. Robinson and his associates fixed him up with a position in a stock broker's office, reading the tickertape and marking the board.[18]

"Don't worry about Percy not returning to Vancouver," said Pat Mulqueen. "He'll be back." Pat was visiting the West Coast city and knew that Vancouverites would be anxious about losing their prize. "That's a very level-headed boy, don't forget. The tumult and the shouting for him has not inflated his cranium. He's just the same modest, likable youth he proved himself at Amsterdam last summer." Then he added: "New York clubs had their men chasing Percy vehemently. It isn't easy for Percy to say no to anybody and he was practically compelled to flee from Buffalo to escape these importunists."[19]

Bright and early on the morning of February 28, Percy put on his suit and strolled down to Roy's auto dealership and punched in to begin his first real job. It would entail more than just driving around — although there would be plenty of that. He had to actually sell cars, and with the help of the old pros in the office he was soon hard at it, meeting a stream of people with their kids in tow, signing autographs and perfecting his spiel. "It's funny selling these cars," he wrote home, "sometimes you just keep on talking and you really haven't the slightest knowledge of what you are talking about." Show me any other car on the market with a seven-bearing crankshaft for the same money, he confidently told one fellow wavering over an expensive Packard. "He admitted he couldn't, so I went on with a flock more good outstanding points. Found out even the Whippets have that kind of crankshaft. Nice day."[20]

Percy eventually lined up a number of prospects, mostly people interested in the Graham-Paige models that Roy carried, the same make of car that Vancouver had given Percy the previous September. (Roy's company motto was, "Ask The Man Who Owns One.") And after two weeks on the job he made his first sale. And then another. And then a third. For someone who was supposed to be painfully introverted and shy, Percy wasn't bad at the sales racket. Roy announced that he would be glad to have him stay on for good.[21]

The Hamilton Indoor Games were now fast approaching and Percy had not done any running since the Buffalo meet nearly one month before, just some skipping and a little stretching and jogging. It was well-known that he didn't like training, and with Bob Granger tied up in New York trying to finish writing his "Life of Percy Williams" for syndication, there was no one around to push him and so he let his conditioning slide. There was also so much to do: the job at Roy's, the endless round of luncheons and functions, driving new cars down for the lot from Toronto, hunting and trap shooting on the weekends, shopping (Percy bought a lever-action Marlin with telescopic scope, a holster and a new pair of outdoor spikes) and visits to Bobby Robinson at his farm — where Bobby's teenaged daughter Edna promptly developed a crush on him.[22] "Should really get licked good and plenty," Percy cheerfully confided in his diary two days before the meet. "No real training so far. Oh well!" He was having too much fun making money to worry about running. He was cleaning up at Roy's and it just seemed to get better, a local businessman offering him a quarter interest in a company that made malted milk. "All I do is advertise it," Percy exulted. "Pretty hot, Eh What!"[23]

It was a hard-fought thing, but Percy did it again, winning his sixty-yard qualifying heat and his final in the Hamilton meet against the likes of Johnny Fitzpatrick and Leigh Miller and Chester Bowman of the Newark AC. In the final they all finished within not much more than a foot of each other, Percy in front in the world-record-tying time of 6 1/5 seconds, Johnny just inches behind in second — *again* — followed by Miller and Bowman. Percy went out after that for a night of carousing with Jimmy Ball, then boarded the train the next day for the long journey home.[24]

"Don't tell anybody that you know when I will be home," he wrote to his mother as the train neared Winnipeg. "Tell them I should be home sometime this month. Either this one or maybe next month. I don't want a crowd down at the station. I've had enough of that for a lifetime." In Winnipeg he followed this up with a cable: "Don't bother to meet me and above all don't tell when you expect me." And then, just to be sure, a note: "Don't forget now! You don't know when I am getting home."[25]

✑

Bob Granger was on the same westbound train and was bursting with plans. First there was the serialization of "The Life of Percy Williams" that he was nursing toward lucrative publication. It had been a lot of work making the rounds of the big newspapers in the East, but he had finally succeeded in securing a tentative $2,800 syndication deal that would see the story published in papers all across North America — assuming he could get the thing written. He wasn't nearly as far along as he hoped and now had to finish it fast, before the excitement over Percy's Eastern invasion died down, or the deal would fall to pieces. He was hoping that once they got back to Vancouver Percy would help.

He was also working on a scheme to put on Vancouver's first big-time indoor track meet, spurred on by what he had seen of the business of meet promotion during his tour of the East. With Percy and Jimmy Ball on board, he predicted, the event would be a "knockout." "Everything depends on you two fellows running at my meet," he had urged in a long, costly cable sent to them in Hamilton the previous month.[26] Whatever their reply was, Bob took it as a commitment and forged ahead with his plans, booking Vancouver Arena, designing a board track that could be built in reusable sections, and sending out invitations to every big-name runner he could think of to appear in his meet alongside Percy Williams. According to the papers, Bob's sporting extravaganza was already an "assured thing."[27]

But it wasn't. After arriving in Vancouver on March 29, Bob was unable to get Percy to commit in writing to his meet and was unable to enlist his help with the writing of his life story either. What was the matter? Percy, he thought, had already agreed. And then, after just one week, Percy was away again, on the train heading back to the East, this time to Montreal for an indoor meet there on April 15, then on to Ottawa for another race two days later, both of which he handily won. It seems the invitations may have been sweetened with a little something extra — but still, was he trying to avoid his coach?[28]

When Percy finally arrived back in Vancouver on April 26, this time to stay, he announced that he would be taking a break from competition. The Los Angeles meet in May was now definitely out, the planned rematch with Frank Wykoff that promoters had been hoping would be the main draw at a "Percy Williams–Paavo Nurmi Invitational." Even a telegram from movie star Harold Lloyd to be his guest while in LA failed to entice him.[29] Nor would Percy make the trip to Berlin for the

July meet promoters were trying so hard to coax him to enter. "I think I'll take a little holiday now and get a job," he said. "That may sound strange, but that's the way I feel. I want a rest, and if I get working I will have a good excuse to decline from taking part in out-of-town meets. These long trips sure take it out of you."[30]

He wouldn't be appearing in Bob Granger's indoor meet either. He "ran out" on the deal, as Bob put it, and the whole project fell to pieces, taking with it everything Bob had invested — which for Bob, impetuous as usual, was practically everything he had. A separate outdoor meet soon began to take shape in its place without Bob's involvement, under the auspices of the Amalgamated Association of Street Railway and Electrical Employees, suggesting a connection with Percy's father Fred, an employee of BC Electric. It would be by far the biggest track meet ever held in the city, and would have as its main event a hundred-yard dash featuring Percy against some of the best in the world. Publicly, Percy would receive a silver watch and a top-notch set of golf clubs if he won. Privately, he would get fifteen hundred dollars just to appear. Something would also be set aside for Fred Williams.[31]

It's hard to say exactly what happened next, and who walked out on whom. The result, however, was that Bob and Percy split up. The tension that had been building between them finally erupted into an open quarrel when Bob asked Percy to write for reimbursement from the Percy Williams Fund for the expenses he had incurred on the Eastern tour. Back in January the money remaining in the fund, $14,500, had been used to set up a trust for Percy, with $750 to be paid annually to Dot Williams for Percy's education and training. Nothing had been set aside for Bob as he had been verbally promised. Had Percy been more supportive of his other schemes, Bob might not have made the request for reimbursement from the fund. But now he did — and Percy told him to "go to Hades."[32]

For Percy, a number of emotions were likely at work. Bob's requests may just have come at the wrong time, when Percy was tired from his long season in the spotlight, his natural amiability pushed to the limit, his patience worn down by Bob being what he called "on the rampage."[33] He may have been offended as well by what he saw as a degree of presumption in Bob's plans. He was now twenty-one, a grown man, and no longer felt like being "Bob's runner." He may also have felt that Bob was trying to use him; that his trusted, self-sacrificing mentor had become like all those other people who were out for a buck, who liked to get close because they *wanted* something. There were plenty of advisers around Percy who were only too willing to encourage these suspicions — amateur sporting bigwigs and city leaders who looked down on Bob, in many ways a bumbler in his life off the track; rival track experts who were just plain jealous; and above all hustlers who saw advantage in moving Percy out of Bob's orbit and into their own. You're a natural, they whispered. You could have done it without Bob. You don't really need him.[34]

As for Bob, it wasn't just about being offended by Percy's rebuff and the anguish of seeing his plans ruined. What really hurt was the lack of gratitude. He had laboured for three years with Percy, three years of training him and caring for him and massaging his legs, three years of spending whatever money he had and asking for not a cent in return. He had bet everything on his conviction that Percy could be the best in the world. And now that he was, it seemed only fair that Bob should get some sort of payoff, that he should be allowed the opportunity to make a return. It was his due. It was the only chance at financial security he had. But Percy seemed intent on denying him this.

The rift between Vancouver's favourite son and its most famous coach was soon common knowledge but little was publicly said. Andy Lytle was the only newsman to mention it in print, informing his readers in his usual blunt way that "The ginger topped coach . . . is out, so far as Williams' athletic activities are concerned, colder than a landlord's ejection."[35] Those close to Percy never doubted the key role Bob had played in his success. Bob was, they were convinced, the only one who could properly handle the runner, getting him out to train and keeping him focused when Percy would have preferred doing other things. They tried to get the pair back together, even offering to pay Bob a small salary. Bob refused. He was angry and hurt. He was through with Percy.

By the time Bob finally finished writing his serialization of Percy's life, too much time had passed and the syndication deal was dead. He sold it to the *Vancouver Sun* instead for a fraction of what he had been hoping to get. It would be published starting in July as "Climbing Olympus: The Inside Story of Percy Williams' Titanic Struggle Against Overwhelming Odds in His Courageous Battle for Fame." In it Bob, billed as "former coach of the world champion," would say only good things about Percy and paint a rosy picture of the triumph they had shared.[36] But privately he was devastated — so much so that he gave up coaching and the sporting life that he loved. As he confided in a letter some months later, the breakup with Percy "finished me with athletics for a while as I nursed him along for 4 years and then just when I could have cashed in, so to speak, I nearly cashed out instead."

Bob resolved instead to get a job — a real job this time, one that paid. He joined the Sun Life Assurance Company where his brother George worked and started selling insurance. And he started out well, signing up Vancouver boxer Jimmy "Baby Face" McLarnin, a top welterweight contender, for an enormous policy. "I . . . started all over again to make my fortune," Bob wrote. "Believe me I'm going to stick with it this time. It is too late to fool around now and you don't get anywhere doing that either. I wouldn't train Percy again unless I either received 4000 or 5000 cash to square me up for what I lost and a good deal of publicity (locally) of course, which would really help me in my insurance work. It makes all the difference in the world if you are really well known."[37]

Yes, Bob was going to turn over a new leaf. He would remake himself completely. He now had a job in which he was determined to prosper. Next he would move out of his parents' Cardero Street house and get a place of his own. He looked around for a while and decided on the frugal expedient of renting a room. He chose one on the other side of town, at 135 Thirteenth Avenue West.

It was in Bobby Gaul's house, just around the corner from Percy's.[38]

∞

The track and field meet set for July 12 and 13 at Hastings Park would be the biggest athletic event ever held in Vancouver, and Percy would be the premier attraction. He had agreed to run the furlong and a hundred-yard dash that was being billed as the "Century of Centuries." Frank Wykoff was coming up from California for the rematch he had been waiting for since Amsterdam. Michigan's Eddie Tolan would be in town as well, and Wykoff's Olympic teammate Henry Cumming of the Newark AC. Claude Bracey of Texas was reportedly signed up, and the great George Simpson of Ohio State, who had just tied the world century mark in April. Charlie Borah had promised to come as well, and Johnny Fitzpatrick, and even Jack Elder, the only runner to have bested Percy in a final on the indoor circuit.[39] Percy promised to turn out and take them on, and anyone else the meet organizers could get. He would do it without Bob. He didn't need Bob.

Or did he?

CHAPTER 17

The Century of Centuries

~

PUTTING ON A BIG-TIME track meet was an expensive proposition and the Vancouver organizers were sweating. It wasn't just a matter of sending out invitations and booking the track. Expense money had to be wired to the athletes as well. Thankfully a number of the American stars were already in Denver for the US national championships, so they wouldn't be claiming for trans-continental train tickets. But still, to bring Eddie Tolan to town was costing $300, Frank Wykoff and his coach needed $350, and that was just the start of the list. It all amounted to what Andy Lytle called "heavy sugar." "Even if you are childlike enough to believe all this running is sport for sport's sake," Andy explained to his readers, "just suppose you had to foot the bills! It runs into big money and the fact that the Employee's Association laid their coin on the line, in advance, means that the only way they can recover is for the public to flock and flock again to Hastings Park this week-end."[1]

Percy would be the star attraction, of course. And in second place for drawing power would be George Simpson, the "Buckeye Bullet," for the Ohio State University speedster had been on a tear all spring. In April he had equalled the hundred-yard world record of 9.6 seconds, in May he had bettered it with a run of 9.5 seconds, and in June he had done an incredible 9.4. Those last two records would not be accepted, the first due to a tailwind, the second because George had used starting blocks, which were unsanctioned.[2] But still, a 9.4-second century — that was *fast*.

But then, at the last moment, came word that George wouldn't be coming. He had pulled a tendon and was out for the season.

That left Eddie Tolan as the man to beat Percy, if anyone could. Just the week before the Vancouver meet Eddie had won both the century and furlong dashes at the national AAU championships in Denver, beating Claude Bracey, Frank Wykoff, Henry Cumming and a slew of others to establish himself as the fastest man in the USA. And on May 25 he had run the hundred in Illinois in 9.5 seconds, breaking Dan Kelly's world mark set all the way back in 1906. It would take a year, but Eddie's new mark would go into the books as official.

Eddie had been born in Denver in 1908, the same year as Percy, and grew up in Detroit. In high school he excelled in football and track, succeeding George "Buck" Hester as Michigan High School Athlete of the Year in 1926 and 1927, and had gone on to the University of Michigan on a football scholarship, scouted for the position of quarterback. But at five-feet-five and 145 pounds he was soon reassessed by the coaches as being too small, and was shifted to track where he proceeded to make a name for himself. He came to be known as the Midnight Express.

Frank Wykoff was in town as well, his coach Normal Hayhurst in tow, and was eager to take on Percy. He had had a rough time over the previous winter, however, and there was still some question as to whether he had fully recovered his form. The trouble had started in December 1928 with an operation to remove his tonsils that went horribly wrong, resulting in a hemorrhage that very nearly killed him. Doctors managed to save Frank's life with two follow-up operations and a series of blood transfusions from his coach and one of his USC friends, but for a while it had been a very close thing.[3] Frank was now back on his feet and looked as strong as ever, but in the nationals in Denver the finishing drive that he had used to blow away the competition at the previous year's Olympic trials seemed to be missing. He had placed fourth in the century and second in the furlong.

Percy, meanwhile, was doing little to get ready, just a bit of starting practice with one of his high school friends helping. He was kept busy with the usual whirl of invitations: out one day to a local gun club to try his hand at trap shooting (he was good; his debut performance made the papers), serving as an official at a high school track meet the next, opening a local rodeo, being adopted into the Squamish Nation as Chief Fleet Foot — "or maybe Flat Foot," he joked.[4] In his quieter moments there was his pup Rusty to look after, and his broken down Graham-Paige coupe to work on, which after just eight months was "on the hog" as he put it, and a flood of track meet invitations to consider. "Just finished a letter to Bobbie Robinson," he wrote in his diary on June 7. "I think I am beginning to weaken. First thing I know I will be taking another trip East. And why not?"[5]

On June 25, with minimum preparation and without Bob Granger, Percy returned to competition in the Police Games at Brockton Point in what would be his only tune-up meet before the big Hastings Park extravaganza, now less than three weeks away. The field consisted mainly of local runners. No handicaps were given but Percy's old Commerce High teammate Wally Scott still gave him a workout in the hundred-yard final, getting a fast break and forcing Percy to extend himself to win in 9 4/5 seconds. Percy also won the two-twenty, in the slow time of twenty-three seconds. It would be one of the last times he would run the longer distance, which he disliked. From now on the hundred yards and the hundred metres would be his focus.[6]

"Gypped!" he wrote in his diary after. "And How. Can't even believe the police. Promised me a set of golf clubs. Did I get them. And How! In the shape and form of two mantle clocks. Refused to take one of them. . . . [Bert] Davison says he will see I get the best set money can buy at Spaldings for July 12th and 13th. I guess all I have to do is win against Simpson etc. Fat chance I have of playing with those clubs. Moral: Believe no one."[7]

Percy wasn't overly confident of his chances against the cream of America's sprinters. At the last minute he headed down to Seattle for three days of training with University of Washington coach Hec Edmundson.

&

The hundred-yard final at the US national championships in Denver had been touted as the "Century of the Century." With Eddie Tolan and other top stars from that race now about to face international champion Percy Williams, an even loftier title was needed. Meet organizers came up with the "Century of Centuries." It would take place over two days, two qualifying heats on Friday, July 12, followed by the final the next afternoon. The cheap seats were going fast at fifty cents, the prime spots for up to two dollars, souvenir programs extra. "Ask Percy," read the ad for Canadian 4X Bread on the inside cover. "He Knows."[8]

Eddie Tolan wasn't impressed with the Hastings Park track. The journalists were clustered round him, firing questions, when he gave his opinion of the rutted, uneven dirt surface on which the sprint crown of the world would be contested. How are you feeling, Eddie, they wanted to know. He had had an infected toenail removed a day or two before, the digit was tender, but he said he was okay.

What do you think of the track, Eddie?

The Michigan star had run on some first-rate tracks in his time and knew a thing or two about cinders. "It's a good track, I guess," he replied in his slow, careful way, ". . . for horses."[9]

Percy drew the first qualifying heat. The field included Frank Wykoff, Henry Cumming of the Newark AC, and Johnny Fitzpatrick. Percy won in convincing style, taking the lead at the ten-yard mark and hanging on to it all the way to the tape. Frank challenged briefly but Percy's finishing surge reopened the gap. When he breasted the tape he was a yard ahead and the crowd was on its feet and roaring so loudly that the official results could scarcely be heard when they were announced over the loudspeakers. But then the buzz spread throughout the stands, people turning anxiously and asking their neighbours: What was that he said about a world record?

Percy, it turned out, had equalled the still-official mark with a time of 9 3/5 seconds. When that sunk in the cheering started again and the pundits had to shout to be heard. And he did it on a horse track, they were saying. That's our Percy! If that had been a decent track, it would have been a new record!

Johnny, fighting hard, managed to claim third and the final qualifying spot. Percy had been saying for months how good Johnny was, and here he had proved it, eliminating Cumming.

Eddie was up next in the second qualifier. Claude Bracey won it in the comparatively slow time of ten seconds, eating up the track with his extra-long stride. He had run second to Eddie at the nationals in Denver and really wanted to beat him. Eddie contented himself with second, casting glances over his shoulder as he neared the tape to make sure he was not being challenged. He was entered in the furlong as well and wanted to conserve his strength.[10]

∽

Saturday afternoon was clear and the track was dry. The six finalists in the Century of Centuries would not have to contend with mud, only ruts and potholes and an uneven surface. Percy by now had a sense of his competition, and in the dressing room in the hour leading up to the race got to know them a little better. Eddie seemed a likeable sort, quiet and polite, and so did Claude Bracey and most of the others. And Johnny Fitzpatrick was of course a good friend. "Only bunch I don't like," Percy observed, "is the LAAC," referring to Frank Wykoff and Milton Mauer and the rest of the athletes affiliated with the Los Angeles Athletic Club. "I hardly think they ever heard of manners."[11]

Race time. Billows of smoke from a waterfront sawmill wafted across the scene in the background. Just beyond lay the waters of Burrard Inlet and beyond that the soaring mountains of the north shore. Percy, clad in a plain white jersey, had drawn lane four. He had now gone several weeks without Bob Granger's regular massages and one of his legs was stiff from the previous day's race. Johnny Fitzpatrick was on his left in lane three, Frank Wykoff in two, Claude Bracey on the inside in one, Frank's LAAC teammate Milton Mauer on the outside in six. And on Percy's right, in lane five, was Eddie Tolan, a big University of Michigan "M" on his chest. Eddie was a couple inches shorter than Percy but carried twenty extra pounds and it was all muscle. His left knee was bandaged, a reminder of an old injury suffered on the gridiron. He continued to wrap it now for all his races. It was for good luck, he liked to tell reporters. It was hard not to notice too the strips of white tape on either side of his head, used to hold his glasses in place as he shot down the track.

Percy's old King Edward High coach, Emslie Yeo, would be doing the starting. It was he who had first spotted Percy's potential four years before and pushed him onto the track team and lent him his first pair of spikes. It was really something for Coach Yeo, seeing how far that scrawny ninth grader had come. It made him feel proud. He directed the runners to the start line and positioned himself on the infield grass, a step behind so that they couldn't see him and possibly take a cue from his movements. As the six finalists settled into their holes a silence descended over the record crowd filling the grandstand, and the sounds emanating from Happyland amusement park momentarily wafted across the track, the rumble of the new roller coaster, the screams of the riders as they crested the rise and then plunged.

Coach Yeo raised his pistol and gave the "Set" command. To the spectators, Bob Granger seated somewhere among them, what came next was a soundless puff of white smoke and the runners rising, followed a split second later by the report of the gun.

The start was good, no need for a recall, and Percy got away well. Perhaps his experience on the indoor circuit had helped. As the pack hurtled down the track he remained with the leaders, no longer aware of the soreness in his thigh, and at the sixty-yard mark was out in front by a yard. The tape drew nearer and it was time for his finishing burst, the strongest part of his race, the time when he surged like nobody else on the planet. But he just didn't seem to be able to put it together. Something was taking the edge off his speed. Instead of shooting ahead and increasing his lead, it was Eddie and Frank who were closing the gap. He's changed his style, Granger thought, noting a slight alteration in Percy's arm swing. He's changed his style and killed his finish.[12] They were almost there now and Eddie was directly beside Percy, Frank just a hair behind.

But Eddie didn't lunge — and Percy did. In his final stride he thrust his chest forward into the tape and that made the difference. The Vancouver Flash, the Canadian Cheetah, Loup Garou, beat the Midnight Express by a few precious inches.[13]

It was a difficult task calling the finish of a sprint in the days before electrically triggered cameras and timers, necessitating a host of officials, each assigned a specific task. First there was the matter of determining the order of finish. This required an official to watch for which runner crossed the line first, another to identity the second-place finisher, and another the third (not much attempt was made to sort out the rest of the field), with a short conference to follow to collate results and resolve any disputes. Then there was the timing, with anywhere from three to seven officials wielding stopwatches, the results of which had to be averaged out when they differed to produce a single time for the first-place finisher alone. It was a difficult job, especially when a race was close, and sometimes took several minutes.

The finish of the Century of Centuries took three minutes to sort out, three minutes in which speculation wafted about in the stands, fuelled by the variety of viewing angles. But only the officials dead in line with the tape were in a position to judge, and to them it was clear that Percy had won, and in a time of 9 4/5 seconds. Eddie accepted the decision. "Percy Williams proved himself in winning today," he said. "He's a great runner."[14] Frank was not so gracious, showing a slight mark on his arm as proof that he had hit the tape first.[15] It didn't mean much and was discounted; in such a close race the string could have whipped across the arm of any of the lead runners as they slowed after the finish. Percy in any event didn't much care. "Won the darned thing," he wrote in his diary. "Not good time, but oh boy, what a race. Merely took a deep breath and won. Wykoff claims he won. Well maybe he did. At any rate I have a nice set of golf clubs."[16]

The visiting American athletes weren't quite as appreciative of their prizes. One of the boys didn't think much of the stick pin he had won in his event and complained to meet organizer Bert Davison, head of the local AAU. "Listen," he said, "there aren't enough people in the United States to make me wear a stickpin."

"Oh well," said Bert, gesturing toward the assortment of knick-knacks lying unclaimed on the prize table. "Pick out what you want from that lot."

Pete Bowen of the University of Pittsburgh was equally unimpressed with the tinny wristwatch he had won in the four-forty. The timepiece that had gone to the Los Angeles runner placing third looked better. "I wouldn't trade you mine for two like yours," the LA athlete was overheard chortling. "No," replied Bowen glumly, "neither would I."

Eddie Tolan received three golf bags for placing second in the century and winning the furlong, three golf bags all exactly alike. He was pondering over the bulky prizes when a stick pin winner ambled over and offered to make a swap for one of the bags. "Okay," said Eddie with a shrug. Then he added with a wave of his hand: "Take the lot."[17]

Otherwise, the Vancouver meet was an unqualified success. The total take, from the two days of ticket sales, the peanuts and popcorn and hot dogs and drinks and souvenirs and cotton candy and everything else, came to twenty-five thousand dollars, the biggest haul ever for a Canadian meet.[18] And as Andy Lytle reported, it was all thanks to the popularity of Percy. "It was Percy Williams' meet," Andy bluntly asserted, "and those who promoted the affair might remember that when it comes to the pay-off."[19]

Andy didn't know about the fifteen hundred dollars Percy received in addition to the golf clubs. The payment was of course made entirely under the table — and would have remained so had not Bob Granger, still bitter over the breakup, let it slip in a personal letter.[20] Two weeks later Percy would lay down the exact same sum to pay off the mortgage on his family's Twelfth Avenue West home, which he would henceforth own. With Grandpa Harry retired from BC Electric, Percy was now the chief breadwinner and head of the household.[21]

Rumours would waft about that Frank Wykoff had received something extra as well, and in May of 1931 the athletic director of Stanford University would appear in Vancouver looking for evidence to use against the runner, the star of rival USC. Meet organizers sent him away empty-handed. They had thrown out all their financial records from the meet, they said.[22]

The Century of Centuries would be Percy's last race for almost a year. Two days later, while warming up at the Seattle meet that he and many of his fellow competitors had gone down from Vancouver to enter, his sore thigh muscle tightened up and he was forced to withdraw. Some of the American runners tried to egg him into running but he refused.[23] Frank Wykoff went on to win it. Eddie Tolan wasn't there; he was on his way east. Percy returned to Vancouver afterward to bid farewell to Johnny Fitzpatrick and Myrtle Cook and the other Canadian athletes who had come out to the coast to compete. Ethel Catherwood, the "Saskatoon Lily," was with them, more beautiful than ever, and more reserved as well, with a touch of sadness. She had been through almost as much as Percy since her Amsterdam homecoming, a clamour that had as much to do with her looks as her high jumping, with a stream of movie contract offers mixed in with the honours, the expectations, the pressure. It was clear she was struggling with it all, trying to find her way through life in the spotlight. Percy felt close to her. He felt close to them all, Johnny and Jimmy and Myrtle and Ethel, his former Olympic teammates. He didn't want them to go.[24]

"I wonder when I will see them again," he confided in his diary. "Hope it will be soon."[25]

∞

In a newspaper column published a few days before the Century of Centuries, Charlie Paddock had picked Percy as the likely winner. Percy possessed a wonderfully well-rounded game, Charlie had written: a strong start, an unusually fast stride, an unparalleled gather and finish — everything perfected to such an extent that he was unlikely to get much better. The one thing Percy lacked was the "superhuman speed" of top American runners like Wykoff and Tolan. He made up for this with fierce competitive instinct, "his greatest asset," an ability to size up the competition before a race and then somehow conjure up just enough speed to beat them.

This natural gift made Percy a strong contender in the next Olympics in 1932. He might even repeat his 1928 gold-medal performance in one or even both of the sprints, something never before accomplished. "But despite this brilliant outlook for his future," Paddock concluded, "I doubt if Williams will ever equal or break the official world's record for the 100 metres, and he may not even tie the present record in the 100 yards. For he is essentially a competitor, and runs just as fast as his opposition forces him to go. He is not a record breaker. . . ."[26]

Percy, in short, might be the World's Greatest Sprinter. But he had yet to prove himself as the World's Fastest Human.

CHAPTER 18

World's Fastest Human

∽

BY THE TIME HE ARRIVED back home in Detroit from Vancouver, Eddie Tolan had changed his mind about the Century of Centuries. He now had pictures, he announced, that proved that *he* had won the race and that Percy's victory had been a biased hometown decision. And indeed, in shots of the finish taken from an angle in front of the tape and from the outside, with Eddie nearest, the advantage of Percy's forward lean could not be perceived and Eddie appeared to be slightly ahead. It was an illusion but it nevertheless had Eddie and his supporters riled. "I have been beaten before," he said, "but never have felt that I was picked second when I actually finished first."[1]

Vancouverites didn't think much of that. The *Sun* said it all in the headline it ran with the story. "Eddie Tolan Squeals About Race Decision," it read.[2]

And then Frank Wykoff and his coach got in on the act, publicly reiterating their claim that *Frank* had won. From the perspective of the finish judges, Coach Hayhurst now claimed, there is a tendency in a close finish to favour the runners furthest away, in this case Eddie and Percy, a tendency exacerbated by the unevenness of the Vancouver track, which Hayhurst asserted slanted a foot upward from the inside to the outside lanes. "The judges could very easily have looked past Frank even if he did hit the tape first," he said. "Williams is a fast little runner, but I doubt if he can beat either Frank or Tolan on a real track with good officials."

A prominent American track official who wished to remain anonymous went even further. "There were thousands of dollars bet by the Canadians," he said. "And the people were betting even money on Williams against the field. Betting is legitimate in Canada. I wouldn't say that any of the officials had money bet on the home town boy, but it could have been done and could have had plenty of influence. We Americans knew that 'Williams against the field' at even money was pretty big odds. It was as the race proved, even though the Dominion people did collect."[3]

It all meant only one thing: There would have to be a rematch.

જ્જ

Up in Vancouver Percy was giving no thought to running. He was done with competition for the rest of the year. He would run just once more in 1929, in an Edmonton exhibition race in October, the deal sweetened with two hundred dollars in addition to travel and living expenses, to be paid in the form of a "souvenir" of his own choosing of comparable value. It wasn't much, but Percy knew that he still had to be cautious. "In accordance with your request, I have destroyed your letter," the meet promoter responded. "You need not have the slightest hesitation in saying anything you like in writing or speaking to me; I give you my word of honor that no one outside of ourselves will know what arrangements are entered into. . . . There isn't a chance in the world of anyone else learning any of the details in connection with your trip."[4]

After putting in his Saturday evening appearance, a half-time dash at a basketball game, Percy returned home to the new job he had just started — the haberdashery idea had been dropped somewhere along the way — as assistant manager at the Western Forwarding Company, handling the paperwork for the loading and unloading of cargo ships in the harbour.[5] He showed up for work on the following Monday, the day bright and sunny. By the time he punched out that afternoon, Wall Street had crashed and the continent had begun its slide into the Great Depression.

Throughout the fall and winter Percy continued to receive invitations to track meets, including one to an indoor showdown in New York between himself and Jack Elder, the only runner to have beaten him the previous year. Percy turned them all down. The Canadian indoor championships came and went and he did not attend. Entreaties to join a European tour were similarly ignored.[6] It wasn't until the spring of 1930 that he finally dusted off his spikes and resumed training.

He did so with Bob Granger again at his side. After months of pressure and coaxing from concerned supporters, the sprinter and his coach had cleared up what was now being called "a series of misunderstandings" that had arisen between them the previous year and got back together, shaking hands on May 20 and vowing not to allow anything to come between them again. Percy expressed satisfaction with the reconciliation, stating that "I have confidence when Bob is getting me into shape," and to everyone's relief the pair got down to work just like in the old days. But things had changed. The closeness and trust that had previously existed between them would never be recaptured. "The one clause in the new agreement of partnership," the *Vancouver Sun* noted, "is that neither one must neglect business for the sake of the other." This was mainly for Bob's benefit, recognition that his priority was his job selling insurance and that he would no longer sacrifice himself financially for Percy. From now on their relationship would be more formal, and strained.[7]

It was no longer the same old Bob that turned out at Brockton Point to resume training with Percy. He had put on weight since the Amsterdam Olympics to the point of being described as "chubby," a middle-aged businessman in a three-piece suit and fedora with a face bearing a resemblance to US president Herbert Hoover. Percy for his part had filled out a little as well, adding nine pounds to his 1928 weight to tip the scales at 134. He had given up slicking his hair back and parting it in the middle like Bob, and was going instead with a part on the left. It was in his face, however, where the change was most telling. The smooth round curves of his teen years were fading. It was now more sharply angled and lean, with lines beginning to show on his forehead, under his eyes and on either side of his mouth. While the papers continued to make frequent reference to his boyish appearance, Percy had started to look like a man.

With careful training and Bob's daily massages, Percy began rounding into condition, his sore thigh muscle and old knee injury no longer a problem. Everything seemed set for the rematch with Wykoff and Tolan, now scheduled for July 1 at Hastings Park. After the aggravation of Eddie's and then Frank's public repudiation of Percy's victory the previous summer, Vancouverites were doubly eager to see their hero deliver to his American rivals a sound and unequivocal beating. The meet therefore promised to be a sell-out. This time, however, organizers would know better what they were doing. There had been too much unguarded talk about the financial arrangements for the "Century of Centuries," talk that had led to criticism of Percy when it came out that money had gone to his father. Even the great Harold Abrahams had taken a swipe.[8] That mistake wouldn't be repeated. Everything this time would be kept completely hush-hush.

To aid with Percy's training, the city assigned a groundskeeper to devote his full attention to the Brockton Point sprint track, watering and rolling it daily to remove any ruts. At Bob's instigation work also was begun on the Hastings Park grounds. "A race such as this one has probably never been run in the history of athletics," he stated, goading the city, "and yet it is proposed to pull it off on a horseracing track!" Within a week a crash makeover project was launched, first scraping and filling guided by surveyors to ensure a completely level surface, then a thorough harrowing and raking and watering and flattening with giant rollers. It was still dirt and not equal to the best in the States, but was nevertheless a considerable improvement.[9]

Bob's main concern now was getting Percy into some tune-up races before the July 1 showdown. This was done at the annual Police Sports on June 25, the hundred-yard dash being made a handicap event to ensure that Percy was properly challenged. The results were entirely satisfactory. In the final, facing runners starting up to nine yards in front, Percy raced down the field to win by a wide margin in 9.6 seconds, a tenth shy of Eddie Tolan's May 1929 mark, which had just been officially accepted as the new world record.[10] That mere tenth of a second, however, represented more than three feet at the finish. And according to the latest reports from LA, Frank Wykoff had just run a century in 9.4 seconds, which as Bob pointed out put him *seven feet* ahead of Percy's 9.6-second personal best.[11] And then there was George Simpson, already on the scene in Vancouver. He too had run a 9.4, albeit with starting blocks and unrecognized as a result. These three American speedsters were taking the short sprints to a whole new level and would only be beaten if Percy ran faster than he had ever run in his life.

Bob was convinced that he would. As every Vancouverite and every Canadian track fan knew, Percy — or "Peerless Percy" as they were increasingly calling him — didn't race the clock. He raced the man, and he had an uncanny knack for taking the lead by the finish. With Eddie, Frank and George pushing him like he had never been pushed before, there was a good chance that he would find an as-yet undiscovered reserve of speed and do something extraordinary. "Despite the marvellous times of the other competitors," Bob predicted, "I still believe Percy will finish in first."[12] Eddie and the others "will have to run their heads off to beat him."[13]

June 19, and reports hit the Vancouver papers that Frank Wykoff was in town. "Percy's Rival Arrives," announced the front page of the *Sun*, together with a large portrait of a smiling Frank. But it was only a rumour. Frank was still at home in California and wouldn't be coming at all. It was a blow, but tickets were selling fast nonetheless. Everything was pointing to a repeat of the previous year's financial success, Depression or not. Then, at the insistence of the visiting American runners, the main event was changed at the last minute from one hundred yards to one hundred metres. Fine. It would just give Percy nine extra yards to work his magic with his sparkling finish. Yes, Eddie Tolan had the 9.5-second century world record. Sure, George Simpson had posted an unrecognized 9.4 with blocks. Percy would beat them just the same, their proven speed only pushing him faster. Percy would win because he *always* won. As an admirer once put it, "He simply can't help it."[14]

Percy lost. In front of eleven thousand fans roaring "Come on! Come on!" the pride of Vancouver was well and truly beaten, placing third behind Eddie Tolan and George Simpson. Eddie had run like a dream, first off the mark and leading all the way to win in a blazing 10.2 seconds, four feet ahead of George and Percy locked in their battle for second. It would have been a new world record had it not been for the invalidating wind to their backs.[15]

The city took the loss hard. After a stunned silence the spectators broke out with a round of applause and cheers for the winner. But it was with long faces and much moaning and groaning that they filed out of the bleachers and made their way home — and, in the more affected cases, out to the bars. One young lady, in describing the grief expressed by her friend at witnessing Percy's defeat, declared that "she wept, and cried, and bellowed!" In the days that followed, such extreme disappoint turned into indignation for a number of fans. Comments were heard about town like: "What was the matter with Williams? He couldn't have been training properly." And: "This will teach him that he cannot sprint without training." Within a couple of weeks a minor storm would blow up when a radio announcer at the "squirms" in Seattle — that's what the scribes called pro wrestling back then — introduced Percy seated in the audience as the "ex" something-or-other.[16]

Percy publicly took the loss in stride and refused to make excuses. Yes, he admitted, he had been taking treatments for a sore leg, but that didn't matter. "There was nothing wrong. Nothing could have beaten Tolan. . . . They beat me and I have no excuses or alibis. . . . If I can't win then they are better than I am."[17] Privately, however, losing came as a jolt. There were times when he thought he no longer cared about running and winning. That was natural for an athlete after a while at the top, the waning of the competitive fire.[18] But now to lose, for only the second time in a final since the nationals in 1927 — there was a timely lesson here, that if he wanted to keep winning, he would have to work harder.

∞

The reporters were still fishing for comments on the loss to Eddie Tolan as Percy boarded the train for Toronto and the Canadian track and field championships scheduled for the second week of August. "That's all over," Percy stated. "I needed just that to prep me. I have improved and am ready to meet the best."[19] Bob Granger wasn't on the train with him. He would follow the next day. Percy slipped into Toronto four days later without any fanfare, no reporters or photographers or fans at Union Station to greet him, not unlike the days when he had come east the first time as a complete unknown.

The anonymity didn't last long. At Varsity Stadium the next day, as he found a secluded corner and began to work out the kinks from the journey, he was recognized by a women's phys. ed. class doing calisthenics on the field. In a flash he was besieged by all three hundred students, urged to give an impromptu talk and a demonstration of racing technique. When he was finally allowed to get back to his training, it was with the entire class lolling on the grass, calisthenics forgotten, indulging in what he had come to hate since the Olympics: staring. He wound things up quickly and retreated to his hotel.[20]

"Things could not be better," he wrote to his mother the next day. "Last night the cars and street cars galloped past making as much noise as possible, and there is a taxi stand across the street where they have a bell that sounds like a fire alarm. This rings every minute for three minutes steady or maybe more. They are tearing a building down across from this room and they start just as soon as it is cool enough to work. This being about six in the morning. Outside of these and a few more things I spent a very quiet night. . . . Oh yes, I nearly forgot to tell you that some darned fool rang up about twelve last night just as I was about asleep and wanted to know if I could go out to some boys camp. By the time I was through talking I think he understood that I meant 'No.'"[21]

He would have one tune-up race before the championships, at the Dominion-wide Police Games at Hanlan Point Stadium on Toronto Island. Bob showed up in the dressing room shortly before the start, said a subdued "Hello," took off his coat and began working on Percy's legs. Percy went on to win the hundred-yard dash with apparent ease in 9 4/5 seconds, running on a slow grass track and leading throughout. "He's in form again," Bob said after. "His legs have stopped troubling him, and I think he's ready to do some serious racing. . . . No one can beat him by any margin when he's right."[22]

They were back on track. If Percy could be kept in condition for the next few days he would be certain to win the championships. And, weather permitting, he might set a new world record. It was thus with intense annoyance that Bob tried to dissuade Percy from going along with Doral Pilling on a speed run on a very choppy Lake Ontario. Budding sports impresario Harold Ballard had invited them out on his racing hydroplane. Nothing doing, Bob fumed. There is no way you're going to risk your legs out on that lake. Percy ignored him and went. "Great!" he and Doral gasped as they stepped back on dry land after an exhilarating ride in the teeth of a squall. "How much do they cost and where can I get one?"[23]

It was still squally two days later at the track and field championships on August 9, a stiff breeze blowing off the lake and across the Varsity Stadium track. The stands sheltered the near portion of the oval where the hundred-metre dash would be run, but occasional gusts swept up the lanes, still wet from the previous day's rain, right into the faces of the runners. For the spectators packing the bleachers it was a cause for concern, for there was a general expectation that today would be the day that Percy Williams would finally go for the record. Meet officials were expecting something special as well. At the finish line they would be using the latest stopwatches that timed to the tenth of a second.

Percy stripped to his Vancouver Athletic Club gear and got to work. He won his preliminary heat with ease, coasting at the finish and still posting the fastest time of 10.9 seconds. Bob had given his legs a thorough rubdown and they felt good. He bore down a bit more to win his semifinal in 10.7 seconds, a tenth off his Canadian record and three-tenths off the world mark. Still no problems. The legs were good. Up in the stands anticipation mounted, for so far Percy had shown no sign of effort and was clearly running well within his limits. As Canada's best sprinters struggled to survive to the next round, he seemed to be still warming up.

Back out on the track for the final Percy lined up alongside his old Olympic teammates Johnny Fitzpatrick and Ralph Adams, and "Buster" Brown, the Edmonton runner he had flipped a coin with at the championships in 1927. Montreal policeman Napoleon Bourdeau and Hamilton running prodigy Bert Pearson made up the rest of the field.

For the first third of the race they all ran more or less even. Then Percy moved into a lead, followed by Johnny and Ralph. At the halfway mark he was a metre ahead. And then he opened up. For the first time since his loss to Eddie Tolan, Percy stepped all the way down on the gas, getting acceleration on demand, rocketing himself further ahead. The fans were on their feet now, clapping and stomping and roaring Go get 'em, Percy! Go get 'em, boy! for they could see that the brakes were off and Percy was making a supreme effort. His lead was two metres now, then two-and-a-half and still growing. They were nearing the tape and, whoosh, they were through, and Percy's eyes were bulging and his mouth was wide open with effort and he was three metres ahead, three whole metres, a whopping margin against the likes of Johnny Fitzpatrick in second.

Percy's face was pale and drawn as he slowed to a stop and the exertion caught up. It bent him over, chest heaving, heart racing, and it was with a pained smile that he accepted the congratulations of the other runners. "I would not want to run like that every day," he joked in the dressing room after. The cheering that had greeted the finish subsided and was replaced by an expectant buzzing as everyone waited for the announcement of the winning time. Down on the field the chief timer could be seen examining each of the stopwatches in turn with a large magnifying glass, making sure of the readings. They were proceeding slowly and carefully, taking no chances. Finally the decision was passed along and the announcer stepped forward. A pause while the big megaphone was swung into place, the whole stadium dead silent.

"Attention please," he began. Then: "The time in the one-hundred metre final: ten and three-tenth seconds — a new world record for Percy Williams!"[24]

It would take nearly two years, but Percy's run that day would be accepted as the official world record, superseding the 10.4-second mark set by Charlie Paddock in 1921. It would stand until 1936, when Jesse Owens whittled off another tenth of a second.

∽

As Torontonians settled down with their papers the following Monday to read about the record Percy had set on the weekend, their attention was diverted by the roar of motors overhead. It was the British airship R-100, more than two football fields long, passing over the city on its trans-Atlantic tour. Posted on a downtown rooftop, CFRB radio announcer Wes McKnight painted a word picture for his audience of the impressive scene. "The great dirigible is coming straight toward us at this moment," he said. "A wonderful sight! For all the world like a great silver fish of the air. Now — now, she is directly overhead — right above us. Your announcer literally has to 'stand on his ear' to observe and broadcast at the same time. She is not more than seven hundred feet above us. It is a thrill worth waiting a lifetime to witness."[25]

Down on Front Street at the Carls-Rite Hotel, Percy managed to scramble up the stairs to the roof with his camera in time to take a picture as the behemoth passed overhead, so big his viewfinder could not contain it, then stood there with the rest of the crowd watching it glide on toward the southwest, the throb of its engines gradually subsiding.[26] She was scheduled to pass over Hamilton next, to commemorate the first-ever British Empire Games to begin the following week. Athletes from all the countries coloured red on the map were at that moment converging on the city, from England, South Africa, Australia and points in between, preparing for their own version of the Olympics.

The seven-day program would culminate with the century dash. It would be the headline event. After Percy's record run in Toronto, hopes were high that he wouldn't just win it, but that he would set another world record, adding the hundred-yard title to the hundred metres he now possessed and proving beyond all doubt that he was indeed the World's Fastest Human.

He seemed to be in the peak of condition, primed and ready to do it. And the track couldn't be better, for Hamilton had one of the best in the country. All that would be needed was a stretch of good weather to ensure that the cinders were dry — and fast.

▲ Percy in his Canadian team sweat suit, circa 1930.
(CITY OF TORONTO ARCHIVES)

▲ Percy after his 10.3-second 100-metre world record, set in Toronto, August 9, 1930. The mark would stand until Jesse Owens ran 10.2 seconds in 1936.
(CITY OF TORONTO ARCHIVES)

▲ Percy winning the 100-yard final at the Empire Games in Hamilton in August 1930, grimacing from the injury that effectively ended his career. (BCSHFM)

▲ Percy, Jimmy Ball, Frank Wykoff and unidentified (right to left) relaxing in the Olympic Village, Los Angeles, 1932. (BCSHFM)

Percy near the end of his athletic ▶ career, wearing his Vancouver Athletic Club jersey. (BCSHFM)

▲ The last race. Percy, in the lane beside Yoshioka of Japan (in headband), is eliminated in the 100-metre semi-finals. Eddie Tolan (in white knee wrap) went on to win gold in both the 100 metres and 200 metres to become the next "World's Fastest Human." (GAMES OF THE XTH OLYMPIAD, LOS ANGELES, 1932, OFFICIAL REPORT)

◀ Percy as a pilot during the Second World War. (BCSHFM)

Bob Granger in later life living alone with his dog. (*Victoria Daily Colonist*, ▼ April 6, 1964)

Percy's grave. His is the small stone set flush to the ground at bottom centre, in front of the larger stone he had arranged for his father. (AUTHOR'S PHOTO) ▼

CHAPTER 19

The Empire Games

❦

PERCY LAY ON HIS IRON cot in a classroom in Hamilton's Prince of Wales school, listening to the rain that had started falling during the night. It was August 23, the final day of the inaugural British Empire Games, and after a week of clear summer weather it had turned wet and cold. The classroom was stark, the desks removed to make way for twenty-four cots, the entire school being turned into billets for the four hundred Empire athletes who had come to the city. Meals were communal, served in the adjacent cafeteria. Shared washrooms with limited bathing facilities were at the end of the hall. It was a Spartan set-up but Percy liked it, tossed in together with all the others, free for the moment from his celebrity status. Until he left the building and walked past the fans, autograph books in hand, clustered round the front entrance, he was just "Perce," just one of the boys.[1]

He had to hand it to Bobby Robinson. The diminutive *Hamilton Spectator* sports editor had really pulled it off. But then nobody could cajole and twist arms quite like Bobby. The idea of a British Empire Games, talked about for nearly forty years, had just been waiting for him to take it by the scruff of the neck and drag it to fruition. He had started laying the groundwork at the Amsterdam Games in 1928, amid the international rivalries and hard feelings and resentments that had become such a feature of the modern Olympics. What was needed, Bobby said, were games solely for the pan-Britannic family of nations where there would be no rivalries, no acrimony, only friendly competition. His pitch sparked a good deal of interest in the project, but it was his promise of financial support that put it over the top, thirty thousand dollars in travel subsidies courtesy of the Ambitious City — Bobby may have gone out on a limb here to personally guarantee that Hamilton would recoup the money — plus free room and board for the athletes once they arrived. And so the nations had come.[2]

Percy got up and rummaged through his bag for clean underwear and socks. There was no privacy here. It was like being in the army. As he was dressing, Jimmy Ball returned from down the hall, gaunt face freshly scraped and scrubbed. He had the cot beside Percy's. Jimmy had had a rough week of it, taking a spectacular tumble in the eight-eighty on the first day of competition, and he still had bits of cinder embedded in his knee. He was going out again today for the final of the four-forty. The track's going to be sloppy, he said, nodding toward the rain pelting against the windows. Then he asked Percy how he felt. It was the question the whole city was asking.

Two days before, Percy had completely blown the start in his qualifying heat of the hundred. The cheering from the packed bleachers encircling the stadium had been so loud that he had not heard the starter's instructions and was still on one knee at the sound of the gun. Despite lagging badly, he caught the field at the halfway mark and from there shot ahead to win in 9.6 seconds, equalling what had been the world record only the previous year. And he seemed to do it with ease.[3]

"Jimmy," he said, straightening up from lacing his shoes, "if my legs hold up, I'll smash the world's record."[4]

∽

The Empire Games had begun the previous Saturday with an opening ceremony modelled after the Olympics. After the march-past of athletes from the eleven countries in attendance, after the speeches and the cannon fire and the singing of "God Save the King," Percy mounted the podium to take the oath on behalf of the athletes arrayed in ranks on the field behind him. Clad in his scarlet Canadian team blazer with a green maple leaf on the pocket, he raised his right arm, bowed his head toward the mike, and in his soft tenor voice repeated the words: "I pledge that I am an amateur and I will maintain the traditions of British sport."[5]

The furlong dash took place that afternoon. Percy wasn't entered. He was saving himself for the century dash that would close out the Games. For the next several days he was free to sit back and enjoy the show — or as much of it as the fans would allow him to see. Whether it was on the track for a morning workout, seated in the stands to watch the afternoon competitions, or just off to the side somewhere reading a book, he would soon be spotted and people would gather until he was completely surrounded.[6]

Still, it was hard not to like these folks. The citizens of Hamilton had gone all out for the Games, decorating their town from one side to the other and throwing their doors open to the visiting athletes, with free admission to movies and shows and anywhere else that they wanted to go. They even dropped by the Prince of Wales school in their cars, offering rides, tours of the city and the surrounding countryside and home-cooked meals — not for money, but just to be hospitable. The whole city was being wonderfully welcoming and generous in what for almost everyone were very hard times.

That's why they started booing in the qualifying heat in the hundred-yard dash immediately following Percy's. A New Zealand runner, Allan Elliot, had made two false starts, violating the rules and being waved off the field by the starter. The other athletes in the line-up didn't like it, and when the fans realized what had happened they loudly joined in. Rules or no rules, it wasn't right to kick a runner out of a race he had travelled halfway round the world to compete in. Let the man have his race, they called out. As the shouts of displeasure filled the air and the other sprinters stood, arms folded, on the sidelines, the harried officials had a track-side consultation and eventually waved Elliot back in. He went on to place third, failing to qualify for the final. But at least he had had his chance.[7]

∽

Additional bleachers had been set up in Scott Stadium for the final day of the Games and now encircled the track. There was seating for eighteen thousand, but it still wasn't enough to satisfy the demand. It had been raining and cold all morning and an ugly leaden sky hung low overhead, yet people continued to clamour for tickets for the privilege of sitting exposed on a wet board bench to watch Percy Williams in the hundred-yard final. By half past two the stadium was packed beyond capacity, the gates were shut and more than a thousand disappointed fans turned away. Some wandered off to hunt up vantage points atop nearby buildings. Others tried buttonholing anyone with a badge or looking in any way official. "What are the chances of grabbing off a couple of tickets?" they asked, with a significant arch of the brow. "Nothing doing" was the invariable reply.[8]

Inside, the crowd sat on newspapers to keep the wet off their bottoms and huddled in raincoats under a sea of umbrellas that looked like a vast ring of mushrooms. Those seated in the press box were the only ones enjoying the luxury of a roof. "Everyone else," sportswriter Lou Marsh gleefully noted, "had to take it and like it." The steeplechase was underway on the track, and on the field the javelin contestants were just warming up. Calgary's Doral Pilling was retrieving his javelin after a practice toss when a cry of "Look out!" arose from the stands. He dropped into a crouch just in time to avoid being skewered by the hurtling spear that had been tossed by a hugely apologetic New Zealand athlete. Then the steeplechasers were nearing the finish and people were pointing and talking and starting to chuckle, for the waistband of one of the Canadian runners had parted and he was racing toward the tape holding up his shorts with one hand.[9]

Then the rain tapered off and the umbrellas came down. After being dripped on and having their view blocked for the past two hours, the umbrella-less found that a particular relief. The hurdles final was now underway, and there was David Lord Burghley, the much-loved, disarmingly down-to-earth British peer whom admirers freely referred to as "Davy." He had spent the past week camped out in the Prince of Wales school, sleeping on a cot without complaint just like everyone else. And he was down there now, smiling brightly and shaking hands after winning his event, a flesh-and-blood example of what the traditions of British sport meant. Humble in victory, gracious in defeat, fair play bred into his bones, the game played with vigour but always kept in perspective, never allowed to dominate his life — *that's* what it was all about. Show me an American runner of equal calibre, knowledgeable fans said, and I'll show you someone who trains twice as hard, three times as hard. Why, Davy makes it look easy. He's just like Percy!

It was chilly in the dressing room under the stands where Percy was getting ready. After Bob Granger finished massaging his legs, Percy put on his sweatsuit and two sweaters to stay warm and filed onto the field with the others. It was remarkably cold outside, more like winter than summer. There were no puddles on the track — an excellent drainage system had been installed underneath — but the surface was soaking wet and that meant the track would be heavy and slow. Just that little bit of extra viscosity of wet cinders sticking to spikes would add a tenth of a second to Percy's race time, maybe even a fifth. Setting a record in these conditions was going to be tough.

With only one event to run, Percy could afford to be generous with his warming up, taking short starts and striding, running on the spot, knees raised high, until he had worked up a sweat and felt in prime condition to race. In the distance he could see people clustered on rooftops, making the most of the hazy view with telescopes and field glasses. Closer in, the telephone poles just outside the stadium wall were decorated with boys and young men, their shirtfronts dirty from the shinnying up.

There was a problem. The earlier rain had delayed some of the events and the century final had to be pushed back. Ten minutes passed. Percy gradually let up on the leg shaking and bouncing and his muscles began

232 / I Just Ran

to cool. Up in the stands Bob Granger started nervously checking his watch. It was now twenty minutes. Then thirty. Then forty.

Finally the race was called. Percy took a flurry of starts and strides and bounces to re-warm his legs and then went to work on his start holes. He had drawn lane four. Johnny Fitzpatrick was beside him in three. The other runners were Stanley Englehart and Ernest Page of England and South Africans Walter Gerhardt and Wilfred Legg. A bit more warming up and the finalists were called to the start line. Percy waited until the last moment before stripping off his sweaters and sweatsuit and settling into his holes. Right away he could feel the cold creeping into his legs.

Another delay. This time it was the medal presentation ceremony for the broad jump. The starter ordered Percy and the others up and off to the side. They all stood there, trying to look respectful as the winner's national anthem was played, discreetly flapping their legs and taking subdued little bounces. Bob Granger had his timepiece back out. Seven minutes passed before the runners were ordered back to the start. "We were all cold," Johnny Fitzpatrick said after. "They kept us there too long."[10]

Gerhardt broke early and the field had to be recalled. They tried again and this time Legg was off before the gun. Again they returned to their marks, the crowd now keyed to a fever pitch of excitement. And then a curious thing: a blimp appeared in the sky overhead, a miniature version of the R-100. Everyone paused and gazed upward as it slowly glided by. Then attention returned to the track.

The third start was good, and for Percy it was a beauty. He was up and away like a bullet, matching strides with Page for the first ten yards before pulling ahead. At the halfway point he was out in front by a full two yards and he hadn't even gone into his surge. Something special was happening. Bob Granger could sense it. The hundred metres a week ago, and the century today. Wet track or no, Percy was on his way to another world record. A few more seconds and he would be the undisputed World's Fastest Human.

It was around the sixty-yard mark that Percy felt something tear in his left thigh, high up near the groin. He would remember the moment distinctly for the rest of his life. "I felt the muscle go," he later recalled. "Two things can happen. The leg collapses and you fall down. Or it keeps flipping and you manage to finish the race. Mine kept flipping. . . ."[11]

It hurt like hell just the same, and got worse with every step. Percy somehow kept going, his face contorted in pain, but his lead was shrinking, Johnny Fitzpatrick and Ernest Page moving up in their battle for second. They were down to the last few yards now and it had gotten so bad that Percy was faltering and had started to veer into Johnny's lane. Johnny knew something was wrong. "I don't see how he ever finished," he would say.[12]

They were a stride from the finish. Percy, his eyes squeezed shut in agony, took a final lurch through the tape to claim first, staggered, and began to fall. Johnny, just missing second, wrapped his arms around him and held him up as they came to a stop. The raucous cheering filling the air continued for a moment, faltered as spectators realized what had happened, then ceased abruptly as concerned officials rushed to Percy and supported him as he hobbled to the sidelines. Percy's hurt, people were saying with anguish. Oh Lord, Percy's hurt.

Bob Granger came hurrying down from the bleachers. A glance at the lump forming on the back of Percy's leg told him the season was over. By the time they carried him to the dressing room it was the size of an egg. It was an hour before Percy, thigh tightly bandaged, could hobble back out onto the field for the flag raising and to acknowledge the cheers.[13]

No one realized at the time just how serious Percy's injury was. It would in fact trouble him for the rest of his running career. "The Canadian team didn't have a doctor there," Percy recalled years later, bitterness seeping into the memory. "Nobody seemed concerned except Bobby Robinson. And his only concern was that he was out the $700 he'd been promised if he delivered me to a meet in Chicago the following week."[14] The Chicago event was a planned British Empire vs. the USA meet that had been scheduled to follow the Empire Games. Percy had been the expected headliner. Now he would miss it.

The more Bob Granger thought about it, the more convinced he became that his boy would have set a world record had he not injured himself. Even with the injury, after all, his winning time had been 9.9 seconds. Taking into account how Percy had faded in the closing yards instead of surging ahead in his usual manner, Bob figured that he would have posted at least a 9.3 had his leg held together.[15]

It was another opportunity lost. But those were the breaks when an athlete pushed his body to the limit, out to the edge where records and injuries lay. There was only one way forward: give Percy another long rest and try again the next year. And after that there was always the next Olympics, the 1932 Games scheduled to be held in LA.

CHAPTER 20

Down the River

A FEW WEEKS BEFORE the Empire Games, Vancouver reporter Robert Elson sat down with Percy and asked him: "Do you want to run anymore?" Percy couldn't give a simple answer but did indicate that he wanted to retire from track as soon as he could. "It's hard to keep in shape and devote full time to the job," he explained. "You can't give your whole time to running and keep a real job — one or the other has to go." While he didn't say so directly, it was clear to Elson that Percy resented how running interfered with his business career and other interests, and that he was staying in the game mainly because that's what everyone expected — at least until the next Olympics, when he would defend the sprint titles he had won in Amsterdam in 1928. "I don't see how I can get out of it before the Olympiad of 1932," he said.

Elson commended Percy for his desire to keep his track stardom from overwhelming his life, preferring instead to focus on his career. "Percy is the only man," he pointed out, "who makes a serious effort towards earning his own living and still continues competition. There is hardly another first-class athlete on this continent who can boast of the same. . . . Percy Williams retains something of a classic amateurism in spite of all temptations."[1] It was a perception that just about everyone still had of Percy, a holdover from his earlier days as the Vancouver schoolboy sensation that the intervening years had done little to change.

It must have been a bit disconcerting to some, therefore, when in 1931 a new friend appeared in Percy's life, a businessman named George Irvine who would be referred to as Percy's "manager."

George was a transplanted Torontonian, unmarried and forty years old. He had come west in the early 1910s to make his fortune, working his way up in the soda pop business until he ran the 7UP bottling plant for the whole of BC. His connection to sports lay mainly in hockey, which he played in his youth and later refereed, and in racing his stable of horses at the local track, where he also owned the snack concession. He didn't know anything about the finer points of sprinting but he did know business, which is likely what drew Percy to him. By the summer of 1931 they had launched a venture together, a barbecue and refreshment stand at Prospect Point in Stanley Park.[2]

This did not sit well with the trustees of the Percy Williams Trust Fund. Percy the co-owner of a business? While that didn't disqualify him from amateur athletics, at the same time it didn't seem quite right. After quiet consultation, it was decided that he no longer needed financial support from the fund, the $750 annual allowance being paid indirectly to Dot Williams. The payments were stopped. Back in the fall of 1928 there had been some public dissatisfaction when it became evident that the fund wasn't going to be given outright to Percy, but used to support others. "The money I gave I forwarded very gladly," stated one disgruntled benefactor. "But it was for Williams. It wasn't for any future athlete who may or may not require financial assistance."[3] Now, more than two years later, passions had cooled and the complete cessation of payments to Percy was hardly noticed. It would be more than a decade before he would see any more of "his" trust fund, and by then it would be greatly reduced.[4]

It was George who arranged for Percy to appear in a much ballyhooed June 18 rematch against Frank Wykoff, this time on Frank's home turf at the Los Angeles Coliseum. They drove down to LA together in George's big Packard, George proclaiming before they set out and in cables sent home along the way that Percy was feeling "great," that he was in "great" condition.[5] But Percy wasn't great at all. His groin injury from the Empire Games hadn't properly healed and had caused him trouble from the moment he resumed training early in May.[6] Bob Granger did what he could with massages and carefully controlled workouts, but there was only so much he could accomplish with Percy unwilling to devote the hours needed for serious training. At Percy's first meet of the season, a May 30 affair in Seattle, he put in a dismal performance, losing an exhibition century to a relatively unknown University of Washington freshman and pulling up short in the furlong to limp off the field.[7]

As Percy and George Irvine made their way south in the Packard, back in Vancouver those presumed to be closest to the sprint star said they were puzzled. They didn't understand why Percy had been so lackadaisical in his spring training, why he was heading off so complacently to this big meet in California, and why he hadn't taken Bob Granger along. It seemed that a certain amount of tension had returned to the relationship between runner and coach, but no one suggested a cause. A family friend observed that Percy simply didn't like running. "He prefers shooting, fishing and fun, and why not? Don't we all?" "I fancy that it is just another little trip for Percy," said King Ed High coach Emslie Yeo. "I hardly think he can expect to beat Wykoff, who is tuned by competition, as he has not done any serious training and, except for that jaunt in Seattle, has had no actual racing."[8]

But if that was the case, if Percy didn't like running, hadn't done any serious training, and didn't have much chance of beating Wykoff, why was he going to LA at all?

No one wanted to say it openly — although Andy Lytle in the *Vancouver Sun* dropped a pretty broad hint — but Percy's trip south had a lot to do with money, quite a bit of money, particularly in the Depression. For the fact was that Ray Barbuti had underestimated how much a track star could expect to make under the table for a meet appearance when he quoted the figure of five hundred dollars in his 1929 exposé. Later that same year Charlie Paddock, still angry over the harassment he had experienced on the road to the Amsterdam Olympics, came out with an exposé of his own in *Collier's* magazine in which he stated that "gifts" of two and even three thousand dollars for a single appearance were not uncommon for a top star who could pull in the fans. (Rumour had it that Paavo Nurmi on occasion charged more than four thousand.[9]) There was usually a learning process involved, Charlie explained, a period when the newly risen star, ignorant of his true worth, was taken advantage of by promoters, but he soon figured things out and began dictating his terms. They all did it sooner or later, assuming their stardom lasted that long. Attracted on the one hand by the temptations of promoters, disillusioned about amateurism on the other by the draconian hand of the AAU with its myriad arbitrarily enforced rules, it was "virtually impossible," Charlie wrote, for the amateur champion to remain "honest."

Of course, in such a shady business, getting the agreed-upon sum to appear at a meet was not always easy. When payment was due, typically just prior to a meet, the promoter might claim financial hardship and make only a down payment, promising to pay the rest later but invariably neglecting to do so. In that case there was little the athlete could do. He couldn't complain to the AAU that he had been bilked out of an illicit payment, and refusing to appear in the promoter's meet meant risking disbarment, the athlete by this time having signed the entry form required at all AAU-sanctioned meets that obliged him to compete.[10]

It was in fact just the sort of business, Charlie might have added, where the guidance of a savvy manager could be very useful.

∽

Percy checked quietly into the Plaza Hotel in Hollywood a week before the big meet and kept a low profile. By the time the local press tracked him down he was being referred to as "The Mysterious Mister X."[11] Once located, the attention and hype were constant. When he showed up at the Coliseum to begin working out the kinks of the journey, a battery of photographers was waiting and began snapping away. The size of the stadium was awesome, the biggest Percy had ever seen, with seating for 105,000 people. A special shot was arranged with Percy, Frank Wykoff and New Orleans sprint star Emmett Toppino all starting together. Toppino had several 9.6-second centuries under his belt, and just two weeks before had run a 9.5. Percy figured he might be the man to beat. "Gangway for the champion," Frank joked as they pushed out of their holes to the sound of clicking cameras.[12]

The press wanted rivalry, a track feud, and Percy obliged. It wasn't all put on either, at least as far as his feelings toward Frank were concerned. Privately, he resented the excuses that had been made for Frank's poor showing at the 1928 Olympics — after all, they amounted to a denigration of his own win — and Frank's protest over his loss in their 1929 Vancouver rematch. And now Percy was finding it irksome how LA seemed to be talking about nothing but "Wykoff, Wykoff, Wykoff," as if Percy with his two gold medals and other honours didn't matter at all. "It seems that the race is already over as far as local fans are concerned," Percy stated. "Naturally, I don't want to disappoint Wykoff's followers, but you can rest assured that Frank will have to run one of his best races to win. Even that may not be good enough, for I like the weather here, and feel that I will be right for Friday evening's effort."[13] In another interview, conducted with Percy and Frank seated side by side, Percy bridled at the question of whether he preferred a soft or hard track. "There have been a lot of dirty cracks taken at me down here by certain people, saying that I can run only on a soft track. I beat every great American runner in the East indoors and the board tracks were not made of sawdust."[14]

This was a new Percy Williams — not cocky, but certainly more forceful in defending his merits. "Looks like great race Friday night," George Irvine wired back to Vancouver. "Percy in great shape, considering short training." Nearly half the Coliseum's seats, George added, had already been sold.[15] In the betting that was going on behind the scenes, the odds that had been running two-to-one in Wykoff's favour shifted closer to even.[16]

The June 18 meet, billed as a "Pre-Olympic Athletic Festival," drew forty thousand ticket-buying fans in what was now the second year of the Great Depression. Expatriate Canadians and Britons alone filled five thousand seats right up along the sprint track, called out by a widely distributed notice proclaiming that "the duty of every Canadian and other Britishers is to be in the British section of the Coliseum to welcome our champion."[17] The show got underway toward sunset with the filming of a staged fifty-yard dash involving Frank and Percy and comedian Joe E. Brown in his trademark round glasses. Joe was declared the winner. It was something for his upcoming movie, *Local Boy Makes Good*. Then, as the sun slipped below the horizon and the sky turned orange and purple, screen legend Mary Pickford stepped forward to throw the switch on the stadium's brand-new fifty-thousand-dollar lights. For most of the people in attendance it was an amazing new sight, their first experience of night turned into day for a sporting event.[18]

It was all in all a strange evening for Percy, not the sort of athletic meet he was used to. Alongside the usual track and field events, the card included a nighttime polo match between teams captained by humourist Will Rogers' son Jimmy and movie producer Hal Roach, amateur boxing refereed by ring legends Jess Willard and Jim Jefferies, and wrestling with Ed "Strangler" Lewis doing the honours in white shirt and bow tie. Then there was the sight of Douglas Fairbanks before the microphone serving as master of ceremonies, and of Harold Lloyd who was helping him out. And when Percy himself stepped out under the lights at nine o'clock for what they were calling the "Race of a Lifetime," it was to the odd sensation of walking at the centre of a star of shadows and of being roared at from tiers of stadium seating that seemed to ascend to the sky. It all made Brockton Point and Hastings Park seem pretty quaint.

They were getting ready to race when a tremendous flash erupted at the far end of the track. A photographer had accidentally ignited a whole bottle of powder while refilling his flashgun to take a shot of the finish. He lay sprawled on the cinders, unconscious, face seared and hands badly mangled. He was quickly hustled away on a stretcher. It was dangerous work, taking flash photos, especially when the flashgun grew hot after a few shots.[19]

Emmett Toppino had a funny way of running. He started out with little stabbing steps, much shorter than Percy's, and sprinted with his shoulders all hunched over. But most noticeable to Percy in the lane beside him was Emmett's vaguely embarrassing huffing and grunting — loud at first as they ran even, then fading as the Loyola University star followed Frank into the lead.

Percy didn't stand a chance. He hadn't done nearly enough training. He finished fourth behind Frank, who won the Race of a Lifetime in 9.5 seconds, Emmett in second, San Francisco sprinter Cy Leland in third.[20] Canada's Olympic champion, concluded the *Los Angeles Times*, was just "a shell of the runner who astounded the world four years ago" and now "seems headed for 'Down the River.'"[21] Back in Vancouver the post-mortems, while not so dismissive, contained a critical edge. Such a loss was to be expected, many said, when Percy took the whole thing so lightly.[22]

∞

Things were not going well for Bob Granger. His role in Percy's life had been significantly curtailed with the arrival of George Irvine, Bob reduced to massaging Percy's legs and offering what guidance he could when his protegé was willing to practise, and beyond that being largely ignored. When he entered Percy in the annual Police Sports for his first competition following the return from LA, Percy didn't even show up. A local newsman who ran into the sprinter at the horse track reported him as saying that he had not agreed to appear and had not signed an entry.[23] Bob was also having trouble sticking with the insurance business that he had resolved two years before to make his career. Increasingly he abandoned the drudgery of the office to spend more and more of his time at coaching, once again becoming a fixture at Brockton Point and Athletic Park, putting a new crop of youngsters through their paces, looking for the next Percy Williams.[24]

In the meantime Percy started rounding into what his supporters were saying was his *real* form for the next big athletic meet being planned for Hastings Park in August, billed as a "Pre-Olympic" meet in imitation of the financially successful June 19 LA extravaganza. A rematch between Percy, Eddie Tolan and Frank Wykoff was at the top of the card. George Irvine had been saying all along that Percy was looking "great," and in the lead-up to the meet others joined in the chorus that he was in "the best form of his career" and "the pink of condition."[25]

Among them was Percy's old high school friend and training partner Pinky Stewart, now graduated from UBC and working as a press agent for the upcoming meet. In the pages of the *Sun*, Pinky related how Percy in his training sessions with Bob Granger was burning up the track, running so fast that Bob could hardly believe it. He had regained his peak Olympic condition, Pinky claimed, and was ready to once again take on and whip all comers.[26]

But what about Frank Wykoff, asked the *Sun*'s Andy Lytle, always eager to stir the pot. He beat Percy pretty handily in LA and had a perfect record of wins for the year. Surely he was a pretty big threat.

"Wait until he meets Percival here next month," Pinky replied with a significant look.

"Okay, Pinkus," said Andy. "We're waiting."[27]

∞

It was a sparse audience that turned up at the downtown Orpheum Theatre for the matinee on August 22 to see a rising vaudeville comedian named Bob Hope, the self-styled Enemy of Depression, sharing the stage with Joe Peanuts and the Brazilian Monkey Jazz Band. All of Vancouver seemed to be at Hastings Park for the Pre-Olympic track meet. "Watch records fall," promised ads in the papers. "Watch Percy Williams, Eddie Tolan and Frank Wykoff dash for the title of 'The World's Fastest Human.'" A new gimmick had been added to the proceedings to draw out spectators. Admission was offered by way of "special privilege tickets" at fifty cents a pop, three for a dollar, one ticket getting you onto the grounds, two into the grandstands. And why not buy a book of five, for each ticket came with a chance of winning prizes such as a world cruise, a motorcycle, and not one car, but two. It was going to be the greatest show in the history of the city, was the promise, one that no one should miss.[28]

The show was mismanaged right from the start. First there was the problem with the programs, someone having neglected to include a schedule of events so that the audience could follow what was going on. "Fifteen cents for this is nothing short of highway robbery," was the generally felt sentiment being muttered in the stands. The oversight left even meet officials in a fog of confusion, scrambling to find a copy of the schedule. Then there was the matter of the numbers that were to be pinned on the athletes' jerseys — the numbers that lay forgotten on a side table, leaving spectators to guess at who might be who. And when the first few races were run, it was without a tape at the finish, no one having thought to bring along a piece of string.[29]

Fortunately Pinky Stewart was at the microphone, keeping everyone as informed as he could and entertained with his snappy, high-speed patter. Now and then he would urge one of the athletes up to the mike to be introduced and say a few words. Phil Edwards took his turn and gave a courtly bow, then Jimmy Ball came up, grinning when Pinky announced that the gangly Winnipegger, Percy's good friend, had just been married. Eddie Tolan, lucky bandage on his knee and glasses taped to his head, was coaxed forward but would only say "Hello everybody." He seemed as shy as Percy. For newspaper audiences south of the border, Eddie's comment would be edited to read: "Man, I sho' does feel fine."[30]

But why hasn't Percy been introduced? the fans started buzzing. They could see him down there, clad in his white track suit with "Canada" on the front, apparently engrossed in warming up. Pinky announced the big race, the hundred-metre main event, and Percy could be seen stripping down to his shorts and flexing his legs and taking a few more half-speed starts. But then, rather than joining Eddie and Frank and the others at the start line, he started conversing intently with a group of older men in suits.

Percy's leg didn't feel right. It was the same old problem, the torn muscle up near the groin. Things had been going well in training since his return from LA, Bob estimating in early August that Percy was more than ready to run a 9.6-second century, and could very well manage a 9.5. Percy's next competition had also gone smoothly, an August 13 affair in New Westminster where he won the dash easily without really testing his leg. But when he tried opening up with some real speed at the BC Track and Field Championships a few days later, the old injury flared up. Percy won the dash but only barely, easing up in the last fifteen yards to cross the finish line at little more than a jog. He didn't want to take any chances with his leg before the upcoming rematch with Wykoff and Tolan, he said. He spent the following week resting and the aggravated muscle seemed to get better. He informed the organizers of the Hasting Park meet that he would run if he could. But the fact that Percy might have to withdraw was largely kept from the public. Without his name to boost ticket sales, the meet would be a financial disaster.[31]

In all the feverish hype in the days leading up to the race, no one took much notice of Bob Granger's comment, out of the blue, that Percy was "through as a sprinter" — and had been ever since the injury he had suffered in Hamilton the previous summer. Before that, Bob stated, he could have whipped all comers, but "he will be lucky if he can come within two yards of either Wykoff or Tolan now."[32] Bob was probably better qualified than any other observer to judge Percy's condition after he had reinjured his groin. But still, it seemed an odd thing to say on the eve of what was being advertised as the biggest race of Percy's life, and suggests the presence of hard feelings, and perhaps jealousy as well. In newspaper accounts of Percy's doings throughout the month of August, it was always George Irvine, "friend, confidante and business partner,"[33] seen at his side, never Bob. Bob was now just Percy's trainer, the fellow who helped out at the star's irregular workouts.

It was George again, not Bob, who was with Percy in the huddle down on the track prior to the Hastings Park race. With them was University of Washington coach Edmundson and Coach Hayward from the University of Oregon, who had come up to the Vancouver meet with some of their boys. Percy wanted to know what they thought about his leg and they were advising him not to run. It isn't worth it, they said. The effort might result in a permanent injury that would put you out of next year's Olympics.

George walked over to Pinky Stewart at the announcer's table and they exchanged a few heated words. "What about this crowd of people?" Pinky hissed. Finally he turned to the mike and cleared his throat.

"Bad news for you, folks. Percy Williams will not start."

Eddie Tolan went on to win the race, tying Percy's still unofficial world record of 10.3 seconds. Frank Wykoff placed second, six feet behind. "I feel pretty good and pretty bad," said Eddie after. "Good because I won, but bad because I was the only one in shape."[34] Frank, it turned out, had not been in the best of condition either. He had in fact been spotted out on the town at two o'clock the previous morning, evidently not too concerned about getting his rest. "You were so far ahead of me it wasn't even funny," he joked with Eddie after catching his breath. A few days later it was reported that he had lost five hundred dollars after the race, somewhere between Hastings Park and boarding the train.[35] The fact that Frank left the meet with such a large roll of bills in his pocket didn't surprise those acquainted with the inner workings of amateur track. They knew the Glendale Greyhound hadn't come all the way up from California for a stick pin.

The Pre-Olympic meet left Vancouverites feeling cheated, with rumours circulating that the whole thing had been a scam; that the organizers had known that Percy wouldn't be running but had kept quiet about it to use his name to sell tickets. The organizers responded by putting all the blame on Percy. Percy, they stated, had promised to run and deserved censure for failing to do so. His manager George Irvine had assured them just the night before the meet that the groin injury wasn't a problem and that Percy would compete. Had they known otherwise, they added, they never would have held the meet in the first place. Percy shot back heatedly that he had never given any sort of unconditional promise. He had only said he would run if he could.[36]

In his office at the *Vancouver Sun*, Andy Lytle figured that something fishy had gone on behind the scenes. "Mr. Pinky Stewart, indeed," he revealed in his column, "mutters darkly of things he could say and of an exposure that would knock us all cuckoo. . . . Having no illusions whatever about the sacred calf called amateurism in these big gate receipts affairs, I sniff a crackerjack of a story should Mr. Pinky carry out his sombre threat."[37]

Pinky never did talk. Neither did anyone else. But then, as Andy himself had observed on several occasions, that was the cardinal rule of amateur sport: make some money, sure, just keep quiet about it.

∞

When Pinky made his announcement at Hastings Park that Percy wouldn't be running, half the audience had let out a sigh of disappointment. The other half didn't hear him. That was the thing about Pinky's machine-gun delivery — it was snappy, but piped through the tinny loudspeakers it was sometimes difficult to catch. Which one's Percy? some of the fans continued to ask, anxious now as the runners went to their marks. With none of the athletes wearing numbers it was hard to tell who was who. That one there, others were saying, pointing to Edmonton's Buster Brown in the outside lane. The runners got set and starter Emslie Yeo sent them away with a bark of the pistol and cries of Come on, Percy! could be heard directed at Buster, loud throaty bellows that rose to desperate shrillness as Buster faded behind Eddie and Frank. Come on, Percy! they were shouting, Come on, boy! not realizing that their Percy wasn't even in the race. He was standing on the sidelines, watching.[38]

CHAPTER 21

The Last Race

∞

IT WAS THE SPRING of 1932 and Percy was already in training. He had begun with a conditioning program in January of daily stretching, push-ups, sit-ups and half-mile jogs to strengthen his legs, and was now well advanced with the sprint work, building up to a peak of speed that, at the age of twenty-four, he should only now be attaining. He seemed committed to running again, committed in a way he hadn't been since his return from Amsterdam four years before. He was at it almost every day.

His dismal record the previous year undoubtedly played a part in the change. It had been a wake-up call that he needed to train more diligently if he was to prove wrong the critics who said he was washed up. And he *wanted* to prove it, because for the first time since the 1928 Olympics he had a clear, simple goal as a runner: to return to the Games and successfully defend his double sprint titles. It was going to be a severe challenge. No Olympic sprint victor had ever returned to the next Games and reclaimed gold in either the one hundred metres or the two hundred and certainly not both. To have any chance at all of prevailing, he would need to attain a level of conditioning he had not had in years. That was why he was out on the track.

And maybe, just maybe, the booing had something to do with it too, the catcalls that for the first time had been mixed with the cheering when Percy was introduced at a hockey game he had attended during the winter.[1] After the fiasco of the previous summer's track meet, some of his fellow Vancouverites had turned against him. Maybe he didn't want to let that stand.

He was training again with Bob Granger, although not on an exclusive basis. For Percy there would be lengthy trips down to Seattle to work out with University of Washington coach Hec Edmundson, while for Bob there was the new flock of young prospects he was now coaching — to the detriment of his increasingly neglected insurance career. It still rankled with Bob that he had never received a cent of the money promised him from the Percy Williams Fund to support his athletic work. In early May, however, he had a brainstorm, a surefire way to raise money. He would organize a sweepstake, promising a cash prize to whoever correctly picked the winner of the hundred-metre dash at the upcoming Los Angeles Olympics. He printed up several boxes of what he called "Olympic Club" tickets and set his stable of young runners to selling them for a quarter a pop.

Sales of Bob's tickets would get a boost when they were mentioned in both the *Sun*'s and *Daily Province*'s sports columns. Getting the word out, that's how you made money. They would get an additional fillip as the BC Olympic trials drew near in June and sports fans started buying them in the mistaken belief that they were good for admission to the meet. That was not quite so lucky, for it annoyed the local AAU branch. Whether Bob realized it or not, he was stepping on toes.[2]

Whatever hard feelings Bob harboured toward Percy were now evidently forgotten. He had come to accept his subsidiary role in the runner's athletic career and the fact Percy now kept him at arm's length. Forgotten too was Bob's prediction the previous August that Percy was "through as a sprinter." In a May 13th article he described Percy's level of fitness as "immeasurably better" than it had been the year before, and flashed some of his old optimism over his protegé's potential. Percy was already hitting a 9.6-second clip in the century in training, Bob revealed, and with more work and a continuing course of massages he would be capable of shattering the world record in both the hundred and the two hundred metres.[3]

It would all depend on his dicky leg. Had the Empire Games injury finally healed? Or would that groin muscle tear again when Percy bore down and pushed himself to the limit? The initial signs were good. At the Police Games at Brockton Point on June 22, Percy's first competition in ten months, the leg held up. Contesting both sprint distances, something he hadn't done in years, he took the century in ten flat and the furlong in twenty-two seconds, respectable times for the start of the season, running smoothly all the way and winning with ease. "Percy Runs as of Old" read the *Sun* headline the following day.[4] "Just breezing," exulted Andy Lytle. "When Percy is right," said another, "no man in the world can beat him."[5]

The BC Olympic trials at Hastings Park fell three days later. Two years had passed since the track was levelled and smoothed prior to the Dominion Day meet of 1930 — two years of horse racing that had left the oval once again a welter of hoof prints. Percy was entered in both the hundred- and two-hundred-metre dashes, but pulled out of the latter after examining the track. On such a rough surface, getting through the hundred alone without injury would be enough of a challenge. Some of the other runners were pulled out by their coaches as well, for the track really was a disgrace. Percy went on to win the hundred in 10.6 seconds, tying the Olympic record and three-tenths shy of his unofficial world mark despite going slow at the start and easing up at the finish. But the effort still cost him, aggravating his old groin tear. His whole upper thigh remained sore to the touch for the next several days, reducing his training to light jogging while Bob continued, a bit more desperately, with his daily massages. A doctor was consulted. He said that an operation immediately after the initial occurrence of Percy's injury two years before would have fixed it completely. Now it was too late.[6]

The next step on the road to the LA Games was the Canadian Olympic trials set for Hamilton in the middle of July. Percy was ready and willing to go and had already written to Olympic Committee chairman Pat Mulqueen saying that he was looking forward to the trip.[7] But this was one trip east that Bob Granger didn't want Percy to make. Bob was worried that Percy's bad leg did not have many races left in it and would be overtaxed by the strain of qualifying at the trials. When Bob made these concerns known, the BC branch of the AAU seized upon them and dispatched a telegram to the Olympic Committee requesting that Percy be exempted from the trials so that he could save his leg for an all-out effort at LA.

The request was denied. It would set a dangerous precedent, the Olympic Committee responded. To soften the blow, they named Percy Olympic team captain. "That gesture . . . doesn't mean a thing," a local AAU man snapped. "Do you suppose the east would take any steps likely to injure a star's chances if the positions were reversed?"[8]

The West-versus-East battle lines were now drawn — and Percy was caught in the middle. A fight had in fact been brewing for several months, ever since Vancouver lost to Hamilton in its bid to host the national trials. Hamilton clearly was more central and had better facilities, but being denied the honour had nevertheless left hard feelings in Vancouver that now steeled the local AAU's position that Percy should be spared the strain of the trip east. "Why sacrifice Percy?" wrote the *Sun*'s Andy Lytle, voicing the Western opinion. "Is the need for Hamilton to show a profit at their Trials greater than the assurance of Percy's perfected condition at the Games if he goes from here direct . . . ? Are our amateur sports conducted for the best interests of the athletes or for the personal and financial aggrandizement of Hamilton promoters and eastern Canadian officials?"[9]

"Let him come down here," shot back Lou Marsh in the *Toronto Star*, "and show that he is not a cripple and that he will be useful to Canada at Los Angeles. In these times Canada has no money to spend on cripples, even though they are Williams."[10]

The controversy and harsh comments hardened Percy's own feelings. He had little inclination to go east now. And he felt even less like going when the Olympic Committee, in trying to appease him, stated that he wouldn't have to compete in Hamilton, just show up. He was needed at the trials, they admitted, to attract fans and sell tickets to help raise money to send the Olympic team to LA. For Percy that was the last straw. Nothing made him angrier than being used to raise money. "I see no reason," he said, "why I should interrupt my whole training schedule to make a long trip at this critical stage, particularly now that Mulqueen says I would not even need to run if I did not feel so inclined."[11]

For a few tense days it was unclear whether Percy would be going to Los Angeles at all. But in the end the Olympic Committee relented. There was really nothing they could do but overlook his now vehement refusal to appear at the trials and let him go to the Games direct from Vancouver. Shortly thereafter a railway representative appeared at the runner's door with a one-way ticket to LA and an envelope containing ten dollars in expense money. Percy brusquely sent him away, stating that he was making other arrangements. He would drive down to California instead with George Irvine and submit a list of his expenses to the Olympic Committee when he arrived.[12]

In Eastern Canada, meanwhile, hard feelings against Percy lingered. Toronto's *Evening Telegram* sportswriter Ted Reeve, who after Amsterdam had used verse to laud the sprinter's achievements, now cobbled together four more stanzas to mock him:

"You are old Percy Williams," the young man remarked,
"You are old and exceedingly weighty.
"Yet on our Olympicing team you are parked,
In this year of our grace, 1980."

"In my youth," Father Williams replied with a bow,
"When I had all the speed of a rabbit,
I won two such notable races that now,
They pick me from sheer force of habit."

"But how," cried the youth, "with your legs in a bend,
And a beard hanging down from your chin,

When races are run to see who they will send,
Pray, how do you manage to win?"

"Why then," said the sage, "though it sounds rather queer,
My sore leg gets worse for a while,
So they bring me along in the hopes every year
I'll return to my '28 style."[13]

One of Percy's friends clipped out the poem and mailed it to him. "Hell," read the comment penned in the margin, "ain't they heard of the Gazelle? Well they soon will, and how!"[14]

∽

Percy arrived in LA feeling "great." At least that's what George Irvine was saying. "Expect Percy to win finals of one hundred," he cabled back to Vancouver. "He is certainly in great shape and working wonderfully well."[15] To leave no doubt of his confidence in Percy, George privately claimed he had placed a heavy bet on the race: five hundred dollars against five thousand that Percy would take the gold.[16]

Percy himself wasn't nearly so self-assured. To the athletes and officials on the Canadian team he appeared worried and moody, and when he resumed his training it was clear he was sparing his leg. "You can take it from me," observed Lou Marsh, who had come west with the team, "that Williams' doubly studded diamond crown, which he wore so jauntily on his return in 1928, has turned to lead. . . . He is living in an inferno of doubt."[17]

The condition of his leg was of course a big worry. In the days prior to the start of competition, Percy did little more on the track than light jogging, fearful that something might give if he attempted too strenuous a burst of speed. His leg, however, wasn't the only thing troubling his mind. Not having Bob Granger along may also have been part of the problem. George Irvine's repetition that everything was "great" just didn't provide the same sort of mental support and focus that Bob had been able to instill at Amsterdam. Then there was the resentment he was still feeling — at the Olympic Committee for trying to get him to appear at the Hamilton trials to raise money, at the criticism levelled against him for refusing, at the trustees of his trust fund for cutting off all support. Just how deeply this had affected him became apparent when he submitted his expenses for the trip down from Vancouver to a team official. When the official gave only a vague assurance of reimbursement, Percy replied sharply that if it wasn't received by opening day, he wouldn't be running.

"We were angry," Percy said later. "The team officials had come in by train from eastern Canada, travelling first class. One of the hurdlers told us the athletes from the east were given a choice: if they rode in the day coach, they could eat in the diner. But if they wanted an upper berth to sleep in, then they'd have to grab their food at the station sandwich counters whenever the train stopped."[18]

At least Los Angeles was doing everything it could to make the athletes comfortable. It had introduced a new concept to the Games with the construction of an "Olympic Village," a fenced compound of five hundred and fifty bungalows that was a tremendous improvement over the catch-as-catch-can accommodation at Amsterdam four years before. And it wasn't going to cost the city a penny, for after the Games the bungalows were to be sold off to the public — assuming they weren't wrecked first. Unfortunately, an Argentine weight thrower had already tossed his hammer through his own roof and the roof of the place across the way, the Finns had burned down their digs with a jury-rigged sauna, and a fellow in one of the American units had thrust his head through a wall. In this congenial atmosphere, akin to a sprawling college campus, with movie stars at the gate and lovesick girls sending in notes which he promptly discarded, Percy began preparing himself for what lay ahead while the rest of the Canadian team speculated on his physical and mental condition.[19]

It was team manager Bobby Robinson who finally put the question to him directly. Percy had just stopped by Bobby's bungalow to say the flannel trousers for his Olympic suit needed shortening, and he seemed willing to talk. "I think I can run as fast as I ever did," he replied when Bobby began probing. "Last year I didn't have the spring in the legs. This year I have it. I'm in good physical condition and as long as my legs stand up I'll be in there at all stages."

"It seems to me, Percy," Bobby pressed, "that the big point is just how much the leg condition is affecting your mental attitude."

"Yes, I realize that. It does give me some worry when I'm playing around, but when I get into my stride and am actually racing I forget all about it." Percy smiled and gave a shrug. "Anyway," he added, "I've got my fingers crossed."[20]

British hurdler David Lord Burghley came in, sprawled into a chair and began expounding on how the Americans were overtraining, just as they had at Amsterdam. "They'll just keep on grinding away," he said, "and by the time that race day comes they'll be burned out. I'm through today. I find I can hold my form for four days and I won't put on my spikes until race day."

He turned to Percy. "What did you do?"

"Oh, Jimmy Ball and I just played around out here on the grass, having a few starts and a few quick bursts of speed."

"That's the idea," replied Lord Burghley with a nod of approval. "These Americans train too hard. They never last. Our system is best."[21]

∽

It was on July 27, three days before Percy was to begin competition, when the clouds that had been following him around finally parted. Perhaps it was the arrival of his 1928 Olympic teammate and friend Doral Pilling. When Doral appeared at the Olympic Village he and Percy greeted each other with unabashed shouts of joy and back slapping. "Why, just the fact Pilling is here will cut a fifth of a second off Percy's time for the hundred," enthused Pat Mulqueen after observing the reunion. That same day Percy unleashed his first real display of speed in training, a thirty-metre burst at the end of a practice hundred that shot him ahead so fast that the whole Olympic Village was buzzing about it. The old Percy was back, people said, the old Percy who could beat *anyone* when he turned on the heat.[22] Up in Canada a collective sigh of relief was heaved from one coast to the other. The *Montreal Star* said it all in its headline spread across the entire sports page: "Percy Williams Is Himself Again."[23]

On July 30 there was more good news: the International Amateur

Athletic Federation at its pre-Olympic meeting had accepted Percy's hundred-metre race in Toronto in 1930, run in 10.3 seconds, as the official world record. It was a mark that probably meant more to Bob Granger than to anyone else. And yet Bob was scarcely able to give it a thought. He had made the front page of the paper himself that day. Percy's long-time coach, Vancouverites were informed, had just been arrested.

∽

It was the sweepstake Bob had been running, the "Olympic Club" tickets he and his band of schoolboy athletes were selling which allowed buyers to bet on the Olympic hundred-metre dash, the outcome of which was now just two days away. Bob had been summoned down to Police Court a few weeks before to answer questions about the tickets, but nothing had come of it and he returned home thinking everything was okay. It wasn't. The police now showed up at his office in the Province Building to arrest him and seize a quantity of unsold tickets. After regaining his freedom on bail, Bob sat down with the lawyer he was obliged to hire and started learning some hard facts.

His sweepstake, the lawyer explained, was in fact a lottery, and lotteries were illegal in Canada. Gambling was illegal too — and betting on the outcome of an Olympic sprint race was gambling. But, Bob said, I see churches holding raffles all the time to raise money. What about that? Yes, said his lawyer, but churches and charities are legally allowed to hold raffles. They're exempt. All right, said Bob, what about all those tickets to the Hastings Park track meet last summer, when they were giving away prizes of a car and a cruise and what have you? That's another exemption, his lawyer replied. Agricultural fairs and exhibitions get them. Well, tried Bob again, what about betting at the horse track? That's legal, and it's sure not church work. The lawyer shook his head. Another exemption, he said.

So Bob was in trouble. As a private citizen he was not free to run a lottery and had broken the law. And then came the real shock, draining the blood from his face, when he asked what the worst was that he could expect.

In the Criminal Code of Canada, his lawyer began, the maximum sentence for running an illegal lottery was two years in prison and a fine of up to two thousand dollars.[24]

∽

There were thirty-two athletes representing seventeen nations entered in the Olympic hundred metres, less than half the number at Amsterdam. It was the Depression that had done it. Some countries had decided to skip the Games altogether and others had drastically reduced the size of their teams. There was still a formidable list of sprint luminaries in competition, however, with the American trio of Eddie Tolan, George Simpson and Ralph Metcalfe at the forefront as the toughest to beat. Frank Wykoff wouldn't be running. A strained back suffered in the spring had thrown him off in the trials. He had qualified only for the relay.[25]

They would be running on an Olympic Stadium track that was being hailed as a beauty. It had a wonderfully fine cinder surface, watered and steamrolled to billiard-table perfection, and an underlying layer of peat that gave what would have otherwise been a very hard surface a pleasant degree of spring. "I can only liken it in texture to a piece of satin and in resilience to a piece of rubber," one of the British runners was quoted as saying. It was also dry as a bone, not at all like the sloppy Amsterdam track, for it almost never rained in LA at this time of year. Fast times were expected.[26]

Round one consisted of seven heats, the first three in each advancing. Percy was in heat four. Running well within his limits to save his leg, he took third behind winner Carlos Luti of Argentina and his 1928 nemesis Helmut Koernig in second. His leg didn't feel great but it was working. He returned to the dressing room satisfied. Don't worry, Canadians seated in the stadium reassured one another. Percy has been saying all along he was going to save himself in the early rounds, running just to qualify, not win. It's all going according to plan. They settled back to watch the next heat end in drama, a Greek runner collapsing on the track at the finish and being carried away on a stretcher, gasping for breath.[27]

Percy was back out for the second round in just under an hour, up against runners from Holland and Mexico, Luti again, and Eddie Tolan. The rumour seemed to be true: the heats were seeded. With a bit of luck, Percy would be able to continue saving his leg and still get through to the semifinals. But Eddie had other ideas. After a first round of lacklustre times, the Midnight Express roared down the track to win in 10.4 seconds, an Olympic record and a tenth shy of Percy's world mark. Seeing Eddie's lead widen alarmingly in the final stretch, Percy instinctively started to drive, giving his leg its first real test. It didn't hold up. He managed to place third and advance, but as he slowed and then trotted back to the start to fetch his gear, even the Canadians in the uppermost tiers could see that the defending champ was in trouble, that he had a perceptible limp.

Later that evening Bobby Robinson found Percy despondent. There had been no driving power in his leg, he said. The old injury was now thoroughly aggravated as well, his upper thigh painful even to walk on. Team trainer Bob Dixon spent an hour massaging it, trying to loosen it up.[28]

Percy drew the first semifinal the following afternoon, another bright and clear southern California day, perfect for racing. After a long session in the change room warming his leg under a heat lamp, he toed the line against Eddie Tolan, Helmut Koernig, the South African Daniel Joubert, Allan Elliot of New Zealand and Takayoshi Yoshioka of Japan, who had a hachimaki headband tied round his head symbolizing perseverance. Eddie, warming up in his baggy blue sweatsuit, was the man to beat. Koernig, who had run a wind-aided 10.3-second hundred earlier that year, might also be a threat. As for Joubert, Elliot and the diminutive Yoshioka in the lane beside him, Percy hardly knew a thing about them.

Eighty thousand spectators looked on from the stands. Percy had never run in front of a crowd like this. Hollywood movie stars were seated up there by the dozen, beneath the balloons holding up advertisements that swayed in the light breeze. Scattered cheering broke out here and there. The Japanese fans were the loudest. They were seated in a block dotted with rising sun flags and parasols and were shouting in unison: "Yo-shi-o-ka! Yo-shi-o-ka!"

Percy lowered himself into his start holes, pain radiating through the back of his thigh. Just surviving to go into the final was going to take a supreme effort. "Oh well," he had said the day before, "if a man can't place among the first three he shouldn't be in the event." That's what he needed now: to place in the first three.

The announcer's voice came over the loudspeakers. "Quiet please. . . ."

The gun sounded and they were away. Percy fought to keep abreast of Eddie but each stride was a torment. Koernig was fading, joining Elliot in last. It was a four-man race.

The halfway mark and Joubert was in the lead, Yoshioka, hachimaki flapping, just inches back, followed by Eddie and Percy, running even. Then Eddie was surging, closing the gap with the leaders while Percy followed behind. Percy looked all wrong. His head was hunched into his shoulders, betraying the pain. They were almost to the finish, the four frontrunners spread out over no more than a yard. Eddie's surge was carrying him forward. He was past the others. Then he was through the tape.

Percy hadn't made it. He placed fourth and was out. Yoshioka, fading toward the end, hung on long enough to edge him out for the last spot in the final. Even before Percy had limped to a stop he knew there would be no point running in the two hundred metres. His leg was shot. He had half-suspected it was no good all along.[29]

He had been wanting out of it all. But there was no sense of relief that it was over, only disappointment. He didn't show it, of course. "Thou shalt not be a bad loser." That was the fourth rule. He started shaking hands, nodding and smiling, taking his elimination like a sport, then returned to the dressing room to shower and change into his street clothes. He was soon joined there by fellow Canadians Harold Wright and Bert Pearson, both eliminated in the second semi. There would be no Canadians going into the final. When they reappeared, Percy hobbling, it was to sit in the grandstand to watch Eddie Tolan win the hundred-metre gold medal by the narrowest of margins. He would go on to win the two hundred as well.[30]

The hurdles followed. Lord Burghley placed fifth.

✺

Bob Granger returned to Vancouver's City Police Court the next day to plead guilty to the charge of conducting an illegal lottery. His lawyer requested an adjournment. He scarcely needed to give a reason: Bob was visibly distraught. The request was opposed by the prosecuting attorney, with the arresting officer adding that since Bob's arrest and subsequent release on bail a number of lottery tickets had been sold. Bob's lawyer may have pointed out that it had simply taken a while for Bob to contact all his boys and put a halt to the selling. Bob was hardly listening. He just sat there and stared at his hands.

The judge denied the requested adjournment. All tickets and related papers seized at the time of Bob's arrest, he ordered, were to be destroyed. He would pass sentence the following Monday.[31]

᷁᷁

Percy ran one more time at the LA Olympics, in the sprint relay. Dropping out of the two hundred gave him a week to rest his leg, and there was a flickering hope in the Canadian camp that he might have enough left to make one last meaningful effort. There were only eight teams entered, necessitating just two rounds of competition, so even with a sub-par Percy there was a slim chance that Canada might snatch up the bronze.

Both rounds were run on the afternoon of Sunday, August 7. The event began with a huge stroke of luck for Percy and his teammates: Mexico and Argentina both withdrew, leaving only two other teams in their heat, the USA and Italy, with all three guaranteed to advance. Percy ran the lead-off leg and took it easy. The Canadians settled for last.

It was clear the Americans would take gold in the final. They were going like blazes. Nothing short of a dropped baton would stop them. But it didn't happen. They passed beautifully, ran superbly, Emmett Toppino grunting his way in the second slot, Frank Wykoff doing the honours as anchor. Percy ran his leg surprisingly well, almost holding even, and so did team anchor Bert Pearson, Canada's newest schoolboy sensation who was said to train in lead-soled shoes. But the best they could do was fourth, just out of the medals. The Germans, led by Helmut Koernig, took silver, the Italians the bronze.[32]

Afterward, one of the Italians jogged over to Percy and took off his team jersey to exchange in the traditional manner. Percy handed over his red maple leaf shirt and the Italian pulled it on and they shook hands and parted. Percy draped the Italian's blue top over his arm. The cheers of the fans filled the air but they weren't for him. They were for Frank and Emmett and the rest of the American team who were celebrating their win. They had done the oval in forty seconds flat, smashing the world record. As Percy walked off the field and disappeared into the tunnel that led to the change rooms, few realized they had just seen him run his last race.[33]

Epilogue

FOLLOWING THE 1932 LA Olympics, Percy Williams disappeared from the spotlight almost as suddenly as he had appeared four years before. Rumours circulated that he might compete occasionally in local meets but he never did.[1] He was through with running. There was talk too that he would begin serious training as a swimmer, pursuing an interest postponed throughout his years on the track, but nothing came of that either.[2] After a stint as volunteer track coach at the University of British Columbia from 1934 to 1936,[3] Percy had nothing more to do with amateur track. He refused to serve on amateur athletic committees and join the ranks of the badgers, would not lend his name to fund-raising efforts and would not even make public appearances at track meets. The Los Angeles Olympic Games was in fact the last meet he ever attended. "It was his nature," says Jack Harrison, a friend of Percy's in the Thirties. "He never got involved." Percy instead developed a preference for golf, and of course there remained his old favourites, horseback riding and hunting. "He was an expert in whatever he did," says Harrison. "I used to go pheasant hunting with him out around Dewdney. I shot at a pheasant or duck and missed it. Percy would bring it down."[4]

Percy's business venture with George Irvine at Prospect Point, the barbecue stand, fared poorly in the Depression. In 1934 he was back in an office, this time selling insurance for the firm of Armstrong and Laing in the Pacific Building downtown, not far from the Capitol Theatre where Dot still worked as cashier. They were hard times financially for him and his family, and in the following year he petitioned the trustees of the Percy Williams Fund to receive his money now that he was finished with competition and his amateur standing no longer an issue. The request was denied. The wording of the trust deed, it was explained, did not allow it. It would take another nine years and a provincial Supreme Court decision to close out the fund and turn the badly depleted proceeds over to Percy, what was left after the default of municipal bond investments and payments to support other BC athletes. It would come to just over three thousand dollars.[5]

Percy would remain an insurance salesman for the rest of his life, moving on to the Riddell Insurance Corporation in the late 1940s, then Armstrong and Taylor in the 1960s, and ending up in a two-man operation with partner George Parks. To Parks it seemed an odd choice of profession for a man of such shyness, good salesmen generally being gregarious fellows. But perhaps it was not so strange. Being an insurance salesman allowed Percy to lead a quiet existence, dealing one-on-one with people, away from large groups, using a gentle touch rather than pushiness to win clients. "He worked hard for his customers," conceded Parks. "And he was conscientious. Very conscientious. He was almost a perfectionist, I would say."[6]

∾

While Percy was working hard to maintain a middle-class living for himself and his mother, his successor as World's Fastest Human, Eddie Tolan, was struggling just to survive. "I know that if I can win the two dash events," Eddie had written from LA to his own mother, a cleaning woman, "our worries will be lessened and some brightness will return to our lives." It didn't happen. There was no free car or trust fund waiting for Eddie when he returned home to Detroit with his two gold medals. And worst of all, there was no work.

Before the year was out Eddie had relinquished his amateur card to appear in vaudeville alongside Bill "Bojangles" Robinson, giving talks on some of his more memorable races. He also sold his story to the Hearst newspaper syndicate. It was his plan now to make as much money as he could with what was left of his fame, enough to support his mother, brothers and sisters and hopefully continue his education. He wanted to become a doctor. But his family was large and the vaudeville work didn't last and he was soon back walking the streets of Detroit, looking for a job. He finally landed a position as a filing clerk and hung on to it for dear life. "I don't have any complaints," he said. "I just don't think I'll ever run again. I'm sticking to my job."[7]

Eddie never did run again. He later became a school teacher. He died of a heart attack in 1967 at the age of fifty-eight.

∽

Percy's return to Vancouver from the 1932 Olympics coincided with the sentencing of Bob Granger on the charge of conducting an illegal lottery, to which he pled guilty. The sentence was to be passed in police court on August 8. Bob didn't show up. His attorney appeared without him, with the curious news that Bob had injured himself in a diving accident at English Bay the previous afternoon and was unable to appear. The case was set aside for one week, then another.[8]

Bob finally appeared on August 22 to be informed of his fate. His case came after the sentencing of an equally downcast fellow to six months in jail for stealing a pair of shoes. When it was Bob's turn, his lawyer was first allowed to speak briefly on his behalf. He pointed out that for the past four years Bob had given up any regular employment to devote himself to the training of young athletes, funding his efforts entirely out of his own pocket. He declared that Bob had been promised financial support from the publicly subscribed Percy Williams Fund but that the fund trustees subsequently refused to give him anything, leaving him to spend his own money on training athletes until he had nothing left. The lottery scheme grew out of the financial distress this had caused him. While clearly a mistake in hindsight, his motives had been sincere. He had simply wanted to raise funds to continue his work as a coach.

The plea struck a sympathetic note with the judge. He delivered a suspended sentence and Bob was released.[9]

Although Bob escaped jail and a fine, his reputation had taken a blow and he would never fully recover. The rest of his life would be characterized by steady decline. He continued to struggle on into the mid-1930s, looking for that next big star, the next Percy Williams. But he never found him.

In early 1936, however, he came very close. The previous fall a Vancouver high school track star named Howie McPhee entered the University of British Columbia as a freshman and was promptly elected captain of the track team, then being coached by Percy Williams in what would be his last season of track involvement. Within a matter of weeks Bob Granger had come onto the scene, talking Howie into accepting him as a private coach and touting him as Canada's hope for the 1936 Olympics. At the Canadian trials that year "Hustling Howie" earned a ticket to Berlin with record-setting wins in the hundred and two hundred metres and was hailed as "a second Williams." For Bob another exciting trip to Europe followed, in many ways a repeat of his first trip with Percy: a scramble to raise money for his ticket; missing his ship in Montreal; finding another route across the Atlantic while the rest of the team wondered where he was; and finally popping up in Berlin unexpectedly to take charge of his boy. But it wasn't to be. Howie never made it past the semifinals. Jesse Owens instead would emerge as the sprint sensation of the Berlin Olympics. Frank Wykoff, now a teacher and school administrator, was one of Jesse's teammates in the sprint relay, winning his third gold medal in three consecutive Olympics.[10]

That was the end of Bob's career as a coach. Later that year his father died, less than twelve months after the death of his mother. The double loss, hard to bear under any circumstances, hit Bob particularly hard, living at home with his parents as he did for most of his life.[11] A few months later an enigmatic note appeared in the UBC student newspaper. "Remember Bob Granger, coach of Percy Williams and our own Howie McPhee?" it read. "Four bits to a doughnut your wildest guess about his whereabouts would be wrong. Bob's speechifying down Arkansas way, yessuh, and as an Evangelist."[12] And that was all.

Throughout these years Bob and Percy never got together, never even saw each other. Their relationship, tense by 1929, had ended completely in 1932. They had a chance meeting at a Vancouver bus stop around 1942. They exchanged awkward pleasantries for a few moments, but outside of track had nothing really to say. They went their separate ways and never saw one another again.

Twenty-eight years later, in November 1970, Percy answered the phone and was startled to hear a voice say: "Percy Williams? This is Bob Granger." It was Bob's nephew, with the news that Bob had just died in a nursing home at Parksville on Vancouver Island.[13] Percy, although he hated any sort of public appearance, went to the funeral and had only good things to say about his old coach to the few journalists present. When asked how much credit he would accord Bob for his Olympic wins, he replied: "Offhand, I'd say a hundred per cent. I'd never have continued running after high school, but for him. I couldn't have cared less about running at the time."

"He was both a conditioner and a teacher," Percy went on, growing unusually talkative, "and that's a rare combination. His theories were his own and he went his own way. He didn't give a damn what people thought of him and he had no regard for money. . . . He was a bit of a maverick, I guess. He didn't want money or fame. He just wanted to be left alone to do the thing he liked best — coaching kids."[14]

For Percy there was real feeling here, and perhaps a touch of guilt at how things had ended. Looking back with the wisdom of age at Bob's guileless hopes and expectations and at his own youthful resentments, Percy would give his old mentor all the recognition he could. "Granger was everything," he said. "*Everything.*"[15]

It was at Bob's funeral that Percy learned the full story of how his coach had ended his days, living in poverty on a meagre senior's pension in the Vancouver Island town of Port Alberni, alone in a ratty apartment over a barber shop. He was occasionally seen walking his mongrel dog Old Yeller or sweeping out the parking lot of a nearby hotel for a meal, a white-haired, somewhat strange recluse. He had nothing left from his days as a trainer, no mementos, no letters, no papers, no clippings. Everything had been lost or discarded along the way. But the poetry remained in his soul. When a local reporter tracked him down in 1964, Bob spoke of his time with Percy as if it had been a wonderful dream. "I wanted to feast my eyes on the sight," he said, recalling that afternoon in Toronto when Percy set the world record in the hundred metres, running into a headwind. "I wanted the finish line to run before him to the ends of the earth. He was thistledown before the summer breeze."[16]

But it was as if the hand of fate had intervened, Bob concluded. It was as if it had been written: "This far and no farther."[17]

∞

In his spare time during the 1930s, when he wasn't playing golf or hunting or looking after the golden retrievers he enjoyed raising, Percy learned to fly. It was a skill that would lead him in an unexpected direction: military service in the Second World War. After signing up in August 1940, he served first as a ferry pilot with Canadian Airways. "I am too old to be a fighter pilot," he said at the time, "so I did the next best thing."[18] Later he became a civilian instructor, training Royal Canadian Air Force recruits in navigation. Being part of the war effort took Percy all across Canada, from BC to Ontario and to postings in Edmonton and Winnipeg in between. It was important work, "the most serious of any at the present time" he would say, and he thoroughly enjoyed it. Forced out of his shyness by the demands of the job, thrown together as part of a team of men who would become like brothers — Percy would look back on these years as the happiest of his adult life.[19]

The war took a heavy toll on the branch of Percy's family that had moved to Washington State. His uncle Lyon Rhodes, Dot's brother, a phone company lineman in Tacoma, lost three sons, two in the Battle of the Java Sea in 1942 and a third in 1945, shot down over Germany.[20] Percy himself survived without a scratch. It was in the months following the war that he very nearly was killed.

It happened on a car trip with George Irvine down to California, to the race track at Santa Anita where George was keeping his horses. They were travelling in George's car, Percy driving, when they ran headlong into an oncoming automobile. The crash put Percy in the hospital for several days, his jaw smashed and several teeth broken. George was thrown through the windshield but escaped with head lacerations. The occupants of the other vehicle, four Mexicans, were more badly injured, three reported as serious, the fourth listed in critical condition.[21]

After a period of convalescence in a California sanatorium, Percy returned to Vancouver and his life as an insurance salesman. Awaiting him there was now only his mother. Grandma Selina had passed away in 1935, and Grandpa Harry, "Old Sport," had followed her three years later. That left only Uncle Archie, who had never left home. He died in 1943, from blood poisoning caused by a small unexplained wound to his scalp,[22] leaving Dot alone and needing her Percy now more than ever. She sold the house on Twelfth Avenue later that year and moved into an apartment on Chilco Street, not far from Stanley Park and the Brockton Point track where Percy had first made a name for himself. Percy joined her there when he returned home in 1945. He was the head of the household, responsible for taking care of his mother. He would remain with her to the end, each the other's closest companion, sharing a very private existence.[23] Years later sportswriter Eric Whitehead would note that stepping into Percy and Dot's apartment was like going back in time. "You were back in the Thirties — the gramophone in the corner, the sheet music on the piano, the furniture."[24]

⁂

In 1950 Percy was named the greatest track and field athlete of the half-century in a Canadian Press poll. It was an easy decision. His double gold performance at Amsterdam remained a shining moment in the country's history. There was also the way he had come figuratively from nowhere, an unknown Vancouver schoolboy with a part-time janitor for a coach; the way he had conquered seemingly invincible American and European opposition, like David against a whole platoon of Goliaths; the way he had even looked the part of a David, so young and slender and boyish, in fact the lightest sprint champion in the history of the Olympics; the way his victory had swept up Canada in a wave of euphoria and launched Percy to stardom. It all amounted to a tremendous story, a glittering sports legend that even Percy himself at times felt was a dream. "Sometimes I look at the clippings," he said, "and ask myself: 'Was that really me or some other guy?'"[25]

Not everyone, however, had unblemished good feelings about Percy. In the amateur sports establishment, among the badgers that Percy now openly disdained, there was a general sense of disappointment in him for turning his back on the track. An athlete, particularly one of his stature, was expected to "give back" to the sport after he hung up his spikes, and Percy wasn't doing that.[26] Even getting him to attend a banquet was a struggle, usually requiring the enlistment of his father Fred, who seemed to be the only one who could get Percy to do something he didn't want to do.[27] If Fred pressed him, Percy would go. But he wouldn't like it. The whole notion of "giving back" to the sport was to him a lot of nonsense, betraying the underlying assumption of amateur athletics that was a source of his own hard feelings: that it was really all about the organization and the officials, with the athletes on hand just to serve them.

With the passage of years Percy had in fact become quite bitter. He now looked back on the adventure of getting to the 1927 trials as an "embarrassing" experience when he was forced to "beg and cadge" for money. He resented the hypocrisy he had to deal with as an amateur star, and how the trust fund collected for him after the Olympics had been taken over, and the way he felt ignored after retiring from competition, his suggestions for reforming Canadian track, the development of indoor meets and an American-style university athletic system, falling on deaf ears.

It all added up to a sizable chip on his shoulder, one that could make him cantankerous and snappish when approached by reporters or athletic officials or city fathers — anyone outside his small circle of friends. Solicit his presence at a public function and if he didn't decline outright he might put you off with "I will have to ask my mother" — right on into his sixties. Presume to ask him about his running career and you were likely to get a curt response.[28] And on those rare occasions when he was in a voluble mood, he was apt to say things that didn't sit well in some quarters. He wasn't at all like his aging rival Frank Wykoff, for example, who said in later life: "The thrills you feel watching the American flag being raised and hearing the playing of the Star Spangled Banner . . . well, that's worth it all."[29] When Percy opened up, it was with statements such as: "I always thought it was a lot of hogwash to say that you ran for your flag and your country. I was out there to beat the guy beside me." And: "They have turned the [Olympic] Games into a joke."[30]

Percy, in short, wasn't what the amateur sports establishment wanted him to be. The dissatisfaction would be made clear in 1954 when Vancouver was looking for a name for the stadium being built to replace the Brockton Point track. A movement was started to name the new facility after Percy, who with difficulty had been brought out to the sod turning. The idea was brushed aside and it was called Empire Stadium instead.

Perhaps it was just as well. As the years slipped by, Percy became increasingly reclusive and found any sort of publicity excruciatingly painful. When his old idea of an annual indoor track meet for Vancouver was finally realized in the 1960s and named the Percy Williams Invitational, meet organizers found Percy so ill at ease when coaxed to attend meetings or appear in public that they decided it would be best to rename the event the following year and allow him to slip back into his very private existence.[31]

∽

There is little doubt that Percy in his later years was unhappy. He had begun to drink heavily somewhere along the way. His insurance partner George Parks would call him a "closet drinker." And it became a

270 / I Just Ran

problem. When Percy formed an attachment to a woman in the 1960s, one of his few close relationships with a woman other than his mother, his drinking ultimately drove her away. Later it cost him his cherished membership at the Capilano Golf Club as well, one of his few remaining sources of social contact, when he started helping himself to the other members' liquor.[32] The embarrassment and loss drove him even deeper into shyness. When he stopped by one day at the home of Harry Warren to drop off a box of mementoes, Harry's wife found him extraordinarily skittish. "I never met a man who was so shy," she would later recall.[33]

In 1976 the Olympics came to Canada and the government invited all the country's gold medal winners to a special ceremony in Montreal. Percy, who had just been named Canada's greatest Olympian, was the only one to decline. "He wouldn't even do it for me," said Harold Wright, Percy's 1932 Olympic teammate and one of his few trusted friends. "He wouldn't do anything that would put him in the limelight."

"He was a real reluctant hero," Wright continued. "I suppose he was just a terribly shy, introverted and lonesome guy. The only way he would come out was if my wife would call and tell him we were picking him up at a certain time. Even then he'd be waiting in the street outside his front door. We'd never go in. He felt people had taken advantage of him during his athletic career and I suppose that was true. But he was a true friend and he didn't have many close friends because of his shyness. But he really was a nice person."[34]

Peter Webster, director of the BC Sports Hall of Fame and Museum in the late 1960s, agrees. Percy, he says, was not the least bit cantankerous or difficult when he felt safe among friends, and was in fact quite willing to drop by the Hall to give a talk to visiting school kids — so long as someone he trusted was there, someone like Harold Wright or Harry Warren or Webster himself. Webster fondly recalls occasions leading school tours through the Hall and stopping in front of the display case containing the things Percy had donated and telling his story. Then he would say: So what do you think it would be like to actually meet Percy Williams? Would you like that?

And the kids would all say: Sure. He's a hero. Of course we would.

Well, Peter would reply nonchalantly, directing their attention off to the side. There he is.

And he would take them over to the little gentleman standing unobtrusively in the corner, hands working nervously, smiling shyly.[35]

∽

In January 1980 Percy's two Olympic gold medals were stolen from the Hall of Fame, removed from the locked display case along with some other medals he had donated fourteen years before. It was suspected at the time, but never proved, that they were taken by a building janitor who left the job shortly thereafter. The theft devastated Hall staff. Percy feigned indifference to the loss but privately it hurt. In the months that followed he would occasionally telephone the photographer who had taken a picture of him at the Hall holding up the medals to request another copy. The call usually came late in the evening, Percy profusely apologetic for causing a disturbance. "I always liked that picture very much," he would say. "And it's the only reminder I have left." Percy's gold medals were never recovered. They were likely melted down for the gold, the skyrocketing price of the metal then being front-page news, spiking at $850 an ounce in the month of the theft. The thief would have been disappointed to discover that they were not gold at all, but rather silver covered with a few grams of gold gilding.[36]

Two weeks later, on January 23, Dot Williams, Percy's mother and lifelong companion, died at the age of ninety-two. Percy buried her cremated remains at Ocean View Burial Park, alongside Grandma Selina, Grandpa Harry, Uncle Archie and actor George B. Howard, the head of the Empress Theatre stock company who had died back in 1921. He did not erect a stone or mark her burial in any way.

Percy himself was just coming up to seventy-two, the age when his father Fred had died back in 1952. And he was now entirely alone. He had no living relations with whom he kept in contact, no close friends, no golf club at which he could while away his afternoons. He was also in pain from arthritis in his ankles and knees, eased only slightly by the daily ingestion of a dozen or more aspirins.[37] He made one reluctant public appearance later that year, in July, at an outdoor ceremony in Stanley Park to receive the Order of Canada, the highest civilian award the Dominion can bestow. After the Governor General had made his speech and placed the beribboned medal around Percy's neck, he gently urged the aging Olympian, paunchy now and slightly stooped, to say a few words. Percy declined. "It was a very great honour," was all he would say after.[38] He returned to his apartment and was not seen in public again.

∽

November 29, 1982, was a Monday, twelve years to the day that Percy had received the call informing him of the death of Bob Granger. He had a doctor's appointment at two o'clock that afternoon, one of the frequent checks he now needed since suffering a stroke five weeks before. He decided he wouldn't go. It was damp and chilly out, the start of another dreary Vancouver winter, and it was aggravating his arthritis. Between that and the stroke he could scarcely get about, scarcely take care of himself. He took another couple of aspirins and, against doctor's orders, had a drink. Then another. He sat quietly in his chair and let the morning slip by, listening to the traffic, the sounds of life passing by on the other side of his wall.

Two o'clock had come and gone when he finally got up and shuffled to the closet to retrieve one of his shotguns. It was a twelve-gauge, given to him back in 1928 in recognition of his Olympic achievements, a favourite weapon in happier times when he had still been able to go hunting. That was long past now. It was hard just to pick the dusty thing up, hard to get the breech open, hard to fumble in a shell.

He hobbled into the bathroom and stepped into the tub and lowered himself onto the cold white enamel.

He had left written instructions. That was all that was needed. No explanations. No excuses. "Thou shalt not alibi." That was rule number two.

He pressed the barrel against his forehead and, using his toe, pulled the trigger.[39]

༝ঌ

At the end of the week when Percy died, as the news filtered out that he had taken his own life, a Member of Parliament rose in the House of Commons and moved that a stamp be issued commemorating the sprinter. The motion was greeted with cries of "Hear, hear!" but failed to get the necessary unanimous approval, a lethargic "No" tossed out from the back benches swatting it down. It was nothing personal against Percy, just how the parliamentary game was played. Every motion brought forward that day by one side of the House was similarly quashed by the other.[40]

It would take another fourteen years but Percy would get that stamp bearing his image. It would be worth forty-five cents. A life-size statue of him in his starting crouch would be placed in front of BC Place Stadium in Vancouver, and a Toronto elementary school named in his honour, Percy Williams Junior Public, the spikes he wore setting the hundred-metre world record on proud display in the lobby. They were stolen in 2005 but fortunately recovered.[41]

Today the name of Percy Williams, once synonymous with speed, is scarcely remembered, even in his hometown of Vancouver. His cremated remains lie in the Masonic Cemetery in Burnaby, BC, up against the fence, overlooked by a telephone pole, cars passing by just a few feet away. According to his wishes he was buried in the same grave as his father, in front of the stone inscribed "Dad" that he had erected for Fred in 1952. Percy's own marker is characteristically modest. "Percy A. Williams, 1928 Olympic Champion, 1908–1982" is all it says. It is not much bigger than the book that you now hold in your hands, set flush to the ground so it will not get in the way when the groundskeeper passes by with his mower.[42]

Acknowledgements

I owe a particular debt of gratitude to Jason Beck, curator of the BC Sports Hall of Fame and Museum, who made me welcome at the Hall for the week I spent there sifting through the Percy Williams Collection and helped me better understand everything from track shoe construction in the 1920s to the arcane use of tension grip blocks. Jason also helped me subsequently find a publisher after the manuscript for *I Just Ran* was shopped around without success by my agent and sat in a drawer for two years.

Peter Webster, the BCSHFM's former executive director, was another wonderful source of information, particularly for his memories of Percy's visits to the Hall in the 1960s and '70s. Thanks are due as well to the staff of the Vancouver Public Library, in particular Andrew Martin, librarian in Special Collections; the staff of the Vancouver City Archives (special thanks to archivist Megan Schlase); athletics historian Fred Hume at the University of British Columbia; Vancouver historian and writer Len Corben; the staff at Vancouver's Masonic Cemetery and Ocean View Burial Park for information on the graves of Percy and his family; and Brenda Waksel, Library Technician and Archivist at St. Michael's University School in Victoria, for information on the summer Percy spent there when he was twelve years old, and for locating the cartoon he drew for the school paper of the lonely boy sitting on the gate.

An early fortuitous encounter I had when researching this book was with Victor Warren, the son of Harry Warren, a former Olympic teammate and lifelong friend of Percy's, whom I tracked down at his home in Fiji. Victor shared his memories and thoughts when I interviewed him over the phone, and he and his sister Charlotte Warren were most generous with their time when I later visited them in Vancouver and we went through Harry's old scrapbooks together. Charlotte also provided me with copies of Bob Granger's letters, written on those little sheets of paper Bob favoured. It was like being handed nuggets of gold. Many thanks, Charlotte.

Thanks are due as well to Glen Pilling and Arta Johnson, the son and daughter of Percy's Amsterdam roommate Doral Pilling; Lee Wright, the son of Harold Wright, Percy's 1932 Olympic teammate and longtime friend; Girija Emery, the daughter of Phil Edwards; Grant D. Fairly, great-nephew of Johnny Fitzpatrick; Murray Fitzpatrick, son of Johnny Fitzpatrick; Peter Dow Granger, great-nephew of Bob Granger, and also Steve Granger, another of Bob's great-nephews; James Worrall, hurdler and flag bearer with the Canadian Olympic team at the 1936 Berlin Games and later president of the Canadian Olympic Association (thanks also to James' wife, Birgitte); Professor Bruce Kidd of the University of Toronto's Faculty of Physical Education and Health; Tanya Magnus, curator at Canada's Sports Hall of Fame in Toronto; Jane Irwin of the Burlington Historical Society, Burlington, Ontario; Burlington historian Emerson Lavender and his wife Madeline; Rebecca Oliphant, Cultural Heritage Special Events Coordinator, Community Services Department, Culture Division, City of Hamilton; and Collections Manager Gloria Romaniuk and Executive Director Rick Brownlee at the Manitoba Sports Hall of Fame for information on Jimmy

Ball; Doug Clement, for his insights into sprinting in Percy's day; Greg Maychak, Supervisor for Sport Development for the City of Hamilton, for information on Bobby Robinson; Megan Cooney at the Bentley Historical Library, University of Michigan, for information on George "Buck" Hester; Gary Cox, University Archives, University of Missouri-Columbia, for a copy of an interview with Jackson Scholz; Earl Zukerman, communications officer with the Department of Athletics at McGill University, and Dennis Barrett, head coach of the McGill track and field team, for information on Phil Edwards; documentary filmmaker Bob Duncan, writer and co-executive producer of *Percy Williams: Running Out of Time*; John Aikman, manager of the Hamilton-Wentworth District School Board's Educational Archives and Heritage Centre, for photos of "Cap" Cornelius; Library and Archives Canada, especially to Gregg J. McCooeye in the Personnel Records Services Branch for documents on Percy's wartime service; and the staff at Queen's University's Stauffer Library, home base for my research.

Finally, I would like to remember Jack Harrison, Vancouver's own "Flying Cop," the only person still surviving when I was doing research for this book who had actually run with Percy Williams and trained with Bob Granger. I spoke with Jack and his wife Marilyn a few months before Jack passed away on September 19, 2008, at the age of ninety-eight. Jack wasn't too impressed when I mentioned there had been another "Flying Cop" back in Percy's day, namely Bowery policeman Bob McAllister. "There was only one Flying Cop," Jack replied. "And that was me."

Notes

ABBREVIATIONS

PWC: Percy Williams Collection
(BC Sports Hall of Fame & Museum, Vancouver)

BE: Brantford Expositor   *NYT: New York Times*
EJ: Edmonton Journal   *TG: Toronto Globe*
GM: Globe and Mail   *TS: Toronto Star*
HS: Hamilton Spectator   *TT: Toronto Telegram*
LAE: Los Angeles Examiner   *VDC: Victoria Daily Colonist*
LAT: Los Angeles Times   *VMS: Vancouver Morning Star*
LFP: London Free Press   *VP: Vancouver Province*
MS: Montreal Star   *VS: Vancouver Sun*
MFP: Manitoba Free Press   *WFP: Winnipeg Free Press*
MG: Manchester Guardian

PROLOGUE

1 *HS*, August 28, 1928, 16; *Maclean's*, October 15, 1928, 60.

CHAPTER 1

1 Photos of Percy as a child, PWC, Photographs, Box 1, 7103.1.2 to 7103.1.23 and 7103.3.33; *VMS*, July 31, 1928, 1–5.

2 *VMS*, July 31, 1928, 1–5; *VS*, April 4, 1938; *Henderson's British Columbia Gazetteer and Directory*, 1901–1904; *Henderson's City of Vancouver Directory*, 1905–1910; Canadian census records, 1901 and 1911; St. John's, Newfoundland baptismal records and British Columbia voter registration records, 1898 (rootsweb.ancestry.com). Starting in 1905 and continuing to his retirement around 1930, Harry Rhodes is listed in Vancouver directories as working at BC Electric variously as a brush hand, painter, car washer, car cleaner and car inspector. His death certificate, Vancouver Public Library, microfilm B13162, registration number 1938-09-541928, lists his occupation as car painter.

3 PWC, Biographical File; Poem signed "Dot Rhodes," dated May 31, 1904, PWC, Written Documents, Box 2.

4 English census records, 1881; Canadian census records, 1901 and 1911; *Henderson's City of Vancouver Directory*, 1905–1910; Fred and Charlotte's marriage certificate, Vancouver Public Library, microfilm B11373, registration no. 1904-09-050829; Postcard from Harry Rhodes Jr. to Lyon Rhodes, December 20, 1909, PWC, Written Documents, Box 2: "Fred Williams the Jock is here and road [sp.] the race to day, but came in last. . . ."

5 *VP*, May 18, 1908, 6 and May 19, 1908, 10.

6 Postcards from Fred Williams to Charlotte Williams, April 26, 1907 and June 1907, PWC, Written Documents, Box 3, black photo album.

7 A description of operations at BC Electric's streetcar repair and maintenance barns where Percy's father and grandfather worked appears in "Behind the Scenes with the B.C. Electric Mechanics," *B.C. Electric Employees' Magazine*, June 1924, 3–6.

8 Correspondence between the author and Brenda Waksel, Library Technician/Archivist at St. Michael's University School, Victoria, August 2008; *School Ties* (St. Michael's University School magazine), Fall 2003, 16; postcard from Percy to Charlotte Williams, April 13, 1920, PWC, Written Documents, Box 2, 985:9:601.

9 *VS*, October 3, 1920, 21, March 18, 1921, 7, March 19, 1921, 7, and March. 23, 1921, 3; *Vancouver Province Magazine Section*, February 26, 1949, 8; *Vancouver Sunday Sun, About BC Feature Magazine*, April 23, 1955, 5; Percy's cartoon portrait of George B. Howard, copied from the *Vancouver Sun* when Percy was twelve, PWC, Written Documents, Box 3. Just what the relationship was between Howard and Percy's mother is not clear. It seems likely, however, that they were close, for he is buried beside her in Ocean View Burial Park in Burnaby, BC, and his name is inscribed on the Rhodes' family stone, above those of Charlotte's grandparents and her brother Archie. Charlotte herself is not named. When she died in 1980, Percy buried her cremated remains in the same grave as Archie — and directly beside George. He did not erect a marker.

10 Divorces were rare in Canada at this time, even in BC, which led the country. In 1925 a total of 551 were granted in the entire country, with BC the leading province with 150, followed by Ontario with 122. (*VS*, May 22, 1926, 9.) It is interesting to note that Charlotte is listed repeatedly as a widow in Vancouver city directories throughout the 1930s and 1940s, even though Fred did not die until 1952.

11 *VS*, December 4, 1982, E3.

12 *Black and Red* (University School magazine), June 1920, 8–12. Percy is also listed as placing second in the obstacle race for boys under fourteen.

13 High school entrance exam results in *VS*, July 28, 1923; *VP*, April 14, 1929, 3.

14 *VP*, December 29, 1962, 12.

15 *GM*, July 29, 1978, 41.

16 "Bounding" as a training technique was first employed by sprint pioneer Arthur Duffy of Boston around 1900, and is still central to sprint training today. Jason Beck, curator of the BC Sports Hall of Fame and Museum, was a valuable source of information on the finer points of construction of track shoes worn by sprinters in Percy's day — and on the pain athlete's had to endure wearing them. The Hall has a pair of Percy's spikes in its collection.

17 *VS*, May 23, 1925, 11; *The Matric Annual, 1925* (King Edward High School yearbook), 74 and 79.

18 Percy's progress through high school can be tracked by the promotion lists published in the *Vancouver Sun* each year in late June. He did well in every year, gaining "honor promotion" along with typically the top third of his class, except in the tenth grade, when he fell into the bottom third and was accorded a "partial," necessitating re-examination in the summer in one or more subjects before he could pass to the next grade.

19 Merv Ferguson, "Notes on Percy Williams," undated typescript manuscript, February 1988, PWC, Written Documents, Box 1. Merv was a King Edward classmate of Percy's.

20 *VP*, May 22, 1926, 26; *VS*, May 22, 1926, 10; *The Matric Annual, 1926*, 74–76.

CHAPTER 2

1 The athletic attainments Bob Granger claimed are enumerated in *The Ubyssey*, January 25, 1927, 4. While many of the stories he told were clearly exaggerated, it wasn't all hot air. His prowess as a swimmer in particular can be verified in old newspaper records. See for example "R. Granger is Winner of Bay-to-Beach Swim," *VS*, July 9, 1917, 8; "Swimming Races Fast; Polo Match Ends Tie," *VS*, July 13, 1917, 6; and "200-Yard Handicap is Won by Granger," *VS*, July 21, 1917, 8.

2 Canadian census records, 1901 and 1911; *Henderson's City of Vancouver Directory*, 1905–1910; *Henderson's Greater Vancouver Directory*, 1911–1922; *Wrigley's British Columbia Directory*, 1923, 1926–1933. Bob is listed in various clerking

positions in Vancouver directories up to 1921. After that no employment information is given — except in 1928, when he is listed as "trainer."

3 In a letter written to Percy following the Amsterdam Games, for example, Bobby Gaul, another of Bob Granger's protégés, sounds almost motherly in his concern for Bob's well-being, urging Percy not to let him pass up any job offers "or I will never forgive you." Bobby Gaul to Percy Williams, August 22, 1928, PWC, Written Documents, Box 1, 985:9:50d.

4 VS, May 22, 1926, 10 and 11.

5 Bob Granger, "The Human Flash. The Story of Percy Williams, Breaker of Speed Records," The American Magazine, November 1930, 63.

6 Bob Granger, "Climbing Olympus: The Inside Story of Percy Williams' Rise to Fame," VS, July 13, 1929, Sunday features section, 1.

7 Granger, "Human Flash," 63.

8 Victor Warren interview with the author, January 11, 2008.

9 The Austrian coach Franz Stampfl, who trained Roger Bannister during his campaign to break the four-minute mile, was one of the first to elucidate on what it actually meant physiologically to "relax" while running in Franz Stampfl on Running: Sprint, Middle Distance, and Distance Events (London: Herbert Jenkins, 1955), 26–27.

10 Granger, "Human Flash," 63. Bob would later say that "Williams runs best when he is completely relaxed and not exerting any forced effort to reach the tape." Unidentified newspaper clipping, May 28, 1930, PWC, large scrapbook.

11 Ibid.; VS, June 26, 1953, 29.

12 Charlie Paddock presents a good explanation of these five stages in Track and Field, 15–27.

13 Ibid., 27–28; VS, July 26, 1929, 19. Dean Cromwell, head track coach at the University of Southern California from 1908 to 1948 and one of the premier track experts in North America, expands of this notion on breathing in Championship Technique in Track and Field (New York: Whittlesey House, 1949), 54–55.

14 According to Paddock, he first got the idea for his trademark finishing move while competing in the California state championships in 1916. He was just breasting the tape to win his race when, out the corner of his eye, he noticed one of the other runners, trailing in fourth or fifth, "suddenly make a frantic leap into the air, as some wild animal might instinctively have done, and land in second place." It set Charlie to thinking. How could he transform that kid's haphazard leap into something controlled and "scientific"? The result was his famous jump finish (Track and Field, 24–27.). For a selection of opinions from the 1920s on Paddock's finishing jump, see Maxwell Stiles, "Paddock's Famous Leap," Back Track.

15 VS, July 20, 1929, 10.

16 VS, July 13, 1929, Sunday features section, 1–3.

17 *VS*, July 13, 1917, 6 ; July 20, 1917, 8.
18 *VS*, June 8, 1926, 10; July 15, 1929, 20.
19 *VS*, June 15, 1926, 10; June 19, 1926, 10.
20 *VS*, July 15, 1929, 20.
21 Ibid.; Granger, "Human Flash," 63; *VS*, June 24, 1926, 13.
22 *VDC*, April 9, 1964, 10; *VP*, April 16, 1964, 11.
23 *VS*, December 3, 1970, 30.
24 Ray Gardner, "How Percy Williams Swept the Olympic Sprints," *Maclean's*, November 24, 1956, 40.
25 Charles Paddock, *The Fastest Human* (New York: Thomas Nelson & Sons, 1932), 10–11.
26 *VS*, August 14, 1926, 11.
27 *VS*, July 17, 1929, 10.
28 Quoted in ibid.
29 *VS*, August 14, 1926, 11.
30 Granger, "Human Flash," 167.
31 *VS*, December 3, 1970, 30.
32 Bob Granger to Harry Warren, November 30, 1926, Charlotte Warren collection.
33 Granger, "Human Flash," 167; *VS*, July 16, 1929, 7 and July 17, 1929, 10.

CHAPTER 3

1 *VMS*, July 31, 1928, 1 and 5; Percy's letters written in Lytton, BC to Charlotte Williams, August 22, 1926, April 14, 1927 and September 19, 1927, PWC, Written Documents, Box 1, 985:9:50r, 985:9:50mmmm and 985:9:50vvvv; Photograph of Percy holding skull, PWC, Photographs, Box 1, 7103.8.89.
2 The entry for Percy in *The Matric Annual, 1927* reads: "Percy Williams — Motocrat Williams. Quick getaway; speed, power; dash — Gas. Prefect, and our star track and field man."
3 Bill and Christine McNulty, *Peerless Percy: The Story of Canada's Greatest Sprinting Legend, Percy Williams* (Vancouver: Bill and Christine McNulty, 1998), 6 and 11.
4 Some of the slang terms Percy uses in his 1929 diary. "And how!" seems to have been his particular favourite. His use of the term "crushed apples" is explained in *VP*, October 5, 1982, A5.
5 *The Ubyssey*, January 25, 1927, 4.
6 *The Ubyssey*, March 15, 1927, 2.
7 *VP*, May 6, 1927, 15.
8 *The Ubyssey*, February 1, 1927, 2.
9 *VS*, July 18, 1929, 10.
10 *VP*, May 6, 1927, 15, May 17, 1927, 22 and May 18, 1927, 22; *VS*, May 17, 1927, 10.
11 *VP*, May 25, 1927, 18–19; *VS*, May 25, 1927, 12–13 and July 19, 1929, 10.
12 *VP*, May 1, 1927, 35. The times required were 10 1/5 seconds for the century or

11 seconds for the 100 metres, and 22 4/5 seconds for the furlong or 22 3/5 seconds for the 200 metres. Metre distances, almost never run in North America at this time, were included because they were the standard at the Olympics.

13 VS, July 25, 1927, 1 and 14.
14 VP, April 30, 1927, 10; TG, August 23, 1927, 8; VP, September 25, 1927, 31.
15 VP, July 23, 1927.
16 VP, July 24, 1927, 30; VS, July 25, 1927, 11.
17 VS, August 12, 1927, 12.
18 VP, July 7, 1927, 14; LAT, July 7, 1927, B1.
19 Cromwell, Championship Technique, 36; LAE, April 23, 1921; Paddock, Fastest Human, 121–122.
20 Jackson Scholz interview from the 1980s, interviewer unknown, audio recording in the University of Missouri archives, collection number C:0/46/41.
21 VS, July 20, 1929, 10; VP, August 10, 1927, 16–17.
22 VS, July 20, 1929, 10; VP, August 14, 1927, 24; unidentified newspaper clipping, PWC, large scrapbook.
23 Bob Granger to Cyril Price, February 18, 1930, Charlotte Warren collection.

CHAPTER 4

1 H. H. Roxborough, "Truth is Stranger!" National Home Monthly, January 1933, 10–11; Henry Roxborough, Canada at the Olympics (Toronto: Ryerson Press, 1963), 73.
2 VS, July 22, 1927, 7.
3 Percy to Charlotte Williams, no date (August 19, 1927), PWC, Written Documents, Box 1, 985:9:50q.
4 WFP, July 3, 1945, 12.
5 George Hester necrology file in the Bentley Historical Library archives, University of Michigan; additional information from the Bentley Library's "History of Michigan in the Olympics" webpage, www.bentley.umich.edu/athdept/olymp2/ol1928.htm; "Michigan High School Athletes of the Year," www.michtrack.org/AOY.htm.
6 Alexander J. Young, "Leigh Miller, Nova Scotia Speed Demon, NASSH Proceedings, 1980, 10.
7 NYT, May 22, 1927, sports section, 4; VP, June 12, 1927, 23.
8 VS, July 22, 1929, 7.
9 VP, August 21, 1927, 23; VS, August 27, 1927, 10.
10 VS, July 21, 1978, C1.
11 HS, August 22, 1927, 16; TT, August 22, 1927; TG, August 22, 1927, 8.
12 HS, August 22, 1927, 16.
13 VP, August 20, 1927, 1 and August 21, 1927, 23; TS, August 22, 1927, 8; TG, August 22, 1927, 8; TT, August 22, 1927; HS, August 22, 1927, 16–17; VS, August 22, 1927, 11; MFP, August 22, 1927, 1 and 6; VS, July 22, 1929, 7;

National Open Track and Field Championships of the AAU of Canada, University of Toronto Stadium, Toronto, Saturday, August 20, 1927 (Percy's copy of the meet program), PWC, Written Documents, Box 2.
14 Granger, "Human Flash," 167; *VS*, July 22, 1929, 7.
15 *HS*, August 22, 1927, 16; *TS*, August 23, 1927, 10.

CHAPTER 5

1 Bob Granger to Cyril Price, Febrary 18, 1930, Charlotte Warren collection.
2 Bruce Kidd, *The Struggle for Canadian Sport* (Toronto: University of Toronto Press, 1996), 69.
3 *VP*, September 1, 1927, 17. Percy was also courted by the University of Oregon, as revealed in a series of letters from G. Richard Eckman to Charlotte Williams and to Percy, May to September 1928, PWC, Written Documents, Box 1.
4 *VP*, September 25, 1927, 31; Merv Ferguson, "Notes on Percy Williams," undated typescript manuscript, February 1988, PWC, Written Documents, Box 1; advertisement for the High School of Commerce, *The Matric Annual, 1927*, 34.
5 *VS*, July 22, 1929, 7 and July 23, 1929, 2; McNulty, 13.
6 *VS*, May 4, 1928, 26 and May 6, 1928, 27; *VP*, May 13, 1928, 33; Telegram from Percy to Charlotte Williams, May 5, 1928, PWC, Written Documents, Box 2; *Ninth Annual Relay Carnival, University of Washington Stadium, May 5th, 1928* (Percy's copy of the meet program), PWC, Written Documents, Box 2.
7 *TS*, September 4, 1928, 5.
8 *VS*, July 23, 1929, 2.
9 *VS*, May 25, 1928, 17.
10 *VP*, June 8, 1928, 20 and 28. Elson is listed in King Edward's *Matric Annual, 1924*, as a "crack miler" and secretary-treasurer of the track and field club.
11 *VP*, August 27, 1927, 7.
12 *VP*, May 8, 1928, 14 and May 22, 1928, 28.
13 *VS*, undated clipping (late May or early June 1928) PWC, large scrapbook.
14 For the 100-metre dash it was 10 4/5 seconds, just a fifth off the Olympic record set by Don Lippincott in a preliminary heat at the 1912 Olympics and tied by Harold Abrahams in the final at the Paris Games in 1924. For the 200 metres it was 22 1/5 seconds, three-fifths off Archie Hahn's longstanding Olympic mark. *VP*, November 20, 1927, 33.
15 *VP*, June 8, 1928, 20 and 22.
16 *VP*, June 5, 1928, 14 and June 10, 1928, 16.
17 *VS*, August 1, 1928, 16. An advertisement for George Spalding Sporting Goods in King Edward High School's *Matric Annual* for 1929 lists two models of track shoe, "a good shoe" for $4.50 and "The Kind that Percy Wore 'Foster's' at $7.50."
18 *VP*, May 20, 1928, 2nd section, 7; Alex Matches, *Vancouver's Bravest: 120 Years of Firefighting History* (Surrey, BC: Hancock House, 2007), 78 and 84.

19 *VS*, August 3, 1929, 25; *VP*, June 15, 1928, 22.

20 Percy to Charlotte Williams, on CPR letterhead, Saturday (June 16, 1928) and Monday (June 18, 1928), PWC, Written Documents, Box 2, 985:9:47h and Box 1, 985:9:50wwwww; Matches, *Vancouver's Bravest*, 78.

21 Gardner, 32 and 42. Gardner evidently had access to Percy's 1928 diary in writing his *Maclean's* article, and quotes liberally from it. Everything subsequently written on Percy that includes quotes from this diary appears to use Gardner's piece as its source. The original diary has disappeared.

CHAPTER 6

1 H. H. Roxborough," Hamilton Sets the Pace," *Maclean's*, September 1, 1928, 17 and 50–52. For a sample of Hamiltonian crowing and Torontonian comebacks, see *TS*, August 17, 1927, 8.

2 Percy to Charlotte Williams, Wednesday (June 20, 1928), PWC, Written Documents, Box 1, 985:9:50w.

3 *VS*, July 24, 1929, 11.

4 Ibid.

5 Roxborough, *Canada at the Olympics*, 73; *TS*, July 3, 1928, 10.

6 *VP*, June 28, 1928, 14.

7 Kidd, 69.

8 *HS*, July 3, 1928, 18 and 19.

9 *VS*, July 24, 1929, 11.

10 Doug Clement, interview with the author, July 31, 2008. Percy's tension grip blocks can be seen in his hands in photographs taken immediately following the Olympic trials 100-metre final. Buck Hester also seems to have had a pair. Percy's are now on display at the BC Sports Hall of Fame and Museum.

11 *VP*, July 1, 1928, 1–2.

12 *VP*, July 1, 1928, 1–2; *HS*, July 3, 1928, 16 and 18; *TS*, July 3, 1928, 10; *TT*, July 3, 1928, 28.

13 Percy's copy of the program for the *Canadian Olympic Trials, June 30, July 2, 1928, The Stadium, Hamilton, Ont.*, PWC, Written Documents, Box 3, 985:9:42e.

14 *TT*, July 3, 1928, 28.

15 *HS*, July 3, 1928, 18; Percy Williams diary, June 30, 1928, quoted in Gardner, 42: "Well, the day of miracles is not passed. I can't quite understand yet but they say winning the 100 metres puts me on the boat for Amsterdam."

16 Percy to Charlotte Williams, 1st (July 1, 1928), PWC, Written Documents, Box 2, 985:9:47i. Percy had already sent a cable to Dot immediately after the race informing her of his victory: "Won hundred metres. New Canadian record. Inform the boys." PWC, large scrapbook.

17 Percy made no secret of his preference for the hundred. Just the day before the trials, he had stated to reporter Robert Elson that he expected "to make his

best showing in the 100 metres, as he finds the 200 metres . . . more difficult."
VP, June 29, 1928, 28.

18 *TS*, July 3, 1928, 10

19 *TS*, July 11, 1928, 10.

20 *HS*, July 3, 1928, 16 and 18.

21 *TT*, July 3, 1928, 28.

22 *VP*, July 3 1928, 15.

23 *VS*, July 25, 1929, 9.

24 Percy to Charlotte Williams, Sunday (July 8, 1928), PWC, Written Documents, Box 1, 985:9:50y.

25 Percy to Charlotte Williams, Wednesday, 2nd (July 2, 1928), PWC, Written Documents, Box 1, 985:9:50u. "[H]ave him up for a Sunday dinner," Percy wrote to his mother of Archie. "He enjoys eating more than anything else."

26 *HS*, July 4, 1928, 19.

27 Roxborough, "Hamilton Sets the Pace," 17 and 50–51.

28 Bob Granger to Charlotte Williams, no date (early September 1928), PWC, Written Documents, Box 1, 985:9:50c.

29 *Hamilton Herald*, November 8, 1919 and *Hamilton Spectator*, July 30, 1923, quoted in Brian Henley, *Henley's People: Fascinating People from Hamilton's Past* (Burlington, Ont.: North Shore Publishing, 1996), 180. Ironically, for all his interest in measurements, Cap himself was not a particularly robust specimen. According to his WWI enlistment papers, he was, at age 31, a shade under six feet tall and had a chest measurement of 33 inches, 35 inches expanded.

30 Percy's copy of the program for the *Canadian Olympic Trials, June 30, July 2, 1928, The Stadium, Hamilton, Ont.*, PWC, Written Documents, Box 3, 985:9:42e. Although written in the third person, the comments are in Percy's own hand. He also commented on some of his fellow athletes. Beside Johnny Fitzpatrick's photo he has written: "Son of a minister but he can run like the devil — a nice fellow 1 year older than Percy." George Hester: "Hester of Michigan looks just like wee Bobbie [Gaul] but he runs like a whippet — just Bobbie's size. 100 yds. 9 4/5 seconds but not fast enough for the Gazelle. Stayed with his wife in same house with Percy." Ralph Adams: "One of Cap Cornelius's pets but a good runner and a nice fellow." Marathon runner Harold Webster: "This old bird is better than he looks even if he does look like Cap." And German middle-distance runner Otto Peltzer: "This fellow never takes a bath so he wouldn't be good company for young Bob's Gyp."

31 *HS*, July 6, 1928, 26 and July 10, 1928, 16; Percy to Charlotte Williams, Tuesday (July 10, 1928), PWC, Written Documents, Box 1, 985:9:50oooo.

32 Percy's copy of the program for the *Canadian Olympic Trials, June 30, July 2, 1928, The Stadium, Hamilton, Ont.*, PWC, Written Documents, Box 3, 985:9:42e; Lou Marsh articles and columns in *TS*, July 9, 1928, 9; July 11, 1928, 9; and July 12, 1928, 14; Girija Emery interview with the author, January 23, 2008.

33 *TS*, July 11, 1928, 9; *VS*, August 17, 1928, 8.
34 Percy to Charlotte Williams, Tuesday (July 10, 1928), PWC, Written Documents, Box 1, 985:9:50oooo.
35 *VS*, July 26, 1929, 7; unidentified newspaper clipping circa 1936, PWC, large scrapbook.

CHAPTER 7

1 *LAT*, April 9, 1927, April 24, 1927, A1 and May 9, 1927, 11.
2 *LAT*, June 2, 1928, 11.
3 Neil Duncanson, *The Fastest Men on Earth: The 100m Olympic Champions* (London: Willow Books, 1988), 40–42. *The Olympic Hero* was later re-released as *The All American*.
4 Maxwell Stiles, "A Calf With Two Heads," *Back Track*.
5 Paddock, *Fastest Human*, 26–27 and 95–96.
6 *LAT*, June 17, 1928, 1–2.
7 *LAE*, June 1928, on-line at frankwykoff.com/plumber.htm.
8 *NYT*, July 6, 1928, 19.
9 *NYT*, July 30, 1928, 12.
10 Robert McAllister, *The Kind of Guy I Am* (New York: McGraw-Hill Book Company, 1957), passim; *NYT*, April 11, 1923, 23; June 7, 1923, 20; August 21, 1924, 2; August 26, 1924, 17; November 14, 1924, 21; November 20, 1924, 1; June 7, 1927, 8 and October 25, 1962, 39.
11 Bob Granger wrote of overhearing McAllister in Amsterdam frequent speak of himself as a "Man of Destiny." *VS*, July 29, 1929, 14.
12 Arthur Duffy, "Wykoff as Good as Our Greatest," unidentified newspaper clipping, July 8, 1928, on-line at frank-wykoff.com/headlines.htm
13 Paddock was sure he had finished second and qualified, and that result was in fact announced to the crowd before being overturned. Paddock, *Fastest Human*, 234–235.
14 *LAT*, July 7, 1928, 7–8.
15 *LAT*, July 8, 1928, 1–2 and July 15, 1928, 2; *NYT*, July 8, 1928, 1 and sports section, 1; Paddock, *Fastest Human*, 235–238.
16 Duncanson, 39–40; Paddock, *Fastest Human*, 164.
17 *VP*, July 10, 1928, 17. Hamilton sports columnist Walter McMullen wrote that the claim that Paddock appeared in *The Olympic Hero* for free "naturally causes one to laugh." *HS*, July 13, 1928, 22.
18 "Dishonorable Trick," *Time*, June 11, 1928; John R. Tunis, "The Olympic Games," *Harper's Monthly Magazine*, August 1928, 316–317. Some Americans felt that Abrahams had jumped the gun in his gold-medal winning race in 1924 and got away with it because the starter was a fellow Englishman. *MS*, September 3, 1928, 12.

19 Early reports of which athletes had been chosen to represent the US at Amsterdam (for example in *HS*, July 9, 1928, 16) in fact listed Locke in place of Paddock in the 200 metres.

20 *LAT*, July 9, 1928, 11.

21 *NYT*, July 27, 1928, 17.

22 "Rah, Rah, Ray, U.S.A.," unidentified Scottish newspaper clipping, July 1928, on-line at http://frankwykoff.com/hussey.htm; *VP*, July 13, 1928, 26. Two other stowaways, students rather than athletes, were discovered just before the *Roosevelt* left New York harbour. General MacArthur let them stay aboard, but promptly put them to work, scrapping paint. William Manchester, *American Caesar: Douglas MacArthur, 1880–1964* (Boston: Little, Brown, 1978), 140.

23 Jackson Scholz interview by unknown interviewer, circa 1980s, audio recording, University of Missouri Library archives, collection number C:0/46/41; Anne Vrana O'Brien interview by George Hodak, October 1987, LA84 Foundation digital archive, Olympian Oral Histories, www.la84foundation.org/6oic/OralHitory/OHVranaOBrien.pdf.

24 *NYT*, July 11, 1928, sports section, 18; *HS*, July 13, 1928, 23.

25 Charley Paddock, "No Son of Mine," *Collier's*, August 1929, on-line at frankwykoff.com.

26 Ernest "Nick" Carter interview by George A. Hodak, June 1987, Santa Barbara, California, LA84 Foundation digital archive, Olympian Oral Histories, www.la84foundation.org/6oic/OralHistory/OHCarter.pdf.

27 Louis S. Nixdorff, Olympic diary, 1928, Archives Center, National Museum of American History, Washington, D.C., on-line at www.americanhistory.si.edu/achives/d9443f.htm.

CHAPTER 8

1 Percy to Charlotte Williams, July 18, 1928, PWC, Written Documents, Box 2, 985:9:47k. This letter was subsequently published in *VS*, August 1, 1928, 3.

2 Doral Pilling interview with Charles Ursenbach, Calgary, 1975; Percy to Charlotte Williams, PWC, Written Documents, Box 1, 985:9:50s; *VP*, July 20, 1928, 15.

3 *HS*, July 19, 1928, 20.

4 *VP*, July 21, 1928, 7; *TT*, August 3, 1928, 19 and August 4, 1928, 19. A photo Percy took looking out his hotel window and into the alley is in the PWC, Photographs, Box 1, 7103.4.1.

5 Ibid.

6 Harold M. Abrahams, ed., *Official Report of the IXth Olympiad, Amsterdam 1928* (London: British Olympic Association, [1928]), 79 and 98.

7 *TS*, July 23, 1928, 2. Percy's wooden shoes are on display in the BC Sports Hall of Fame and Museum; Jimmy Ball's, signed by Percy and others, are in the Manitoba Sports Hall of Fame.

8 Percy to Charlotte Williams, July 21, 1928, PWC, Written Documents, Box 1, 985:9:50yyyy.

9 Doral Pilling interview, 1975.

10 M. M. Robinson, ed., *The Official Report of the IXth Olympiad, 1928* (Hamilton, Ontario: Canadian Olympic Committee, 1929), 22.

11 *VP*, July 21, 1928, 9.

12 *VP*, July 24, 1928, 1 and 4.

13 *VP*, December 3, 1970, 23.

14 Bob Granger to Charlotte Williams, no date (early September 1928), PWC, Written Documents, Box 1, 985:9:50c. Charlotte Williams publicly explained how the fund for Granger was raised in a letter in *VP*, August 1, 1928, 23.

15 *VS*, July 26, 1929, 7; Bob Granger to Cyril Price, Febrary 18, 1930, Charlotte Warren collection; Harry Warren comments in *VP*, December 2, 1928, C2. In later retellings of the story, Bob would come to be described as working his way across the Atlantic on a "cattle boat," an often-repeated embellishment that would come to be accepted as fact. The *Minnedosa* in fact was not a cattle boat or even a freighter, but a passenger liner, much like the *Albertic*, and Bob paid for his passage aboard her — albeit in the cheapest berth he could get.

16 *HS*, July 25, 1928, 18; *TS*, July 27, 1928, 2; *Vancouver Province, B.C. Magazine*, September 3, 1955, 6; *VS*, July 28, 1978, C2. Phil Edwards was similarly left to his own devices, and Jimmy Ball managed to slip out of some of the training as well.

17 *VS*, July 26, 1929, 7.

18 Granger, "Human Flash," 8.

19 *VP*, January 26, 1929, 7.

20 Percy Williams to "Mes Chers Enfants," July 21, 1928, PWC, Written Documents, Box 2, 985:9:47m.

21 *HS*, July 25, 1928, 18.

22 *HS*, July 21, 1928, 22.

23 Bobby Kerr, "Canada at the Olympics," *Maclean's*, October 1, 1928, 17.

24 *TS*, July 27, 1928, 1–2.

25 Ibid., 1.

26 *TS*, July 26, 1928, 2; *Time*, August 13, 1928, 28.

27 *Manchester Guardian Weekly*, August 3, 1928.

28 *TS*, August 11, 1928, 4.

29 Robinson, 22–25; *VS*, July 28, 1928, 1; *VP*, July 28, 1928, 1;

30 Manchester, 140.

31 *HS*, July 27, 1928, 22.

32 *TS*, July 25, 1928, 11.

33 *HS*, July 28, 1928, 22.

34 Gardner, 42.

CHAPTER 9

1 Robert Elson, "The Fastest Human: How Percy Williams Plus Bob Granger Won for Canada a Dual Olympic Championship," *Maclean's*, October 15, 1928, 9, 59–60.

2 *VS*, July 27, 1929, 22.

3 *HS*, August 28, 1928, 16.

4 *TS*, July 30, 1928, 24.

5 *VS*, July 27, 1929, 22.

6 Gardner, 42.

7 McAllister, 268.

8 Ibid., 269.

9 *VS*, July 29, 1929, 14.

10 Ibid.

11 *HS*, July 30, 1928, 1; *VS*, July 30, 1929, 16.

12 According to the *New York Times*, McAllister had a "usual custom of disconcerting his opposition with genial comment upon their infirmities" (July 30, 1928, 12.).

13 Figures obtained from speed tests conducted on Percy at the time of the Amsterdam Olympics on an indoor track outfitted with a series of electrical timing devices. Percy in his three runs obtained the highly consistent maximum speeds of 11.42, 11.41 and 11.41 yards per second. C. H. Best and Ruth C. Partridge, "Observations on Olympic Athletes," *Proceedings of the Royal Society of London, Series B, Containing Papers of a Biological Character* 105, no. 737 (September 1929): 325 and 329.

14 Robinson, 41; Abrahams, 107–108; McNulty, 28–29; McAllister, 270–271; *VP*, July 30, 1928, 1–2; *VS*, July 30, 1928, 1 and 16, July 31, 1928, 10 and July 30, 1929; *HS*, July 30, 1928, 1, 14 and 16; *TS*, July 31, 1928, 3; *TG*, July 31, 1928, 1 and 8; *LAT*, July 31, 1928, 1 and section 3, 1; *NYT*, July 31, 1928, 1 and 19.

15 McAllister, 271.

16 *VS*, July 21, 1978, C1.

17 *TS*, September 4, 1928, 5.

18 *HS*, July 30, 1928, 1; Elson, 60.

19 Ibid.; *TS*, July 31, 1928, 3; *HS*, July 31, 1928, 16; *TT*, July 30, 1928, 1 and 13; *VP*, August 2, 1928, 22. The track shoes Percy wore at the 1928 Olympics and the trowel he used are on display at the BC Sports Hall of Fame and Museum.

20 *VS*, July 30, 1929, 16.

21 Elson, 9; *HS*, August 28, 1928, 16; *VS*, July 21, 1978, C1.

22 Gardner, 43.

23 Victor Warren interview with the author, January 11, 2008; *VP*, December 2, 1982, C2.

CHAPTER 10

1 *VS*, July 24, 1928, 1 and 9; Alan Morley, *Vancouver: From Milltown to Metropolis* (Vancouver: Mitchell Press, 1961), 164–165. The BC Airways plane would crash into Puget Sound a month later, claiming six lives. *VP*, August 26, 1928, 1.

2 *VS*, July 30, 1928, 1; *VP*, July 30, 1928, 1.

3 *VS*, July 30, 1928, 1.

4 *VMS*, July 31, 1928, 1 and 5.

5 *TG*, August 1, 1928, city news section, 1.

6 *VP*, August 4, 1928, 6.

7 *HS*, August 1, 1928, 16.

8 Unidentified, undated newspaper clipping, PWC, large scrapbook.

9 *NYT*, July 31, 1928, 1. The "nine firsts" MacArthur spoke of were the 100- and 200-metre dashes, 110- and 400-metre hurdles, long jump, high jump, discus, hammer, and pole vault.

10 *NYT*, August 1, 1928, 16.

11 *TS*, August 2, 1928, 10.

12 *Evening Standard*, August 2, 1928, 1.

13 *TS*, August 2, 1928, 10.

14 *VP*, August 2, 1928, 3.

15 *MG*, July 31, 1928, 6. Percy would say much the same thing in an article he wrote for the *Seattle Post-Intelligencer* in September 1928, "Williams Lauds US," PWC, large scrapbook: "If I were to pick out the athletes who were outstanding in good sportsmanship," he wrote, "as a whole the American team would rank first. . . . If any hard feeling was created at the games it was among the spectators and press representatives."

16 Louis S. Nixdorff Olympic diary, July 30, 1928.

CHAPTER 11

1 PWC, large scrapbook, contains many of these telegrams; *HS*, July 31, 1928, 16; *VS*, August 2, 1928, 1; *VP*, August 7, 1928, 13. Lee Millar Jr., aka Spuddie, went on to work in radio and television in the 1950s and '60s, notably as the announcer on *I Love Lucy* and, together with his mother Verna Felton, as one of the voices in Disney's animated film *Lady and the Tramp*.

2 *VP*, September 3, 1955, 6.

3 "Two Minutes to Glory," *Time*, August 2, 1928.

4 Paddock, *Fastest Human*, 100; Robinson, 43.

5 *TT*, July 31, 1928, 17.

6 *VP*, August 1, 1928, 23.

7 *HS*, July 31, 1928, 16; Victor Warren interview by the author, January 11, 2008.

8 *VS*, August 1, 1929, 3; Percy Williams, "Williams Lauds U.S.; Star Sends Message," *Seattle Post-Intelligencer*, September 1928, PWC, large scrapbook; Gardner, 43.

9 Robinson, 66–67; Gibb, 46–48.

10 Robinson, 66–67; *NYT*, August 1, 1928, 1 and 16; Gibb, 46–48; *TS*, August 1, 1928, 2; Ethel Smith interview, 1978.

11 "People don't believe me when I tell them," Percy later said, "but I didn't know any of those people I ran against. I didn't even know what they looked like until I saw them on the track. And certainly very few people over there could recognize me." *VS*, July 21, 1978, C1.

12 *VP*, August 1, 1928, 19.

13 *VS*, August 1, 1929, 3.

14 Gardner, 43.

15 *VP*, August 1, 1028, 19.

16 *TT*, August 1, 1928, 24.

17 *HS*, July 31, 1928, 17.

18 Paddock, *Fastest Human*, 239; *NYT*, August 1, 1928, sports section, 16 and August 2, 1928, 17.

19 Elson, 60; *HS*, August 1, 1928, 7.

20 Gardner, 43–44.

21 *HS*, August 1, 1928, 1 and 7; *TS*, August 1, 1928, 2.

22 *NYT*, August 2, 1928, 17 and August 27, 1928, sports section, 21.

23 Charley Paddock, "Failure in 200 Meters Ends Career," unidentified newspaper clipping, PWC, large scrapbook; Paddock, *Fastest Human*, 238–239.

24 *TS*, August 1, 1928, 2.

25 *VS*, July 28, 1978, C2.

26 Elson, 60.

27 *TS*, August 1, 1928, 1–2; *TT*, August 2, 1928, 18; *VP*, August 1, 1928, 1 and 20; *TG*, August 2, 1928, 6; *HS*, August 2, 1928, 16–18; *NYT*, August 2, 1928, 1 and 17; Elson, 60; Robinson, 43–44.

28 Kerr, 52.

CHAPTER 12

1 *HS*, August 2, 1928, 18; *LAT*, August 2, 1928, 11; *TT*, August 2, 1928, 43 and August 4, 1928, 29.

2 *TS*, August 1, 1928, 1 and 2; Elson, 60.

3 Gardner, 32.

4 *VP*, August 2, 1928, 3.

5 Percy to Charlotte Williams, August 4, 1928, PWC, Written Documents, Box 1, 985:9:50pppp.

6 *VS*, August 1, 1928, 3.

7 *VS*, August 1, 1928, 10; Percy to Charlotte Williams, Tuesday (June 26, 1928), PWC, Box 2, 985:9:47j.

8 *VP*, August 1, 1928, 1, August 2, 1928, 1 and August 14, 1928, 1.

9 *VS*, August 1, 1928, 1.

10 VP, August 2, 1928, 1; VS, August 2, 1928, 1; MS, August 2, 1928, 27.
11 VS, August 4, 1928, 6.
12 Telegram, Frank E. Woodside to Percy Williams, no date (around July 31, 1928), PWC, large scrapbook; VP, August 1, 1928, 21.
13 VP, August 2, 1928, 3.
14 Duncanson, 60.
15 VS, August 3, 1929, 25.
16 VP, August 1, 1928, 1.
17 TS, September 4, 1928, 5.
18 VS, August 4, 1928, 1 and 8; VP, August 4, 1928, 19; VMS, August 4, 1928, 1 and 5.
19 VS, August 21, 1928, 1.
20 "Fair Play" to Charlotte Williams, August 6, 1928 and Anonymous to Charlotte Williams, no date (August 1928), PWC, Written Documents, Box 1, 985:9:50e and 985:9:50eeeee.
21 HS, August 28, 1928, 16; Elson, 60.
22 TT, August 3, 1928, 19.
23 Percy to Charlotte Williams, August 9, 1928, PWC, Written Documents, Box 1, 985:9:50eeee.
24 TS, September 4, 1928, 10.
25 A good 1920s description of relay-running technique is found in Paddock, Track and Field, 65–74.
26 Robinson, 56; MS, August 6, 1928, 18; HS, August 7, 1928, 16; TS, August 7, 1928, 2.
27 VP, August 6, 1928, 2; HS, August 7, 1928, 10 and 16; TG, August 6, 1928, 9.
28 George Hester alumni file, Bentley Historical Library, University of Michigan.
29 VS, August 1, 1928, 3.
30 MS, August 2, 1928, 27.
31 Percy to Charlotte Williams, August 9, 1928, PWC, Written Documents, Box 1, 985:9:50eeee.
32 HS, August 13, 1928, 16. In Percy's papers is the menu from the banquet held for the American and British Empire athletes following the meet. Bob McAllister has signed it: "On the Menu of the Champion of Champions I sign my name. Bob McAllister, the Flying Cop, New York Police Dept." PWC, Written Documents, Box 2.
33 Percy to Charlotte Williams, Sunday (August 12, 1928), PWC, Written Documents, Box 1, 985:9:50xxxx and Box 2, 985:9:47d (the two pages of the letter have become separated and are filed in different boxes); TS, August 14, 1928, 13; VS, August 2, 1929, 4.
34 LAT, August 13, 1928, 11 and 13; NYT, August 13, 1928, sports section, 18; VP, August 13, 1928, 2.

35 Bob Granger to Charlotte Williams, no date (early September 1928), PWC, Written Documents, Box 1, 985:9:50c; *HS*, August 27, 1928, 18. Before being plucked clean Bob had tried to repay Percy the sixty dollars he owed him, but Percy had thrust it back in his pocket. "If he had taken the money," Bob ruefully wrote to Dot Williams, "that would have saved that much of it at any rate."

36 Bob Granger to Cyril Price, February 18, 1930, Charlotte Warren collection.

37 *VP*, August 18, 1928, 1 and September 9, 1928, 1.

38 Bob Granger to Charlotte Williams, no date (early September 1928), PWC, Written Documents, Box 1, 985:9:50c.

39 Percy to Charlotte Williams, about Friday (August 17, 1928), PWC, Written Documents, Box 1, 985:9;50ffff.

40 Percy Williams, "Inside Dope on Harry Warren Is Given by Famous Sprinter," *The Ubyssey*, November 2, 1928, 3. This is one of the very few things Percy ever wrote for publication. He also penned an article for the *Seattle Post-Intelligencer* in September 1928 ("Williams Lauds U.S.; Star Sends Message," PWC, large scrapbook), and a piece for the *Vancouver Sun* on September 8, 1945 ("On the Sunbeam"), filling in for vacationing columnist Alf Cottrell.

41 *VS*, August 2, 1928, 4; Doral Pilling interview, Calgary, 1975. A detailed synopsis of the post-Olympics tour is given in Robinson, 88–92.

42 Menu for the S.S. *Doric*, September 1, 1928, PWC, large scrapbook.

43 *HS*, August 28, 1928, 16; *VP*, September 2, 1928, 1.

44 *VS*, August 15, 1928, 19.

45 *VS*, September 13, 1928, 3.

46 *VS*, August 15, 1928, 20 and September 6, 1928, 16.

47 *VS*, August 4, 1928, 7.

48 *VP*, August 31, 1928, 32; *HS*, August 31, 1928, 20.

CHAPTER 13

1 *VP*, September 14, 1928, 20.

2 *VS*, September 14, 1928, 1 and 4.

3 *MS*, September 3, 1928, 4 and 11.

4 *MS*, September 3, 1928, 1.

5 *TS*, September 4, 1928, 5.

6 *MS*, September 3, 1928, 1 and 11; *VS*, July 28, 1978, C2.

7 *TS*, September 4, 1928, 5.

8 *MS*, September 3, 1928, 12.

9 Bobby Gaul to Percy, August 22, 1928, PWC, Written Documents, Box 1, 985:9:50d.

10 Telegram, Charlotte Williams to Mrs. H. Rhodes, September 4, 1928, PWC, Written Documents, Box 1, 985:9:50gggg; *TS*, September 5, 1928, 3.

11 HS, September 1, 1928, 24 and September 4, 1928, 18 and 20; TS, September 4, 1928, 5.
12 MFP, September 6, 1928, 20, September 7, 1928, 11 and September 10, 1928, 1 and 18; VS, August 2, 1929, 4.
13 VP, September 11, 1928, 2.
14 Typescript of songs sung at Percy's homecoming, PWC, Written Documents, Box 2.
15 VS, September 14, 1928, 23.
16 In Percy's 1929 diary in the British Columbia Sports Hall of Fame, on some blank pages beginning under the date September 30, is a list of everything he had received to date, under the heading, "Presentations, Prizes and What Have You."
17 VS, January 22, 1929, 14.
18 VS, September 14, 1928, 1, 4, 15 and 23; VP, September 14, 1928, 1 and 20; VMS, September 15, 1928, 1, 5 and 16. "Would you run one hundred yards in your Olympic outfit," Graham Bruce had cabled Percy in Toronto. "No watches. Will arrange so things won't be too hard." Graham Bruce to Percy Williams, September 8, 1928, PWC, large scrapbook.

CHAPTER 14

1 VP, September 29, 1928, 24.
2 VS, September 24, 1928, 1.
3 VS, September 19, 1928, 10 and September 24, 1928, 1; VP, September 24, 1928, 21.
4 VS, September 22, 1928, 4; VP, September 29, 1928, 22 and September 28, 1928, 27; The Ubyssey, September 28, 1928, 6; McNulty, 41.
5 "Percy Likes His Graham-Paige Auto," clipping from unidentified newspaper, no date, PWC, large scrapbook.
6 VP, September 15, 1928, 2.
7 VS, August 22, 1932, 5.
8 The Ubyssey, October 12, 1928, 2.
9 The Ubyssey, October 2, 1928, 6.
10 The Ubyssey, October 12, 1928, 3.
11 VS, September 19, 1928, 2; The Ubyssey, October 5, 1928, 6 and October 12, 1928, 4.
12 The Ubyssey, October 16, 1928, 2.
13 Bob Granger to Cyril Price, February 18, 1930, Charlotte Warren collection.
14 Jackson Gaines, Choctaw County Training School, Lisma, Alabama, to Percy Williams, February 4, 1929, PWC, Written Documents, Box 1; letters from young fans in Norway asking for Percy's autograph, PWC, Written Documents, Box 2.

15 "Percy Slated for Fame on Movie Screen," unidentified newspaper clipping, PWC, large scrapbook. The Hollywood representative was Charlie Royal, the former manager of the Empress Theatre and an old friend of Charlotte Williams. He was now based in LA and part-owner of Consolidated Sound Pictures.

16 VS, March 21, 1929, 14.

17 Percy's enigmatic diary entry for April 9, 1929, for example, suggests that he felt he understood the inner workings of amateur athletics, and regarded fellow track star Jimmy Ball as rather naïve. "Arrived Winnipeg," Percy writes, en route to Montreal to an indoor meet he was to headline. "Got in touch with Jimmy. He still believes in papers. Finally convinced him to leave work and catch same train. I really believe he thinks there is a Santa Claus."

18 Bob Granger, for example, would state in a personal letter that Percy received $1500 to run in Vancouver in July 1929, a particularly big pay-off. (Bob Granger to Cyril Price, February 18, 1930, Charlotte Warren collection.) Correspondence from Percy Page to Percy Williams regarding arrangements for Percy to run an exhibition race in Edmonton in October 1929 contains assurances that he would receive $200 in addition to his travel expenses, to be presented in the form of a "souvenir" of his choosing "to satisfy the curiosity of the Amateur Athletic officials" (Percy Page to Percy Williams, September 30 and October 7, 1929, PWC, Written Documents, Box 2, 985:9:47r and 985:9:47p.).

19 VS, February 5, 1929, 10.

20 VS, February 15, 1929, 18 and February 25, 1929, 14.

21 NYT, March 1, 1929, 19, March 2, 1929, 10, March 8, 1929, 19 and April 4, 1929, 24; VS, April 4, 1929, 18; "Questions," Time, April 22, 1929.

22 NYT, October 23, 1929, 32 and January 30, 1929, 21.

23 VP, December 7, 1928, 34.

24 VP, December 8, 1929, 18.

25 VP, December 9, 1928, 1.

26 VS, December 10, 1928, 1 and 4.

27 Gardner, 32; VP, September 14, 1928, 29, September 23, 1928, 31 and September 29, 1928, 8.

28 As Robert Edgren put it earlier that summer, the AAU was "a business organization for the control of amateur sports." VS, August 23, 1928, 15.

29 Lou Marsh, "With Pick and Shovel," TS, undated clipping, PWC, large scrapbook.

30 Maxwell Stiles, "Amsterdam: Before . . . And After," Back Track.

31 LAT, December 6, 1928, B3.

32 VP, January 6, 1929, 28; The Ubyssey, January 8, 1929, 4.

33 Percy Williams diary, January 14, 1929, British Columbia Sports Hall of Fame and Museum, PWC, Written Documents, Box 1, 985:9:40a (hereafter Percy Williams diary).

CHAPTER 15

1 *VS*, July 21, 1978, C1.

2 Percy Williams diary, January 17, 1929.

3 Ibid., January 18–21, 1929.

4 Ibid., January 24–28, 1929; Telegram, Alexandrine Gibb to Percy, January 22, 1929, PWC, Written Documents, Box 1, 985:9:50hhhh; Percy to Charlotte Williams, January 27, 1929, PWC, Written Documents, Box 1, 985:9:50xxxx.

5 *VP*, January 26, 1929, 7.

6 Newspaper clippings in PWC, large scrapbook: "Canadian Stars Reach Boston," *Boston Globe*, January 31, 1929, 19; "Cupid Can't Catch Up With Williams," *Boston Advertiser*, January 31, 1929; Frank Ryan, unidentified Boston newspaper clipping, January 31, 1929; Tom McCabe, unidentified Boston newspaper clipping, January 30, 1929; R.E. Knowles, unidentified Boston newspaper clipping, no date.

7 George Grimm article in unidentified Boston newspaper clipping, PWC, large scrapbook.

8 *TS*, September 4, 1928, 5.

9 *VP*, January 16, 1929, 24.

10 *VP*, January 31, 1929, 16.

11 Arthur Duffy, "Williams Class of Sprint World," *Boston Post*, February 9, 1929, clipping in PWC, large scrapbook; *VP*, January 24, 1929, 14.

12 Paddock, *Track and Field*, 162; *VP*, January 26, 1929, 7.

13 *VP*, December 31, 1928, 7.

14 For example *NYT*, February 2, 1929, 12. One Boston newspaper concluded on the eve of Percy's indoor debut: "We believe it will be a miracle if he wins the 40-yard sprint Saturday night. One cannot step from the cinders to the short spikes in a day or a week and have his full speed. This dash business that Williams must face is a question of the start. Forty yards is all start and Williams is much like Charley Paddock was, a rather clumsy starter. It is in the finish that Williams shines." Unidentified Boston newspaper clipping, no date (around January 30, 1929), PWC, large scrapbook.

15 Letter from "Connecticut Yankee" received January 1929 and published in *VP*, February 10, 1929, 27.

16 J. P. Abramson's account of the Boston meet in the *New York Herald Tribune*, reprinted in *HS*, February 5, 1929, 19.

17 *NYT*, February 18, 1929, sports section, 19.

18 *TS*, February 4, 1929, 10.

19 *VP*, February 3, 1929, 1, February 4, 1929, 10 and February 6, 1928, 14; *NYT*, February 3, 1929, sports section, 1; *TS*, February 4, 1929, 10; *VS*, February 4, 1929, 11; *The Boston Athletic Association Fortieth Annual Games, February 2, 1929* (official program) PWC, Written Documents, Box 2.

20 Percy Williams diary, February 2, 1929.

21 *TS*, February 4, 1929, 10.

22 *VP*, February 4, 1929, 10.

23 Telegram, Pat Mulqueen to Percy, February 3, 1929, PWC, large scrapbook.

24 *TS*, February 4, 1929, 10; Percy to Charlotte Williams, February 11, 1929, PWC, Written Documents, Box 2, 985:9:47b.

25 Bob Granger to Cyril Price, February 18, 1930, Charlotte Warren collection.

26 Percy Williams diary, February 3–5, 1929; Percy to Charlotte Williams, February 4 and 7, 1929, PWC, Written Documents, Box 2, 985:9:47a and Box 1, 985:9:50gggg.

27 Percy Williams diary, February 6, 1929.

28 *VP*, February 8, 1929, 26; *TS*, February 8, 1929, 8; *NYT*, February 8, 1929, 17; *HS*, February 8, 1929, 22; *VMS*, February 8, 1929, 1.

29 Percy Williams diary, February 8, 1929.

30 *NYT*, February 18, 1929, 19.

31 *VP*, February 9, 1929, 7.

32 *NYT*, January 7, 1929, 26 and February 3, 1929, sports section, 4.

33 *TS*, February 13, 1929, 8; *NYT*, February 18, 1929, 19; Percy Williams diary, February 8, 1929; Percy's copy, his name signed on the cover, of the program for the *Ontario Track and Field Championships and Provincial Olympic Trials, University of Toronto Stadium, June 23, 1928*, PWC, Written Documents, Box 3. "The Ten Commandments of Sport" are printed on the inside of the front cover.

34 *VP*, February 10, 1929, 1–2.

35 *TS*, February 11, 1929, 8.

36 *NYT*, February 9, 1929, 10 and February 10, 1929, sports section, 1; *TS*, February 11, 1929, 8; *TT*, February 11, 1929, 28; *VP*, February 10, 1929, 1; *VS*, February 11, 1929, 10; *VMS*, February 9, 1929, 8 and February 11, 1929, 7.

37 Percy to Charlotte Williams, February 11, 1929, PWC, Written Documents, Box 2, 985:9:47b.

38 *NYT*, February 13, 1929, 29; *TG*, February 12, 1929, 10; *HS*, February 12, 1929, 20 and February 15, 1929, 24; *TT*, February 13, 1929, 30; *TS*, February 13, 1929, 8; *VMS*, February 13, 192, 7.

39 Percy Williams diary, February 16, 1929.

40 *VP*, February 18, 1929, 12.

41 *VP*, February 16, 1929, 1 and February 17, 1929, 1; *NYT*, February 17, 1929, sports section, 1; *VMS*, February 18, 1929, 7; *The World* (New York), February 17, 1929, sports section, 1.

42 Percy Williams diary, February 16, 1929.

43 Percy to Charlotte Williams, February 11, 1929, PWC, Written Documents, Box 2, 985:9:47b; Percy Williams diary, February 14, 1929.

44 Bob Granger to Cyril Price, February 18, 1930, Charlotte Warren collection.

45 *VP*, February 18, 1929, 12; *LAT*, February 23, 1929, 11.

46 HS, February 19, 1929, 16; VP, February 19, 1929, 18.

47 Percy Williams diary, February 18, 1929; NYT, February 19, 1929, 24; TG, February 19, 1929, 10; HS, February 21, 1929, 20; VMS, February 19, 1929, 1.

48 VS, February 20, 1929, 6 and February 23, 1929, 14; VP, February 21, 1929, 1; VMS, February 20, 1929, 8.

49 NYT, February 22, 1929, 24.

50 Telegram, Graham Bruce to Percy, February 18, 1929, PWC, large scrapbook; Telegram, Charlotte Williams to Percy, February 21, 1929, PWC, Written Documents, Box 2; Telegram, "Olive and Billy" to Percy, February 22, 1929, PWC, Written Documents, Box 3, black photo album, 985:9:65.

51 The influence that Fred Williams had over Percy was suggested to the author by Lee Wright, son of Percy's 1932 Olympic teammate Harold Wright and himself a later friend of Percy's, in an interview on January 15, 2008.

CHAPTER 16

1 VP, February 22, 1929, 28.

2 Percy Williams diary, February 21, 1929; TS, February 21, 1929, 12.

3 HS, February 21, 1929, 20.

4 Percy Williams diary, February 20, 1929; TS, February 12, 1929, 12.

5 VP, February 21, 1929, 24; VMS, February 21, 1929, 1–2; TS, February 21, 1929, 12; TT, February 21, 1929; NYT, February 21, 1929, 23.

6 TT, February 22, 1929.

7 TS, February 22, 1929, 10.

8 HS, February 26, 1929, 18.

9 Percy Williams diary, February 21, 1929.

10 TG, February 22, 1929, 1.

11 TS, February 22, 1929, 10; TT, February 22, 1929; TG, February 22, 1929, 1–2; VP, February 22, 1929, 28; VS, February 22, 1929, 16; VMS, February 22, 1929, 1–2.

12 VP, February 23, 1929, 7.

13 NYT, February 23, 1929, 21.

14 Percy to Charlotte Williams, February 23, 1929, PWC, Written Documents, Box 1, 985:9:50xxxxx.

15 Telegram, John Leslie, Hon. Sec. AAU of C, and Sam B. Ferris, President, Club of Edmonton, to Percy Williams, March 22, 1929, PWC, Written Documents, Box 1, 985:9:50nnnnnn.

16 Telegram, Charles Keppen, LAAC, to Percy Williams, March 12, 1929, PWC, Written Documents, Box 3: "Will you come airship for meet March twenty-third run in open hundred. Borah and Wykoff not running, with understanding you compete against one or both of them here May fourth." Percy's reply is penciled on the back: "Never accept invitation with strings attached. Thanks a lot."

17 Percy to Charlotte Williams, February 27, 1929, PWC, Written Documents, Box 2, 985:9:471.
18 Percy Williams diary, February 26, 1929; *HS*, March 13, 1929, 22.
19 *VS*, March 9, 1929, 12.
20 Percy to Charlotte Williams, March 6, 1929, PWC, Written Documents, Box 1, 985:9:50ttttt; Percy Williams diary, March 2 and 6, 1929.
21 Percy Williams diary, March 8, 9, and 11, 1929; *HS*, March 11, 1929, 16.
22 Greg Maychak interview with the author, November 27, 2007.
23 Percy Williams diary, March 15 and 18, 1929.
24 *HS*, March 21, 1929, 24–26; *VS*, March 21, 1929, 14; *VP*, March 21, 1929, 26; Percy Williams diary, March 20 and 21, 1929; *Official Program Tenth Annual International Indoor Track Games* (Percy's copy of the meet program), PWC, Written Documents, Box 3.
25 Percy, aboard a CPR train, to Charlotte Williams, March 22, 1929, PWC, Written Documents, Box 1, 985:9:50aaaa; Telegram, Percy to Charlotte Williams, March 25, 1929, PWC, Written Documents, Box 1; Percy, aboard a CPR train, to Charlotte Williams, no date (around March 25, 1929), PWC, Written Documents, Box 1, 985:9:50z.
26 Telegram, Bob Granger to "Jimmy Ball, or Percy Williams, Royal Connaught Hotel, Hamilton," February 25, 1929, PWC, large scrapbook.
27 *VP*, March 27, 1929, 32.
28 Percy, Windsor Hotel, Montreal, to Charlotte Williams, Friday (April 12, 1929), PWC, Written Documents, Box 2, 985:9:47c. On his way east Percy stopped off in Winnipeg and talked Jimmy Ball into accompanying him on the trip. "Finally convinced [him] to leave work and catch same train," Percy wrote in his diary. "I really believe he thinks there is a Santa Claus." Percy Williams diary, April 9, 1929.
29 Telegram, Harold Lloyd to Percy, March 14, 1929, PWC, large scrapbook. "Oh Yez!" Percy wrote in his diary the following day. "Received a nice telegram from Harold Lloyd asking me to be his guest in Los Angeles. Pretty hot, Eh what!" Percy Williams diary, March 15, 1929.
30 *VP*, April 26, 1929, 34.
31 Bob Granger to Cyril Price, February 18, 1930, Charlotte Warren collection; *VS*, May 10, 1929, 2 and May 18, 1929, 14; W. A. Hewitt, "Sporting Views and Reviews," *TS*, undated clippings (1929), PWC, large scrapbook.
32 Bob Granger to Cyril Price, February 18, 1930, Charlotte Warren collection.
33 "Granger over last night. I was out. I guess he is still on the rampage. Oh well." Percy Williams diary, June 6, 1929.
34 According to Andy Lytle, "There are those who hold that Granger didn't have much, if anything, to do with Percy's success. Others, who were close to the pair in days of adversity, say the reverse is true. Write your own ticket." *VS*, June 15, 1929, 15.

35 Ibid; *VS*, May 21, 1930, 20.
36 Granger's "Climbing Olympus," serialized in twenty chapters, appeared in the *Vancouver Sun* from July 13 to August 3, 1929.
37 Bob Granger to Cyril Price, February 18, 1930, Charlotte Warren collection.
38 Bob Granger's movements can be tracked in *Wrigley's British Columbia Directory* for 1930, 1931 and 1932.
39 *VP*, June 15, 1929, 3. An attempt had been made in April to entice Percy into a rematch against Jack Elder. He turned it down. Telegram, W. D. Griffith, Director, Ohio Relays, to Percy Williams, April 11, 1929, PWC, Written Documents, Box 2.

CHAPTER 17

1 *VS*, June 28, 1929, 16 and July 10, 1929, 13.
2 In the late 1920s starting blocks were not regarded as giving a runner an especial speed advantage. Many runners after trying them claimed to prefer holes. The initial impetus for the use of blocks was rather that they kept a track in better condition, precluding the need for constantly digging start holes into the cinders.
3 *LAT*, January 4, 1929, 10; *NYT*, January 4, 1929, 17 and January 5, 1929, 17.
4 *VP*, May 6, 1929, 14 and May 23, 1929, 16; Percy William diary, May 24, 1929.
5 Percy Williams diary, May 13–June 7, 1929.
6 *VS*, June 27, 1929, 14; *VP*, June 27, 1929, 18.
7 Percy Williams diary, June 26, 1929.
8 *Mid-Summer Carnival and Grand Amateur Athletic Meet, Hastings Park, July 12–13, 1929*, PWC, Written Documents, Box 2.
9 *VS*, July 16, 1929, 10.
10 *VP*, July 13, 1929, 1 and 13; *VS*, July 13, 1929, 1 and 13; *VMS*, July 13, 1929, 1, 3 and 11; *NYT*, July 13, 1929, 11; *LAT*, July 13, 1929, 9.
11 Percy Williams diary, July 12, 1929.
12 Bob Granger to Cyril Price, February 18, 1929, Charlotte Warren collection; *VP*, August 17, 1930, 4–5.
13 *VP*, July 14, 1929, 1 and July 15, 1929, 20; *VS*, July 15, 1929, 1 and 12; *LAT*, July 13, 1929, 9.
14 *VP*, July 19, 1929, 32.
15 *VS*, July 15, 1929, 12; *Glendale News Press*, July 24, 1929, on-line at frankwykoff.com.
16 Percy Williams diary, July 13, 1929.
17 *VS*, July 16, 1929, 10.
18 Bob Granger to Cyril Price, February 18, 1930, Charlotte Warren collection.
19 *VS*, July 15, 1929, 13.
20 Bob Granger to Cyril Price, February 18, 1930, Charlotte Warren collection.
21 Percy Williams diary, July 30, 1929. Percy's exact diary entry reads: "Sunk

1500 in Mort. Should . . ." — and here he switches to Pitman shorthand — "be cleared up tomorrow and how." Percy is listed as the "householder" and owner of 196 Twelfth Avenue West in *Wrigley's British Columbia Directory* starting in 1931. Prior to this Charlotte is listed as head of the household.
22 *VS*, May 13, 1931, 14.
23 *Glendale News-Press*, July 24, 1929, on-line at www.frankwykoff.com
24 *LAT*, July 16, 1929, A9; *VS*, July 16, 1929, 10; *VP*, July 15, 1929, 20 and July 16, 1929, 18; Diane Eileen Ransom, "The Saskatoon Lily: A Biography of Ethel Catherwood" (Master's thesis, University of Saskatchewan, Saskatoon, 1986), 135–188. Ethel would give up her Canadian citizenship and become an American and settle in California. Reporters who tracked her down in later life would find her fiercely protective of her privacy and uncommunicative when pressed. "You just try it," she barked at one Toronto writer who suggested coming out to California to see her. "I have a big hurricane fence around my house, you wouldn't get close" ("Muddy York," *Toronto Life*, May 1928, 15.).
25 Percy Williams diary, July 17, 1929.
26 *VP*, July 11, 1929, 3.

CHAPTER 18

1 *TS*, July 19, 1929, 8.
2 *VS*, July 19, 1929, 18.
3 *Glendale News-Press*, July 24, 1929, on-line at www.frankwykoff.com.
4 Percy Page to Percy Williams, October 7, 1929, PWC, Written Documents, Box 2, 985:9:47p; *EJ*, October 26, 1929, 1.
5 Percy Williams diary, September 3, 1929; H. F. Mullett interview with Percy in *EJ*, October 26, 1929, 1 and 19; "Praises Elevator on Fraser River," clipping from unknown newspaper, November 5, 1929, PWC, large scrapbook. The clipping notes that Percy was overseeing the uploading of a shipment of corn from the freighter *Brandanger*, "having charge of the checking out of the cargo."
6 McNulty, 58.
7 *VS*, May 21, 1930, 20.
8 W. A. Hewitt, "Sporting Views and Reviews," *TS*, undated clipping (1929), PWC, large scrapbook.
9 *VP*, June 5, 1930, 24, June 6, 1930, 28 and June 22, 1930, 16.
10 *VP*, June 24, 1930, 20 and June 26, 1930, 26. The record progression for the sprints in the early 20th century can be confusing because of the delay that typically occurred between when a record-breaking performance was run and when it was recognized as official. In the century dash, Eddie Tolan set his record of 9.5 seconds in May 1929, breaking Dan Kelly's previous mark of 9.6 seconds set in 1906, but it wasn't recognized by the International Amateur Athletic Federation until May 1930. Frank Wykoff's mark of 9.4 seconds, set

in May 1930, was recognized by the AAU later that year in November and by the IAAF in July 1932. It would stand until 1948, when Mel Patton ran a nine-point-three.

11 *VP*, June 29, 1930, 11; *VMS*, July 1, 1930, 12.

12 *VP*, June 29, 1930, 10–11.

13 *VS*, May 21, 1930, 20.

14 Montreal politician and sportsman Louis Rubenstein, after Percy's performance at the Canadian Olympic trials in July 1928. *MS*, July 31, 1928, 22.

15 *VS*, July 2, 1930, 16 and 17; *VMS*, July 2, 1930, 1 and 7; *International Track Meet, 1930* (Percy's copy of the meet program), PWC, Written Documents, Box 3.

16 *VS*, July 3, 1930, 12 and July 12, 1930, 12; *VMS*, July 3, 1930, 6.

17 *TS*, August 5, 1930, 10.

18 A couple weeks earlier Frank Wykoff had been quoted as saying that prior to breaking the world century mark in May 1930 he had "felt a distinct lack of interest in the procedure. I didn't care whether I ran or not." *Des Moines Tribune-Capitol*, June 11, 1930, on-line at frankwykoff.com.

19 *VS*, August 2, 1930, 14.

20 *VS*, August 6, 1930, 10.

21 Percy to Charlotte Williams, August 5, 1930, PWC, Written Documents, Box 1, 985:9:50i.

22 *TS*, August 7, 1930, 10; *TG*, August 7, 1930, 14.

23 *TS*, August 9, 1929, 12.

24 *TS*, August 11, 1930, 8; *TG*, August 11, 1930, 1 and 5; *TT*, August 11, 1930; *HS*, August 11, 1930, 16–18; *VS*, August 9, 1930, 1.

25 *TG*, August 12, 1930, 1.

26 The photo Percy took of the R-100 is in the PWC, Photographs, Box 2, 7103.18.114.

CHAPTER 19

1 Cleve Dheensaw, *The Commonwealth Games: The First 60 Years, 1930–1990* (Victoria, BC: Orca Book Publishers, 1994), 15; *TS*, August 23, 1930, 11.

2 Dheensaw, *Commonwealth Games*, 7–10. According to Greg Maychak, a friend of Bobby Robinson's daughter Edna, Edna would in later years tell how her father personally raised $30,000 to help fund the games (without ever telling his wife), confident that he would recoup the money from the resulting profits. Fortunately he did. Greg Maychak interview with the author, November 27, 2007.

3 *VP*, August 22, 1930, 1; *VS*, August 21, 1930, 1; *VMS*, August 22, 1930, 6; *HS*, August 22, 1930, 18; *TG*, August 22, 1930, 28; *LFP*, August 22, 1930, 12; *BE*, August 22, 1930, 13.

4 *VS*, July 28, 1978, C2.

5 McNulty, 62.

6 *HS*, August 19, 1930, 16.
7 *HS*, August 22, 1930, 18–20; *MS*, August 22, 1930, 24.
8 *HS*, August 22, 1930, 5 and August 25, 1930, 16.
9 *TG*, August 25, 1930, 11; *TS*, August 25, 1930, 8; *MS*, August 25, 1930, 22.
10 *VP*, August 24, 1930, 32.
11 *VS*, July 21, 1978, C1.
12 *NYT*, August 24, 1930, S1.
13 *HS*, August 25, 1930, 16 and 19; *TS*, August 25, 1930, 8; *LFP*, August 25, 1930, 10; *MS*, August 25, 1930, 22; *TT*, August 25, 1930, 16; *TG*, August 25, 1930, 1 and 11; *VP*, August 23, 1930, 1 and August 24, 1930, 1 and 32; *VS*, August 23, 1930, 1; *VMS*, August 25, 1930, 6 and 11; Duncanson, 61; *The Official Program of the British Empire Games, 1930* (Percy's copy of the meet program), PWC, Written Documents, Box 2.
14 *VS*, July 21, 1978, C1.
15 *VP*, August 29, 1930, 30.

CHAPTER 20

1 *VP*, August 17, 1930, 2nd section, 4–5. The second of this two-part feature on Percy appeared in *VP*, August 24, 1930, 2nd section, 4–5.
2 *Who's Who in British Columbia, 1942–43* (Vancouver: S. Maurice Carter, 1943), 160–161; *VS*, September 2, 1930, 12, June 22, 1931, 10 and July 5, 1954, 3; *VP*, July 5, 1954, 10; PWC, Biographical File and Written Documents, Box 3, unidentified clipping in "Ledger." There is a photograph of George and Percy's refreshment stand in the PWC, Photographs, Box 1, Photo number 7103.7.3.
3 Andy Lytle, "Sport Rays," undated *VS* clipping, PWC, large scrapbook.
4 *VP*, May 22, 1935, 1. In denying a request in 1935 from Percy for the remaining money in the trust fund, it was "pointed out that the trustees, under the deed as it exists, can not give any further money to Williams or to his mother, because the purpose for which the payments were authorized, Williams' education and training, has passed. The result is no payments have been made from the fund for some time."
5 *VS*, June 9, 1931, 10 and June 22, 1931, 10.
6 *NYT*, May 12, 1931, 33.
7 *VS*, June 1, 1931, 13; *VP*, June 2, 1931, 20; *TS*, June 1, 1931, 8.
8 *VS*, June 17, 1931, 14 and June 22, 1931, 10.
9 *VS*, January 27, 1932, 14.
10 Charley Paddock, "No Son of Mine," *Collier's*, August 1929, on-line at frankwykoff.com.
11 *LAT*, June 11, 1931, 11 and June 13, 1931, 7.
12 *VS*, June 27, 1931, 14.
13 *LAT*, June 16, 1931, A11.
14 *LAE*, June 15, 1931.

15 *VS*, June 17, 1931, 14; *VP*, June 17, 1931, 27.
16 *TT*, June 17, 1931.
17 *VS*, June 17, 1931, 14.
18 *Helms Athletic Foundation Newsletter*, 1957, on-line at frankwykoff.com.
19 *LAT*, June 20, 1931, A1; *VP*, June 20, 1931, 7.
20 *LAT*, June 20, 1931, 5; *VP*, June 20, 1931, 7; *VS*, June 20, 1931, 14; *VMS*, June 20, 1931, 6; *TS*, June 20, 1931, 12.
21 *LAT*, June 21, 1931, F2.
22 *VS*, June 22, 1931, 10.
23 *VP*, June 22, 1931, 8, June 23, 1931, 20 and June 25, 1931, 22.
24 *VS*, July 7, 1931, 10.
25 *VP*, August 9, 1931, 27 and August 13, 1931, 18. After returning home from LA, Percy won the 100-yard-dash main event at the Caledonian Games in 9 4/5 seconds, reigniting the hopes of his supporters. He travelled to Victoria for another meet later that month, but refused to run due to the poor condition of the track. *VMS*, July 2, 1931, 6 and July 21, 1931, 6.
26 Pinky Stewart's write-ups in *VS*, July 25, 1931, 11 and *VMS*, August 21, 1931, 6.
27 *VS*, July 11, 1931, 12.
28 *VP*, August 16, 1931, 19.
29 *VP*, August 24, 1931, 8.
30 *VS*, August 25, 1931, 10; *LAT*, August 22, 1931, 5–6.
31 *VP*, August 13, 1931, 18 and August 16, 1931, 26; *VS*, August 13, 1931, 12 and August 17, 1931, 12; *VMS*, August 13, 1931, 9.
32 Bob's comments were noted in *TS*, August 21, 1931, 8 and August 24, 1931, 8, and in *VMS*, August 22, 1931, 8.
33 *VS*, August 25, 1931, 10.
34 *VP*, August 24, 1931, 8; *VS*, August 24, 1931, 10–11; *LAT*, August 23, 1931, F1.
35 *VP*, August 25, 1931, 19; *VS*, August 25, 1931, 11 and August 27, 1931, 14; *VMS*, August 24, 1931, 6.
36 *VS*, August 24, 1931, 1 and 14; *TS*, August 25, 1931, 8.
37 *VS*, August 27, 1931, 14.
38 *VP*, August 24, 1931, 8; *VMS*, August 24, 1931, 7.

CHAPTER 21

1 *VS*, July 20, 1932, 12.
2 *VP*, May 14, 1932, 7, June 1, 1932, 26 and June 17, 1932, 22; *VS*, June 7, 1932, 10.
3 *VP*, May 13, 1932, 18.
4 *VS*, June 23, 1932, 13.
5 *VS*, June 24, 1932, 16.
6 *VP*, June 26, 1932, 1 and 17; *VS*, June 27, 1932, 10–11, June 30, 1932, 10 and July 21, 1978, C1.
7 *HS*, July 13, 1932, 18.

8 *VS*, July 7, 1932, 12; *VP*, July 7, 1932, 16.

9 *VS*, July 6, 1932, 14.

10 *TS*, July 8, 1932, 8.

11 *VS*, July 6, 1932, 15; *VP*, July 8, 1932, 1.

12 *VS*, July 21, 1978, C1.

13 *TT*, July 13, 1932.

14 PWC, Written Documents, Box 2.

15 *VS*, July 30, 1932, 16.

16 *TS*, July 27, 1932, 10. The article attributed this bet to a "Vancouver man who came down with Williams."

17 *TS*, July 26, 1932, 8.

18 *VS*, July 21, 1978, C1.

19 *TT*, July 28, 1932, 2nd section, 2; *VP*, August 1, 1932, 1; John Cooper, ed., *Shadow Running: Ray Lewis, Canadian Railway Porter and Olympic Athlete* (Toronto: Umbrella Press, 1999), 52–53.

20 *HS*, July 28, 1932, 20.

21 *HS*, July 29, 1932, 20.

22 *MS*, July 27, 1832, 18.

23 *MS*, July 27, 1932, 16.

24 *VS*, July 30, 1932, 1; *VP*, July 30, 1932, 16; Section 236, *The Criminal Code and Other Selected Statues of Canada, 1927* (Ottawa: F. A. Acland, 1928), 78–79.

25 *LAT*, July 10, 1932, E4 and July 16, 1932, 6; *NYT*, July 15, 1932, 20 and July 19, 1932, 24.

26 British 800-metre runner Tommy Hampson, interviewed by Roger Bannister on the BBC radio program *London Calling* in 1956, transcript in "The Olympics: Six Interviews Given by Roger Bannister," *Bulletin du Comité International Olympique No. 58*, May 1957, 72.

27 *HS*, August 9, 1932, 26.

28 *HS*, August 2, 1932, 16; *VS*, August 2, 1932, 11.

29 W. A. Fry, ed., *Canada at the Tenth Olympiad, 1932* (Dunhill, Ontario: Dunhill Chronicle, [1933]), 38–39 and 102; *The Games of the Xth Olympiad, Los Angeles, 1932: Official Report* (Los Angeles: Xth Olympiade Committee, 1933) 402–405; *TS*, August 2, 1932, 12; *LAT*, August 2, 1932, 9–10; *NYT*, August 2, 1932, 1 and 12; *VS*, August 2, 1932, 10; *VP*, July 29, 1932, 20 and August 1, 1932, 1; *TT*, August 2, 1932, 18; *HS*, August 2, 1932, 16.

30 *TS*, August 3, 1932, 12.

31 *VS*, August 2, 1932, 5; *VP*, August 2, 1932, 10.

32 Fry, 54–55; *Games of the Xth Olympiad*, 439–440; *HS*, August 8, 1932, 14–16; *LAT*, August 8, 1932, 9; *TT*, August 8, 1932, 2nd section, 2; *VP*, August 8, 1932, 8–9.

33 *HS*, August 8, 1932, 16.

EPILOGUE

1 *HS*, August 11, 1932, 20.

2 *VP*, May 13, 1932, 18.

3 *The Ubyssey*, November 27, 1934, 4, February 26, 1935, 6, October 4, 1935, 4 and April 28, 1936, 4; *VS*, January 15, 1936, 14.

4 Jack Harrison reminiscences in McNulty, 102.

5 *VP*, May 22, 1935, 1 and December 10, 1942, 13; *VS*, December 10, 1942, 10 and December 13, 1946, 17.

6 George Parks interview in the History channel documentary *Percy Williams: Running Out of Time*, written by Robert Duncan, directed by Annie O'Donoghue, 1998.

7 *NYT*, November 29, 1932, 21 and January 24, 1933, 24.

8 *VP*, August 8, 1932, 2; *VS*, August 9, 1932, 16.

9 *VS*, August 22, 1932, 5; *VP*, August 22, 1932, 18.

10 *VS*, July 13, 1936, 1–2, July 14, 1936, 16, July 15, 1936, 18, July 18, 1936, 12, August 3, 1936, 1 and August 5, 1936, 1. Percy, who had trained Howie at UBC, would say after the Olympics that Howie, facing tougher opponents in Berlin than he had ever faced before, had likely tried too hard and "tighten[ed] up," losing "the smooth, flowing motion so essential to sprinting." Unidentified newspaper clipping circa 1936, PWC, large scrapbook. Howie died in 1940, just a few months after graduating from UBC, from what was believed to be a brain aneurism.

11 *VS*, December 7, 1936, 2.

12 *The Ubyssey*, October 26, 1937, 4.

13 *VP*, December 3, 1970, 23.

14 *VS*, December 3, 1970, 30.

15 *TS*, December 5, 1982, E12.

16 Dennis Orchard interview with Bob Granger, 1964, in Bruce Levett, "Percy Williams: Reluctant Runner," *Winners: A Century if Canadian Sport* (Toronto: Grosvenor House, 1985), 16–18.

17 Dennis Orchard, "The Road Back from Olympus Led to Lonely Alberni Room," *VDC*, April 9, 1964, 10. Orchard wrote a similar piece on his interview with Granger that was published in *VP*, April 16, 1964, 11. There is a copy of it among Percy's papers, but with a sentence carefully cut out, leaving a rectangular hole in the paper. The missing lines, which apparently offended Percy, read: ". . . he quit in 1932 after a dismal showing at the Los Angeles Olympics." PWC, Written Documents, Box 3, ledger.

18 Leo Russell, "Percy Williams Digs His Spikes into Bigger Task," unidentified clipping, PWC, Scrapbook 985:9:55; *NYT*, March 13, 1942, 26.

19 "Olympic Star is Now Bomber Pilot in City," unidentified newspaper clipping, PWC, Written Documents, Box 3, ledger; *Percy Williams: Running Out of Time*; NcNulty, 77. Percy's wartime service records were destroyed when

he turned seventy, as is required for the records of civilian instructors attached to the military. The only official document the author was able to obtain from Library and Archives Canada concerning Percy's service was a copy of his attestation paper, dated August 19, 1940.

20 Unidentified newspaper clipping, 1945, PWC, Written Documents, Box 3, ledger.

21 *VS*, December 31, 1945, 1 and January 2, 1946, 6; *VP*, December 31, 1945, 3; *NYT*, January 1, 1946, 32.

22 Death certificate for Archibald Rhodes, Vancouver Public Library, microfilm B13179, registration number 1943-09-623085.

23 Percy supported his mother throughout the war with monthly checks, and his letters to her contain a good deal of financial instructions and advice. PWC, Written Documents, Box 1.

24 *VS*, December 4, 1982, E3.

25 PWC, Biographical File, unidentified clipping.

26 *VS*, June 26, 1953, 29.

27 According to Lee Wright, son of Percy's 1932 Olympic teammate and long-time friend Harold Wright, "If there was a special banquet or Olympic event in Vancouver, Percy Williams' father would be the one that would get Percy to come. He was obviously the only person who could get him to come to any sort of event." Lee Wright interview with the author, January 15, 2008.

28 *VS*, December 4, 1982, E3. When asked in 1976 to fill out a questionnaire for the upcoming publication of a *Who's Who in Canadian Sport*, Percy listed "tennis, squash, shooting, riding" under "Athletic Achievements," and under "Other Awards" wrote only: "A few." PWC, Written Documents, Box 2.

29 *Los Angeles Herald Examiner*, August 20, 1972, on-line at frank-wykoff2.com.

30 *GM*, December 1, 1982, S5; Don Carlson sports column, unidentified newspaper clipping, August 5, 1948, PWC, large scrapbook.

31 Doug Clement interview with the author, July 31, 2008. The meet was re-named the Achilles Indoor Games.

32 *Percy Williams: Running Out of Time*.

33 Charlotte Warren interview with the author, January 11, 2008.

34 Duncanson, 62.

35 Peter Webster interview with the author, July 9, 2008.

36 Correspondence between the author and Jason Beck, BC Sports Hall of Fame and Museum curator, June 2008; Peter Webster interview with the author, July 9, 2008; "Materials Stolen from Percy Williams Showcase," typewritten manuscript, PWC, Biographical file; *VS*, January 15, 1980, A3 and December 2, 1982, A3; International Olympic Committee, "Composition of the Medals of the Olympic Games," September 2004, at www.hesge.ch/heg/vous_etes/doc/stages/2004/ sta04_schnyder_annexe1.pdf. Solid gold medals were last awarded at the 1912 Stockholm Olympics. According to Beck, six of the stolen

sixteen medals belonging to Percy were later discovered among the possessions of a person deceased in the interior of BC and were anonymously returned to the Hall of Fame in 1996. Percy's Olympic gold medals are still considered missing stolen property and remain on the books with Interpol and other organizations.

37 *VS*, July 21, 1978, C1.
38 McNulty, 80.
39 The author is grateful to James Worrall, former president of the Canadian Olympic Association, for copies of Percy's funeral service, Harold Wright's eulogy, and various clippings and other materials relating to Percy that were helpful in piecing together the later years of his life.
40 *VS*, December 2, 1982, C2 and December 4, 1982, A8; *House of Commons debates for Dec. 3, 1982, House of Commons Debates, First Session, 32nd Parliament*, vol. 19 (1982), 21 and 248.
41 *TS*, March 22, 2005, B4.
42 Percy and Fred Williams are buried in the southwest corner of the Masonic Cemetery, in section A, plot 121, grave 1.

Bibliography

UNPUBLISHED MATERIAL

Beck, Jason. Correspondence and telephone interview with the author, June–July 2008.

Carter, Ernest "Nick." Interview with George Hodak, June 1987, Santa Barbara, California, LA84 Foundation Digital Archive, Olympian Oral Histories, www.la84foundation.org/6oic/ OralHistory/OHCarter.pdf.

Clement, Doug. Telephone interview with the author, July 31, 2008.

Cornelius, John Richard ("Cap"). Letters and photos in the Educational Archives of the Hamilton-Wentworth District School Board, Hamilton, Ontario.

Emery, Girija. Telephone interview and correspondence with the author, Jan. 2008.

Granger, Robert D. Letters in the possession of Charlotte Warren, Vancouver, BC.

Harrison, Jack and Marilyn. Telephone interview with the author, Feb. 2, 2008.

Hume, Fred. Correspondence with the author, Jan. 2008.

Johnson, Arta. Correspondence with the author, Oct. 2007.

Maychak, Greg. Telephone interview with the author, Nov. 27, 2007.

Nixdorff, Louis S. Olympic diary, 1928. Archives Center, National Museum of American History, Washington, D.C., www.americanhistory.si.edu/archives/ d9443f.htm.

O'Brien, Anne Vrana. Interview with George Hodak, Oct. 1987, Tustin, California, LA84 Foundation Digital Archive, Olympian Oral Histories, www.la84foundation.org/6oic/OralHistory/OHVranaOBrien.pdf.

Osborne, Robert F. "Canada's Reluctant Hero: A Look at the Life of Percy Williams." Handwritten manuscript. Biographical file, Percy Williams Collection, BC Sports Hall of Fame and Museum, Vancouver.

Pilling, Doral William. Oral history. Interview with Charles Ursenbach, Calgary, Alberta, 1975. Typescript. Oral History Program, Historical Department of The Church of Jesus Christ of Latter-Day Saints, Salt Lake City, Utah.

Scholz, Jackson. Telephone interview with unknown interviewer, c. 1980s. Audio recording in the archives of the University of Missouri Library, collection number C:0/46/41.

Smith, Ethel. Interview with T. West, 1978. Typescript. Canada's Sports Hall of Fame, Toronto.

Waksel, Brenda, Library Technician/Archivist, St. Michael's University School, Victoria. Correspondence with the author, Aug. 2008.

Warren, Charlotte. Telephone interview with the author, Jan. 11, 2008.

Warren, Victor. Telephone interview with the author, Jan. 11, 2008.

Webster, Peter. Telephone interview with the author, July 9, 2008.

Williams, Percy A. Diary, 1929. BC Sports Hall of Fame and Museum, Vancouver, BC, Percy Williams Collection, Written Documents, Box 1, accession number 985:9:40a.

Worrall, James. Telephone interview with the author, Jan. 28 and Feb. 9, 2008.

Wright, Lee. Telephone interview with the author, Jan. 15, 2008.

NEWSPAPERS

The Citizen (Ottawa)

The Evening Telegram (Toronto)

The Gazette (Montreal)

The Globe (Toronto)

The Hamilton Spectator

The London Evening Free Press (London, Ontario)

The Los Angeles Examiner

The Los Angeles Times

The Manchester Guardian Weekly

The Manitoba Free Press

The Montreal Daily Star

The New York Times

The Ottawa Journal

The Star (Johannesburg)

The Sunday Province (Vancouver)

The Times (London, England)
The Toronto Daily Mail
The Toronto Daily Star
The Ubyssey (University of British Columbia)
The Vancouver Daily Province
The Vancouver Morning Star
The Vancouver Sun
The Victoria Daily Colonist

DIRECTORIES

British Columbia and Yukon Directory, 1934–1948
Henderson's British Columbia Gazetteer and Directory, 1901–1904
Henderson's City of Vancouver Directory, 1905–1910
Henderson's Greater Vancouver Directory, 1911–1922
Vancouver City Directory, 1949–1982
Wrigley-Henderson Amalgamated British Columbia Directory, 1924–1925
Wrigley's British Columbia Directory, 1923, 1926–1933

BOOKS AND ARTICLES

Abrahams, Harold M. *The Official Report of the IXth Olympiad, Amsterdam 1928*. London: British Olympic Association, [1928].

Amateur Athletic Union of Canada. *First National Indoor Track Championships, Conducted by Amateur Athletic Union of Canada, Ontario Branch [at the] Coliseum, Exhibition Park, Toronto, Canada, Thursday, February 21st, 1929*.

Batten, Jack, ed. *1896–1996 Canada at the Olympics: The First Hundred Years*. Toronto: Infact, 1996.

———. *The Man Who Ran Faster than Everyone: The Story of Tom Longboat*. Toronto: Tundra Books, 2002.

Best, C.H. and Ruth C. Partridge. "Observations on Olympic Athletes." *Proceedings of the Royal Society of London, Series B, Containing Papers of a Biological Character* 105, no. 737 (Sept. 1929): 323–332.

Buchanan, Ian and Bill Mallon. *Historical Dictionary of the Olympic Movement*. Lanham, Maryland: Scarecrow Press, 1995.

Cooper, John, ed. *Shadow Running: Ray Lewis, Canadian Railway Porter and Olympic Athlete*. Toronto: Umbrella Press, 1999.

Cromwell, Dean B. *The Sprint Races*. Indianapolis: International Sports, Inc., c1939.

———. *Championship Technique in Track and Field*. New York: Whittlesey House, 1949.

Dheensaw, Cleve. *The Commonwealth Games: The First 60 Years, 1930–1990*. Victoria, BC: Orca Book Publishers, 1994.

————. *Olympics 100: Canada at the Summer Games*. Victoria: Orca Book Publishers, 1996.

Duncanson, Neil. *The Fastest Men on Earth*. London: Willow Books, 1988.

Elson, Robert T. "The Fastest Human: How Percy Williams Plus Bob Granger Won for Canada a Dual Olympic Championship." *Maclean's*, Oct. 15, 1928, 9, 59–60.

Findling, John E. and Kimberly D. Pelle, eds. *Historical Dictionary of the Modern Olympic Movement*. Westport, Connecticut: Greenwood Press, 1996.

Fotheringham, Allan. "In Praise of Percy Williams." *Maclean's*, Oct. 18, 1999, 96.

Fry, W. A., ed. *Canada at the Tenth Olympiad, 1932*. Dunhill, Ontario: Dunhill Chronicle, [1933].

Galloway, Hap. "The Fastest Human Being on Earth." *1981 B.C. Elementary School Relay Championships*, 27–31.

The Games of the Xth Olympiad, Los Angeles, 1932: Official Report. Los Angeles: Xth Olympiade Committee, 1933.

Gardner, Ray. "How Percy Williams Swept the Olympic Sprints." *Maclean's*, Nov. 24, 1956, 32–46.

Gibb, Alexandrine. "Canada at the Olympics: The Story of How Six Canadian Girls Won the Women's Track and Field Championship of the World." *Maclean's*, Oct. 1, 1928, 16, 46–50.

Granger, Bob. "Climbing Olympus: The Inside Story of Percy Williams' Rise to Fame." *Vancouver Sun*, July 13–Aug. 3, 1929 (a 20-chapter serial).

————. "The Outdoor Boy." *The Country Gentleman*, April 1930.

————. "The Human Flash: The Story of Percy Williams, Breaker of Speed Records." *The American Magazine*, Nov. 1930, 63 and 167–68.

Guttmann, Allen. *The Olympics: A History of the Modern Games*. Urbana, Illinois: University of Illinois Press, 1992.

Hayes, Derek. *Historical Atlas of Vancouver and the Lower Fraser Valley*. Vancouver: Douglas and McIntyre, 2005.

Heath, Eric. "'You Don't Have to be a Scotsman': Sport and the Evolution of the Vancouver Caledonian Games, 1893–1926." MA thesis, Simon Fraser University, 2005.

Henley, Brian. *Henley's People: Fascinating People from Hamilton's Past*. Burlington, Ontario: North Shore Publishing, 1996.

Kearney, Jim. *Champions: A British Columbia Sports Album*. Vancouver: Douglas and McIntyre, 1985.

Kerr, Bobby. "Canada at the Olympics: An Expert Records the Achievements of the First Canadian Olympic Team to Produce a Double First." *Maclean's*, Oct. 1, 1928, 17 and 50–52.

Kidd, Bruce. *The Struggle for Canadian Sport*. Toronto: University of Toronto Press, 1996.

Kloppenborg, Anne, Alice Niwinski and Eve Johnson. *Vancouver's First Century: A City Album, 1860–1985*. Vancouver: Douglas and McIntyre, 1985.

Levett, Bruce. "Percy Williams: Reluctant Runner." *Winners: A Century of Canadian Sport*. Toronto: Grosvenor House, 1985, 16–18.

Lowe, D.G.A., and A.E. Porritt. *Athletics*. London: Longmans, Green and Co., 1929.

Lucas, John A. "USOC President Douglas MacArthur and His Olympic Moment, 1927–1928." *Olympika: The International Journal of Olympic Studies* 3 (1994): 111–115.

Macdonald, Bruce. *Vancouver: A Visual History*. Vancouver: Talon Books, 1992.

MacDonald, Rob. "The Battle of Port Arthur: A War of Words and Ideologies Within the Canadian Olympic Committee." *Proceedings of the First International Symposium for Olympic Research*, Feb. 1992, 135–152.

Manchester, William. *American Caesar: Douglas MacArthur, 1880–1964*. Boston: Little, Brown, 1978.

Magnusson, Sally. *The Flying Scotsman*. New York: Quartet Books, 1981.

Matches, Alex. *Vancouver's Bravest: 120 Years of Firefighting History*. Surrey, BC: Hancock House, 2007.

The Matric Annual. Vancouver: King Edward High School, 1926–1929.

McAllister, Robert, with Floyd Miller. *The Kind of Guy I Am*. New York: McGraw-Hill, 1957.

McNulty, Bill, and Christine McNulty. *Peerless Percy: The Story of Canada's Greatest Sprinting Legend*. Vancouver: Bill McNulty and Christine McNulty, 1998.

McWhirter, Ross, and Norris McWhirter. *Get to Your Marks! A Short History of World, Commonwealth, European, and British Athletics*. London: Nicholas Kaye, 1951.

Meyer, H.A., ed. *Modern Athletics, by The Achilles Club*. London: Oxford University Press, 1964.

Morley, Alan. *Vancouver: From Milltown to Metropolis*. Vancouver: Mitchell Press, 1961.

Morrow, Don. "Peerless Percy: A Study of the Interrelationships Among Coaching/Training, the Media and Personality." *Proceedings of the 6th Canadian Symposium on the History of Sport and Physical Education*, June 1988, 1–9.

———. "Grace Without Pressure: Canadian Scintillation and the Media in the Amsterdam Olympic Games." *Proceedings of the First International Symposium for Olympic Research*, Feb. 1992, 125–134.

Mussabini, S.A. *The Complete Athletic Trainer*. London: Methuen and Co., 1913.

Netherlands Olympic Committee. *The Ninth Olympiad. Being the Official Report of the Olympic Games of 1928 Celebrated at Amsterdam*. Amsterdam: J. H. De Bussy, 1928.

"The Olympic Story." *The Canadian Athlete*, Nov. 1928, 7–9.

Paddock, Charles W. "No Son of Mine." *Collier's*, Aug. 1929.

———. *The Fastest Human*. New York: Thomas Nelson & Sons, 1932.

———. *Track and Field*. New York: A.S. Barnes and Co., 1933.

Percy Williams: Running Out of Time. Video recording. Written and directed by Robert Duncan. Edmonton, Alberta: Faces II Productions, 1998.

Radcliffe, Ted. "Fifty Years Ago, Percy Williams Won Two Olympic Golds." *Athletica*, Aug. 1978, 26.

Ransom, Diane Eileen. "The Saskatoon Lily: A Biography of Ethel Catherwood." Master's thesis, University of Saskatchewan, Saskatoon, 1986.

"Replay." Two-part radio show on Percy Williams, originally broadcast on Vancouver radio station CHQM, June 1979. (Audio cassette, item # C-45-3, in the Percy Williams Collection, BC Sports Hall of Fame and Museum, Vancouver.)

Robinson, M.M., ed. *The Official Report of the IXth Olympiad, 1928*. Hamilton, Ontario: Canadian Olympic Committee, 1929.

Roxborough, Henry H. "Hamilton Sets the Pace." *Maclean's*, Sept. 1, 1928, 17 and 50–52.

———. "Are the Olympics Worthwhile?" *Maclean's*, Nov. 1, 1928, 8–9 and 52–55.

———. "Truth is Stranger!" *National Home Monthly*, Jan. 1933, 10–11 and 48.

———. *Canada at the Olympics*. Toronto: Ryerson Press, 1963.

Roy, Patricia E. *Vancouver: An Illustrated History*. Toronto: James Lorimer and Co., 1980.

Schaffer, Kay and Sidonie Smith, eds. *The Olympics at the Millennium: Power, Politics, and the Games*. New Brunswick, New Jersey: Rutgers University Press, 2000.

Scholz, Jackson Volney. *Split Seconds: Tales of the Cinder Track*. New York: William Morrow, 1927.

Stampfl, Franz. *Franz Stampfl on Running: Sprint, Middle Distance, and Distance Events*. London: Herbert Jenkins, 1955.

Stewart, V. L. ("Pinky"). "Western Sport Arrives." *Maclean's*, July 15, 1931, 14 and 48.

Stiles, Maxwell. *Back Track: Great Moments in Track and Field*. Los Angeles: Track and Field News, 1959 (on-line at http://www.trackandfieldnews.com/general/back_track).

Waites, Kenneth Arthur, ed. *First Fifty Years: Vancouver High Schools, 1890–1940*. Vancouver, 1940.

Warren, Harry V. "Olympic Memories." *OCC Communiqué*. No. 3 (1979).

Whitehead, Eric. "Percy Williams: World's Fastest Human." *Vancouver Province, B.C. Magazine*, Sept. 3, 1955, 6.

Wise, S.F., and Douglas Fisher. *Canada's Sporting Heroes*. Don Mills, Ontario: General Publishing Co., 1974.

Worrell, James. *My Olympic Journey: Sixty Years with Canadian Sport and the*

Olympic Games. Toronto: Canadian Olympic Committee, 2000.

Yeo, E.L. "Percy Williams." In *The Matric Annual, 1929,* 48–49. Vancouver: King Edward High School, 1929.

Zeiler, Lorne. *Hearts of Gold: Stories of Courage, Dedication, and Triumph from Canadian Olympians.* Vancouver: Raincoast Books, 2004.

ABOUT THE AUTHOR

∽

Samuel Hawley was born and grew up in South Korea, the son of missionary parents. After earning BA and MA degrees in history from Queen's University, he returned to East Asia for two decades to teach English, first in Japan and then Korea, retiring in 2007 as an associate professor at Yonsei University in Seoul. He additionally served for three years as head of Yonsei's Communicative English Department and as editor of the Royal Asiatic Society's *Transactions*, the oldest Korean studies journal in the world, a position he continues to hold.

It was in Japan that Samuel started writing for magazines and newspapers on topics ranging from travel and Japanese fashion to sumo wrestling and urban fishing. By the late 1990s he had turned his attention to books, most notably *The Imjin War*, a seven-hundred-page account of Japan's sixteenth-century invasion of Korea and attempted conquest of China, a conflict vastly larger than European wars at that time and yet little known today in the West. He followed this with two volumes on George Foulk, Washington's chargé d'affaires in Seoul in the 1880s: *America's Man in Korea* and *Inside the Hermit Kingdom*.

Samuel switched his focus to popular nonfiction after returning to Canada in 2007. His first work in this new vein was *Speed Duel*, about the epic rivalry on the Bonneville Salt Flats between Craig Breedlove and Art Arfons in which they pushed the land speed record from 394 to 601 mph — with some of the fastest crashes in motor sport history along the way. He lives in Kingston, Ontario.

Index

RECYCLÉ
Papier fait à partir
de matériaux recyclés
FSC® C103567

Marquis imprimeur inc.

Québec, Canada
2011

Imprimé sur du papier Silva Enviro 100% postconsommation
traité sans chlore, accrédité ÉcoLogo et fait à partir de biogaz.